The Excess of Heroism in Tragic Drama

The Excess of Heroism in Tragic Drama

~

Leonard Moss

University Press of Florida

Gainesville/Tallahassee/Tampa/Boca Raton
Pensacola/Orlando/Miami/Jacksonville

Copyright 2000 by Leonard Moss
Printed in the United States of America on acid-free paper
All rights reserved

05 04 03 02 01 00 6 5 4 3 2 1

Library of Congress Cataloging-in-Publication Data
Moss, Leonard, 1931-
The excess of heroism in tragic drama / Leonard Moss.
p. cm.
Includes bibliographical references and index.
ISBN 0-8130-1759-9 (cloth: alk. paper)
1. Tragedy—History and criticism. 2. Heroes in literature. 3. Courage in literature.
4. Pride in literature. I. Title.
PN1892 .M67 2000
809.2'51209352—dc21   99-088037

The University Press of Florida is the scholarly publishing agency for the State University System of Florida, comprising Florida A&M University, Florida Atlantic University, Florida International University, Florida State University, University of Central Florida, University of Florida, University of North Florida, University of South Florida, and University of West Florida.

University Press of Florida
15 Northwest 15th Street
Gainesville, FL 32611–2079
http://www.upf.com

for
Shaoping and Eli

One feels the man's power as an augmentation of his character; he cannot make an empty gesture or say a word that is not listened to. He knows it, and the knowledge gives him more reality than most people own: a solidness of being, a substantiality, a human grandeur.

Ursula K. LeGuin, *The Left Hand of Darkness*

It is as if the souls of men floating on an abyss and in touch with immensity had been set free for any excess of heroism, absurdity, or abomination.

Joseph Conrad, *Lord Jim*

Contents

Preface ix

The Treason of Stereotypes
1. Hegel's Theory 3
2. The Male Model 9
3. Women 32
4. The Sequence of Athenian Tragedy 47
5. Shakespeare's Fatal Female 57

The Flux of Metaphor
6. Nietzschean Dream Imagery in Aeschylus and Seneca 73
7. Nietzschean Dream Imagery in Strindberg and Kafka 85

The Duplicity of Rhetoric
8. Plato's Distrust 103
9. Milton's Single-mindedness 114
10. Shakespeare's Trickery: Piling up Nothing 122

Summary and Speculation 155
Notes 161
Further Reference
The Theory of Tragedy 183
Plato and Aristotle on the Craft of Literature (Annotated) 200
Index 213

Preface

Impressed by the many admirable qualities shown by tragic characters—especially their eloquence—and saddened by their misfortune, we may overlook their responsibility for the suffering they bring to themselves and others. Yet they *are* responsible even though they often deny it or shift the blame elsewhere. One purpose of this book is to account for their complicity, to get beyond hero worship and see the sinister side of tragedy, the "excess of heroism, absurdity, or abomination," as Conrad put it.

The Greek dramatists understood this destructive potential. "Your anger has made a savage of you," a friend tells Sophocles' Philoctetes; and at Colonus, Creon informs Oedipus that "anger has always been your greatest sin!"[1] This accusation surfaces in any number of Athenian plays. Aeschylus, Sophocles, and Euripides took their cue from Homer's *Iliad* when they exposed their heroes' intemperate response to insult. In the *Iliad*, Patrocles contrasts the incorrigible Achilles with warriors whose injuries have taught them the benefits of compromise: "while they try to heal their wounds, you, Achilles, remain intractable. Heaven preserve me from the vindictive feelings you cherish, warping a noble nature to ignoble ends."[2]

Shakespeare's noble protagonists too transform themselves into ignoble victims of a fixation on power and perfection. Their one constant turns out to be inconstancy, the bane of their aristocratic standard of conduct; they vibrate in contradiction; they dis-integrate. What causes so surprising and so deadly a metamorphosis? Shakespeare and the Athenians were delivering a radical critique of stereotypical notions about masculine excellence. They were pointing not merely to the self-destructiveness of particular characters but to the inconsistency of a value system. The system seemed logical, workable, and necessary: exceptional characters demanded unconditional validation from peers and leaders, intimates and followers, and in return for unlimited respect they were expected to support those allies in war and governance. But this arrangement failed, and when it did the tremendous energy these models of manhood had generated to enlist public or private approval pushed them to defend their status at any cost, the usual consequences being violence, madness, isolation, and death. They fluctuated between great strength and great shame, irrationality, and impotence. Their illustrious careers became weapons for murder and suicide.

They approached chaos in an orderly way, however: like jugglers in a circus, the authors of tragic drama neatly balanced the antitheses of integrity and dissolution. Those authors skillfully controlled ethical contraries with literary mechanisms that gave a concrete shape to the treason, flux, and duplicity residing in models of manhood—mechanisms such as a narrative vehicle that carried the irony of self-defeat, a two-faced imagery that pictured extreme alterations of personality, and speech that could sound elaborately weighty but be deceptively hollow. Truth to the first playwrights was composed of polarities, so they conveyed it through double-voiced dramatic messengers. And when later generations of authors revisited the critique, their artistic innovations reflected an equally ambiguous outlook.

My intention, then, is to relate a broad philosophical and moral issue to specific literary techniques, to describe a contradiction in values embodied in technical procedures fashioned by the three Athenian dramatists and recast by Shakespeare and other writers. These writers were playing variations on a single theme. In the first five chapters, I call upon twenty-two well-known Athenian and Shakespearean plays to illustrate the theme as expressed by a recurring narrative pattern. But this is not a historical survey: to explore more subtle techniques, involving metaphor and rhetoric, I forgo the quantity of examples that was appropriate while reconstructing a story framework and instead reach for depth of detail in several comparative studies.

We shall ask three heroic theorists—Plato, Hegel, and Nietzsche—to help guide us through these intricacies (Aristotle's *Poetics* will be discussed in connection with Plato's attitude toward poetry but does not play a major role here). These philosophers offer invaluable but contrasting insights; our mission is to adapt those insights and integrate them in order to support a conclusion based upon our observation of tragic drama. Without them we would be half blind, yet without learning how to use them effectively we will end up just as shortsighted.

We must, therefore, report our strenuous objections to and modifications of the seminal proposals advanced by Plato and Hegel as well as our profound indebtedness. Hegel taught us that the tragic tale centers on a struggle between competing principles, a lesson we can profit from once we revise it. I acknowledge a less qualified sympathy toward Nietzsche's comments on tragedy, though they do need to be organized a bit to bring out their relevance to both ancient and modern literature. If Hegel emphasized the endurance of heroic integrity, Nietzsche emphasized the dissolution of integrity. If Hegel's theory is particularly applicable to the narrative structure of tragic works, Nietzsche's theory is most relevant to symbolic transformations, changes visualized in images generated by classical playwrights like Aeschylus and Seneca, as well as by modern authors like Strindberg and (in nondramatic tragedy) Kafka.

Plato might seem to be unhelpful because of his hostility to poetic methods, yet he conceived an essential distinction. Poets, he wrote early in the *Republic,* can devise versions of either elevated or debased manhood: he detested the latter, but we find a dual potential to be at the heart of tragedy, the double-edged (ambiguous) rhetoric that he distrusted being a suitable conveyance for a double-edged standard of excellence. We may compare Platonic (*un*ambiguous) rhetoric in Milton's *Samson Agonistes* with the more complex speech constructions in *King Lear.*

I am reaching for unity, trying to reconcile the ethical insights presented by three major philosophers with each other and with the technical resources displayed in notable examples of the tragic form—an ambitious enterprise! As a guide for further reading, I append two reference lists, one on the theory of tragedy in the twentieth century, the other on the attitudes of Plato and Aristotle toward the art of literature.

Tragic literature and theories explaining it have intrigued me for nearly half a century. Here are the preliminary studies, aside from my dissertation in 1959, in the order they will be developed:

"The Unrecognized Influence of Hegel's Theory of Tragedy." *Journal of Aesthetics and Art Criticism* 28 (1969): 91–97.

"The Critique of the Male Stereotype in Greek Tragedy." *Soundings* 68 (1985): 106–30.

"The Conservative Temper in Greek Tragedy." *Virginia Quarterly Review* 49 (1973): 38–45.

"The Critique of the Female Stereotype in Greek Tragedy." *Soundings* 71 (1988): 701–18.

"Light and Darkness Imagery in Aeschylus and Seneca." *Athena* (University of Athens) 76 (1977): 267–78.

"Strindberg's Nietzschean Dream Play." *Mosaic* 12 (1978–): 119–29.

"A Key to the Door Image in 'The Metamorphosis'." *Modern Fiction Studies* 17 (1971): 37–42.

"Plato and the *Poetics.*" *Philological Quarterly* 50 (1971): 533–42.

"The Rhetorical Style of *Samson Agonistes.*" *Modern Philology* 62 (1965): 296–301.

"Rhetorical Addition in *King Lear.*" *Language and Style* 20 (1987): 16–29, 171–84.

"A Check List on the Theory of Tragedy, 1900–1970." *Bulletin of the New York Public Library* 77 (1974): 407–17.

I am grateful to the journal editors for welcoming ideas that have been revised and unified here. My thanks also to Professor Saul Levin, State University of New York at Binghamton, for the sharp perception, kindness, and good humor he has extended through the years.

The publishers of the following works have generously granted permission for extensive quotation:

David Grene and Richmond Lattimore, eds., *The Complete Greek Tragedies*, 4 vols. (Chicago: University of Chicago Press, 1959).

William Shakespeare, *The Complete Pelican Shakespeare*, gen. ed. Alfred Harbage (Baltimore: Penguin, 1974).

G. W. F. Hegel, *Aesthetics: Lectures on Fine Art*, 2 vols. (Oxford: Clarendon Press, 1975).

The Treason of Stereotypes

I
Hegel's Theory

How can we describe the contest of tragedy? Aristotle had been the traditional guide until Hegel became the master of tragic theory for a hundred years. Hegel's *Aesthetics* influenced most debates after its publication in 1835. For example, at the beginning of the twentieth century, A. C. Bradley, the best-known disciple writing in English, erected his famous study of Shakespeare on a Hegelian foundation,[1] and in 1945 Kenneth Burke, to name another notable follower, attributed his alliterative formula, "Purpose, Passion, and Perception," to "the Hegelian dialectic."[2] Nowadays such formulas are considered obsolete. "There was a time when it would have been essential to discuss Hegel," D. D. Raphael observed in 1960, "but I think there is no need now."[3] While a few supporters in Britain and the United States maintained their allegiance,[4] they were outnumbered by critics and theorists who disparaged Hegel's interpretation of literature, or ignored it, or else borrowed liberally from it without recognizing their source. Occasionally an author employed Hegel's terminology in order to dismiss it vehemently.[5] Yet to deny the relevance of this comprehensive interpretation would be to waste an invaluable resource. Can we reevaluate the great evaluator? Students of tragedy faced with the intricate arguments of original thinkers must perform a juggling act of their own.

Hegel commented on drama and the other arts in an exhaustive series of lectures delivered from 1820 to 1829 and published after his death in 1831. His key explanation distinguishes between subjectivity and objectivity in literature. *Subjective* refers to the ardent pursuit of gratification and authority by unique individuals. In contrast, the term *objective* or *substantive* denotes "absolute spirit," the universal and enduring content of family, national, and religious principles.[6] Such principles, which are more than formal rules governing relations within social organizations, embody a sacred impulse that creates and justifies them. They serve as the highest goals of "idiosyncratic" personal life; in the most serious drama, intense subjectivity forgoes its self-centeredness, expands its awareness, and strives to realize vital truths. The eternal wisdom informing all moral and legal abstractions may express itself concretely through individual conscience and collective altruism, controlling "the contingent affairs of worldly existence." "Art belongs to the same province as religion and philosophy" (*Aesthetics* 1: 94). "In general terms, we may say that the proper theme of the original type of tragedy is the Divine . . . made real in the world" (2: 1195).

Tragic theater exhibits characters whose personalities intrigue us but who make claims that go beyond their private desires and "unique" traits. According to Hegel, their animal energies fuel a drive to attain both renown and rationality through the medium of substantive codes: "The true content of the tragic action is provided, so far as concerns the *aims* adopted by the tragic characters, by the range of the substantive and independently justified powers that influence the human will: family love between husband and wife, parents and children, brothers and sisters; political life also, the patriotism of the citizens, the will of the ruler; and religion" (2: 1194). Hegel concedes that some legendary tales featured rugged heroes like Heracles, who showed "individuality as a law to itself," but such laws were not "genuine" since they only served male vanity. Those early heroes lived without reference to civilized values dictated by social institutions (1: 185–89). In tragedy, Hegel insists, a protagonist enjoys the opportunities presented by ethical obligation.

To mobilize the greatest possible force, tragic characters center their passions upon a narrow front, "inseparably identifying themselves with some single particular aspect of those solid interests" (2: 1195). They inevitably take their "particular" grasp of truth for the whole, and so oppose those trying to fulfill other "interests" (other standards sanctified by clan, community, or church). Hegel sees their collision as the central action—a duel between conflicting defenders of justice, each one-sided in outlook (ethically nearsighted) but wholly virtuous: "The original essence of tragedy consists then in the fact that within such a conflict each of the opposed sides, if taken by itself, has *justification;* while each can establish the true and positive content of its own aim and character only by denying and infringing the equally justified power of the other" (2: 1196). Moral commitment provides the dramatic precondition; conflict of commitments, the dramatic event.

Eventually this spiritual division gives way to reunification, or reconciliation. When standpoints compete they are in actuality attesting to a comprehensive reality that encompasses them both but manifests itself through their incomplete assertions and antagonism:

> However justified the tragic character and his aim, however necessary the tragic collision, the third thing required is the tragic resolution of this conflict. By this means eternal justice is exercised on individuals and their aims in the sense that it restores the substance and unity of ethical life with the downfall of the individual who has disturbed its peace....
>
> The true development of the action consists solely in the cancellation of conflicts *as conflicts*, in the reconciliation of the powers animating action which struggled to destroy one another in their mutual conflict. Only in that case does finality lie not in misfortune and suffering but in the satisfaction of the spirit, because only with such a conclusion can the necessity for what happens to the individuals appear as absolute rationality, and only then can our hearts be morally at peace: shattered by the fate of the heroes but reconciled fundamentally. Only by adherence to this view can Greek tragedy be understood. (2: 1197, 1215)

Tragedy cancels the one-sidedness, or exclusiveness, of values, not the values themselves; the antagonists locate for the spectator the complementary poles of a total structure of inferred meaning, just as polar landmarks locate the boundaries of a sphere.

Hegel's theory, presenting tragedy as more than a jungle of self-will and revenge, seems wonderfully plausible, but critics have lost patience with its bias. Contrary to the inclination of many twentieth-century English and American commentators, not to mention nineteenth-century German rebels like Nietzsche, Hegel attaches the highest importance to an impersonal holy "power." His insistence on definitive rationality, these authors complain, glosses over the impact of anarchy and ambiguity, mutability and contingency. "His solution," Sidney Hook writes, "attempts to console man with a dialectical proof that agony and defeat are not really evils but necessary elements in the goodness of the whole. The position is essentially religious."[7] Hegel disregards, as Bradley put it, the individual's "noble endurance of pain."[8]

If the subordination of suffering individuals to objective order has put off English-speaking critics, starting with Bradley, the demotion of Shakespeare has infuriated them. Discussing the history of tragedy, Hegel finds his conception nicely executed by the Athenian dramatists (with some qualification concerning Euripides), but not as well by dramatists during and after the Renaissance. "What principally counts in Greek drama, whether tragedy or comedy," he states,

> is the universal and essential element ["substantive content"] in the aim which the characters are realizing. . . . Therefore neither the various descriptions of the human heart and personal character nor particular complications and intrigues can find their place completely in Greek drama; nor does the interest turn on the fate of individuals. Sympathy is claimed above all not for these particular and personal matters but simply for the battle between the essential powers that rule human life and between the gods that dominate the human heart, and for this battle's outcome. (2: 1206)

Characters in "modern" (postmedieval) literature, though they might sometimes possess "a noble will and deep soul," remain dedicated to self-indulgence, bound by "capriciousness and contingency," their notion of honor lacking ethical insight: "For honour's fight for personal independence is not bravery defending the common weal and the call of justice in the same, or of rectitude in the sphere of private life; on the contrary, [their] honour's struggle is only for the recognition and the abstract inviolability of the individual person. . . . Everything drawn into this sphere proves to be inherently dissoluble owing to the shape and standing given to it by its subjective opinion, mood, and originality" (1: 553, 595). The "romantic" character opts for unrestricted self-expression even if he must enact terrible crimes to achieve it, and when duties like family loyalty or patriotism do attract him they serve only to enhance his unfettered personality. In Shakespeare's plays "we have individuals before us resting independently on themselves alone, with particular ends which are their own, prescribed by their individuality alone, and which they now set themselves to execute with the unshakable logic of passion, without any accompanying reflection or general principle, solely for their own satisfaction" (1: 577–78). Shakespeare plumbed the depths of "idiosyncrasy" in brilliant amoral portraits that lack ultimate authority. They leave the spectator unsettled, not pacified by any intimation of "eternal justice" and the "inner rationality of its sway" (2: 1230).[9]

To correct the bias in these lines, and to address the objections raised by Hegel's critics, we can modify this invaluable but lopsided theory. While it would have been a logical impossibility for Hegel, we may see ethical antagonism occurring within the subjective sphere, discordant values originating in and tearing apart an ancient program combining a desire for "recognition" with a *principle* of individual "inviolability" or "personal independence." The Athenian playwrights no less than Shakespeare examine in their plays an undying thrust toward glorious personal achievement blessed by public approval, a problematic standard of honor that brings together an ideal of ego elevation and an ideal of social or religious accommodation.

A few characters are able to carry off a successful merger, but tragic protagonists usually come to grief when their two intentions create internal—not only social—disharmony. They fail to integrate traditional rules encouraging self-promotion with traditional rules dictating accord with their peers, leaders, and dependents. The passionate individual may indeed act blindly, but he can be blinded by principle, not guided by it, misled by an excess rather than an absence of idealism. Greek as well as later dramatists conceived the psychological arena as a crucial location for value conflict, subject to the same substantive self-division Hegel locates in the larger arena of "political life" or "family love" or "religion." Tragic drama, of course, may involve feuds between competing social factions, each sustaining an undisturbed allegiance to some partisan faith. But, with some exceptions, tragedy focuses on collisions between disparate orientations toward honor manifested by one individual committed to a self-contradictory moral scheme.

This internal duel (or dualism), furthermore, is not resolved rationally. In Hegel's view, an incomplete value proves its validity by engaging with another incomplete value; since justice can be claimed by both sides, Hegel supposed that the battle between them posited an ethical totality from which each drew sustenance. But if dramatic conflict announces the disunity of a single code of masculine achievement, then mutual mutilation by opposing principles will more likely be the outcome than mutual validation. Psychological and social discord lead not only to value *collision* but also to value *collapse*, signaled by disenchantment, alienation, and criminality—symptoms experienced by characters with a defective, not unified, regimen.

Along with many other European scholars of his time, Hegel favored classical drama because he did not perceive in it the turbulence[10] induced by self-centered characters who, under the stress of challenge, forfeit or contaminate their social viability. He assumed that Greek tragic figures acted with uncompromised honesty and good faith. But in fact their immoderate "indulgence" in self-pity, fear, and anger (to use Aristotle's terms), warps their loyalties and endangers all parties on the stage. Classical tragedy, in common with Shakespearean tragedy, envisioned a nightmarish divorce, not a divine marriage, between propriety and pride, the pride of aggressive egos vying for the unconditional confirmation called for by their rationale but at the same time refuting the political or religious criteria necessary for that confirmation. If Hegel denied "substantive content" to Shakespearean drama, which in fact *does* temper a drive toward self-glorification with "objective" codes aiming to integrate the outstanding individual with his society, he also refused to admit the destabilizing effect of the "abstract inviolability of the individual" in Homeric epic and Athenian drama. Believing, with good reason, that equity could never rest upon such an unsteady foundation, he overstated the ethical consistency of the earlier theater and underestimated it in the later.

Hegel found backing even in the *Poetics* for his doctrine on the "might of the ethical order, . . . that eternal and inviolable something" (2: 1198). But Aristotle did not rise to such heights, preferring instead to sketch the artistic aims and plot mechanics involved in producing a change from good to bad fortune. For the audience, Greek or English, theatrical turmoil was probably ameliorated less by stoic reassurance concerning some overriding spiritual harmony than by emotional discharge, as Aristotle suggested.[11] Fascinated by "that eternal something"— spiritual well-being and wholeness—Hegel misjudged the power of *negation,* the corrosive *nothing.* He misjudged the destructive capability of the vulnerable and volcanic, honor-loving and honor-killing, self-justifying and self-nullifying *I,* and so described neither the Athenian nor the Shakespearean protagonist with complete accuracy.

And yet his thought lives! The narrative format in which he cast tragic action can be recast to accommodate the fluctuations of degradation and resurgence. His dogma on the noble stance and the collision of laws needs to be modified, but it has contributed an indispensable vocabulary, as this study may show. Assertions delivered by passionate defenders of high principle, Hegel said, are inevitably countered by contrary assertions; all idealistic acts, therefore, are ironic, and in this he was correct. The most skilled dramatists pinpointed a strange reality: the defending champion and his opponent come from the same moral source. And there is an even deeper irony: that source is less than the sum of its parts! A defaulting tragic figure defeats pride in the name of pride, victim of a fatal discrepancy inherent in the noble stereotype. Tragedy dramatizes a fall from certainty, a loss of "solidness," and to understand that symbolic event we can profit by adapting Hegel's concept so as to describe an inconsistency that split in half a foundation stone of Western secular belief—the male model.

2
The Male Model

Perfection Can Be Unreliable!

The Athenian empire in the fifth century B.C. was menaced by political and military issues severe enough to inhibit its affair with democracy and encourage a nostalgic yearning for the stereotypical strongman, immune to weakness, impervious to corruption, competent to meet every danger to the state. Tragedy exposed the risk in that yearning. We may never know exactly how far politics motivated Aeschylus, Sophocles, and Euripides, but we can see how skeptical they were regarding the doctrine that places every hope in one brilliant commander. We can see their skepticism if we put aside the persistent Hegelian proposition that they wrote to praise famous men as examples of overenthusiastic but commendable and enlightened conduct. No, on the contrary, the tragedians conceived the masculine model they dealt with to be functionally deficient. Differing only in their degree of cynicism, they concluded that the impressive stereotype Athens had inherited from legend and Homer's epics was in their contemporary perspective untenable for individuals and catastrophic for communities.[1]

The stereotype of manhood evaluated by the playwrights embodied self-contradiction when the aristocratic protocol mandating personal achievement crashed headlong into a wider social policy mandating fraternal conformity. Belonging to an elite male superclass, obeyed by allies and kinsmen, deferred to by women, commoners, slaves, and foreigners, and deferring only to higher authority or to gods or to no one, some illustrious figures drawn from mythology presumed that they were superior to other nobles. Lineage and upbringing, possessions and estate, family and followers verified their high caste and justified their self-esteem; courageous confrontation with enemies elevated them still further, publicly demonstrating perfection of body, mind, emotion, and will. They aspired to combine physical strength, skill, and endurance with an ability to think coolly, speak commandingly, and act consistently under stress—the highest standards of bravery, constancy, and self-reliance.[2]

And they demanded respect for their prowess: their aim, as Hegel saw, was usually moral preeminence rather than military conquest, recognition rather than domination, the playing field their own country more often than a foreign city. These glory-hunting nobles, although they were thoroughgoing egoists publicizing self-confidence as their prime attribute, revealed a compulsive, sometimes pathetic craving for favorable peer appraisal—high reputation—preferring to die for a good name if forced to live without it. Social reception, the shadow cast by their accomplishments, could magnify or shrink their worth: the perception of their matchless quality by all classes was as important as its attainment, and they assumed that the two roads to fulfillment were indivisible.

In Euripides' *Hecuba*, Odysseus explains this goal:

> There is a principle at stake
> and one, moreover, in whose neglect or breach
> governments have fallen and cities come to grief,
> because their bravest, their most exceptional men,
> received no greater honor than the common run.
>
> (trans. William Arrowsmith, *CGT* 3: 307–9)

Imperishable respect, Odysseus continues, ought not be diminished even by death:

> Tell me, what conduct could be worse
> than to give your friend a lifetime of honor and respect
> but neglect him when he dies?
> ... honor in the grave
> has eternity to run.
>
> (311–12, 319–20)

Unfortunately, the intense drive for recognition brought out their self-centered competitiveness in extreme measure and perverted their need for accommodation. Aeschylus describes soldiers in *Seven against Thebes*:

> Never a word of pity was in their mouths.
> Their spirits were hard as iron and ...
> war looked through their lion-eyes.
>
> (trans. David Grene, *CGT* I: lines 51–53)

"Some fury put it in their hearts ... / to itch for power," Ismene says of her brothers in *Oedipus at Colonus*, "for seizure of prerogative and throne"

(371–73). This aggressiveness turned gifted men into ruthless, shortsighted generals or kings who dignified the "itch" for special status with the rules of revenge or martial engagement. They were driven by an insatiable appetite for precedence among other willful contestants also asserting precedence. The need for support in such an enterprise should have urged them to cooperate with their peers, but an uncontrollable ambition to *compel* respect for their considerable talents tended to close down rational policies and make adversaries out of friends.

They were always, therefore, vulnerable to judgment by others. A prestigious individual could be disgraced at any moment, a possibility that bred excruciating insecurity among contentious personalities unable to abide any abridgment of "prerogative." The foremost competitors went to outrageous extremes to solidify a reputation for excellence that would never be questioned or qualified. Yet neglect or humiliation was inevitable in a game played by enhancing one's status and curtailing that of one's fellows; injustice viewed as improper evaluation or insufficient support came to be the trigger of tragic action. As Hegel pointed out, certain self-reliant mythological heroes like Heracles predated the concept of mutual dependence and civic feuds, but most protagonists in tragedy (and Homer's Achilles) exhibit a painful sensitivity to real or imagined insults. Sometimes, during their disputes over the privileges of rank, the fear of public devaluation served as a check on pride. "When a man is moved by wholesome fear and shame," Menelaus announces in Sophocles' *Ajax*, "you may know that combination makes for safety [for the state]" (trans. John Moore, *CGT* 2: 1079–80). More often, an intolerance of restriction, subordination, or criticism impelled them to defend fiercely their inflated sense of stature. Confirmation was their need, but deference was not their habit.[3]

They would go to any length to avenge an injury, and that was suicidal. "You will tear your heart out in remorse for having treated the best man in the expedition with contempt," Achilles tells his colleagues in the *Iliad*, the bible of protocol in wartime; "my blood boils when I think of what happened, and the vile way in which Atreides treated me in public, like some disreputable outcast" (Rieu 29, 178). In tragedy as in this epic, hypersensitive nobles responded to offense by lashing out at their leaders, peers, or family members, which did irreparable damage to their "public" image, contrary to what they had intended. At those times, their tough constancy and limitless self-regard worked against their pressing desire for endorsement; the double commitment to brilliant accomplishment and brilliant reputation fell apart, the break causing loss of control, paralysis of thought, and disillusion.

Their emotional gymnastics exaggerated their victimization: immense self-pity and fear arose from shame or even the possibility of humiliation, at the same time that their outrage absurdly compelled them to renew their claim to eminence. Distress frustrated the ambition to realize a praiseworthy vision of manhood, pushed them into revenge, suicide, or insanity, turned champions into killers, and threw their homeland into chaos, jeopardizing any hope of reinstatement and terminating the Hegelian union of passion with community-directed principle. They were terribly punished—or they punished themselves terribly—for following the injunction to be extraordinary; self-esteem, their strength, became the agency for their fall from favor. The tragic moment arrived when the model universally acclaimed to be the best—the individual expected to mesh an ideal of narcissism with one of communal leadership—ended as the worst, the first ideal canceling the second.

What part did divinity play in this deadly masculine game? Although Athenian drama generally concentrates on its human characters, the gods often acted as referees and coaches or else as players, themselves competing in the contest for respect. As mediators, they occasionally tried to ease the severe stress built up by heroic adversaries. But as players they were prone to the same rash and contradictory behavior that typified the human participants, who commonly blamed their transgressions on the influence of these anthropomorphic deities. If anything, gods sometimes magnified such behavior and presented an even more unrestrained image of self-will. Whether supernatural intervention ameliorated or aggravated the outcome, a tragic division of values, an internalized version of Hegel's factional warfare, remained the central issue.

The unphilosophical activists of Athenian tragedy made few reasonable comments about their dilemma. Unphilosophical?[4] Yes—their unawareness was remarkable. Despite their obvious, often insane, exaggerations, they rarely admitted to inconsistency or complicity in their defeat, staunchly upholding a godlike innocence with the single-mindedness that excited Hegel, who took at face value (as it were) their justifications. Hegel's sympathy was understandable: Athenian protagonists do not lack admirers on or off the stage because they defend their positions with their lives, an impressive nonintellectual argument. Their fanaticism is awesome, and it has continued to enchant us in its many reincarnations down through the centuries. However mixed the response might be among their peers, they compel *our* respect as spectators for their implacable determination to carry out magnificent if contradictory commandments.

Yet our response is mixed too, for they elicit our horror at the suffering they inflict as well as our sympathy for the suffering they endure. An audience can be moved to both pity and impatience by the sight of such superlative quality coming to so catastrophic an end. Tragedy exploits this contrast between great expectation and pitiful, fearful conclusion, between inspiring motives and irrational conduct. In their critique of the stereotypical male, the Greek dramatists evoked wonder at his daring, sorrow for his agony, and terror at his intemperance.

Pride and Propriety, Contingency and Security

The pressure to conform to the dictates, evaluations, and needs of others, pressure exerted by gods, rulers, peers, and dependents and then transformed into shame as an inward control, is the enemy of pride. In tragic drama, the rivalry for precedence among heroic adversaries stands out as the melodramatic focus, but the influence of collective norms of justice pervades all such confrontations. Because the Athenian chorus articulates those conservative norms clearly and at great length, Hegel adored it. Cautious and pious, it seemed to him to have incorporated the spiritual "substance" sought by the rivals, "the one and undivided consciousness of the Divine" (*Aesthetics* 2: 1210). The chorus achieved, he said, "the equilibrium of a stable life secure against the fearful collisions to which the energies of individuals in their opposing actions must lead" (2: 1211).

Now, Hegel was right in assigning to the choruses in Athenian tragedy a single viewpoint celebrating stability. Different as they may be in composition and activity, they are united as they express that common viewpoint through song, speech, and dance: the kind of security they favor makes an obvious contrast with the self-glorification favored by the protagonist. But it too remains an almost unreachable destination. Far from having realized immunity to contingency, they must solicit (and advise others to solicit) protection from or redress for the shocks delivered by nature, bad luck, angry deities, and self-seeking aristocrats. "Man's fate sets a true / course," the elders declare in Aeschylus' *Agamemnon*, "yet may strike upon / the blind and sudden reefs of disaster" (trans. Richmond Lattimore, *CGT* 1: 1005–7). Rarely blessed with Olympian ("Divine") insight or might, they expound a style of conduct (we may label it "choric") that people of every class hope will enable them to cope with disaster, yet is as limited and fallible as the protagonist's (customarily labeled "heroic").

If some aristocrats respond to the threat of mutability with rigid protests, the choruses without exception respond by recommending patience, humility, adaptation, and obedience to law. If the rash nobleman covets unrestricted freedom to extend his exceptional abilities, the wise chorus member—whether noble, common, or immortal—counsels practical, safe use of finite abilities. The first strives for omnipotence, the second pursues political correctness, expedience, moderation, unanimity with those equal in rank, and submission to those superior. One conceives justice as success in achieving imperishable celebrity or revenge for dishonor; the other, as success in achieving group survival through social and religious accommodation. While the elitist may insist on being the sole judge of his rewards, the chorus believes that judgment should be conditioned by communal interests. Sane men, the chorus maintains, will yield to or placate greater force, however arbitrary. Even the Furies in *The Eumenides* of Aeschylus and the disciples of Dionysus in *The Bacchae* of Euripides—two choric groups that do not strike a modern audience as noticeably temperate—argue for modesty in human affairs, consideration for the welfare of the whole society, and reverence toward divinity.

That dogma, however, though eminently reasonable, was not sufficient in times of crisis: the contrasting stereotypes depended upon each other. "Humble men without their princes / Are a frail prop for a fortress," the chorus of sailors says in *Ajax;* "They / Should be dependent upon the great, / And the great be upheld by lesser ones" (158–61). Yet balance is difficult to attain. Ajax finds it impossible, and after his suicide the chorus can only repeat to his enemies and allies the barren hope shared by other choruses: "I wish you both might learn a moderate mind!" The shifts of chance, which can annul every accomplishment, are compounded rather than alleviated by erratic "princes" who in their stampede to enforce their reputations and get back at foes neglect their obligation to "lesser ones." Their tenacity may be laudable, but the choruses would prefer them, for the benefit of all, to submit to higher rank, city laws, cultural traditions, and divine directives. Choric types do not ask noblemen to give up their competitive behavior, just to curb its wild excesses in order to take the strain off the bond that links their fortunes in a very wobbly class hierarchy.

In general, choric personalities need help to guarantee public order because of their inferior capabilities or secondary dramatic roles. Over half of the thirty-four Athenian choruses are composed of females with small standing—young women, servants, captives, refugees, and aliens. Elderly male citizens, whose age rather than gender signals their subordinate place, make up the next most frequent membership, supplemented by sailors, soldiers, and huntsmen, among others. These choruses must rely on divine agencies or on the heavyweights governing their kingdoms to deal with war and civic disturbance. And choric *gods,* like their human counterparts, also appeal to dominant personalities (stronger gods) for aid in stabilizing social order.

The choruses are joined in their conservative lifestyle by secondary characters—common people (workers, messengers, slaves), wisdom figures (seers, or kings, officials, and gods performing as counselors), and aristocrats whose age, sex, or circumstance has curtailed their influence. These characters are particularly vocal in the plays of Euripides. "The ways of life that are most fanatical," the nurse states in *Hippolytus*, "trip us up more, they say, than bring us joy" (trans. David Grene, *CGT* 3: 261–62). The nurse in *Medea* summarizes a guideline evident in every Athenian tragedy:

> How much better to have been accustomed
> To live on equal terms with one's neighbors.
> *I* would like to be safe and grow old in a
> Humble way. What is moderate sounds best,
> Also in practice *is* best for everyone.
> Greatness brings no profit to people.
>
> (trans. Rex Warner, *CGT* 3: 123–28)

As the helpless heroine exclaims in *Iphigenia in Aulis*, "It is better that we live ever so / Miserably than die in glory" (trans. Charles R. Walker, *CGT* 4: 1251–52). Heroic Heracles in Euripides' *Alcestis* scoffs at this philosophy—the conviction that "life is not really life but a catastrophe" (trans. Richmond Lattimore, *CGT* 3: 802). Nevertheless, most individuals too old, battered, friendless, subservient, or smart to take an aggressive part in the action consider the highest virtues to be patience and reverence. Leery of their world's unpleasant changes or untrustworthy leaders, choric personalities offer a glamorless but safer alternative to great expectations.

The founders of tragedy, then, dramatized the deadly consequences engendered by obstinate males seeking "greatness" in a community seeking order. Fixed upon self-justification, the man of honor cannot hear the ever-present refrain on safety first. But when he disregards social security—self-control and awareness of his dependence—he disregards a value inescapably operating upon his moral makeup. He dismisses at his peril a principle that he supposedly shares with the chorus and choric characters—the principle of responsibility, the obligation to establish appropriate precedence through accurate, not headstrong, judgment. Overcome by dreams of immovable self-sufficiency and yet sensitive to peer insult and group disapproval, oblivious of this incongruity and unable to receive pedestrian advice on caution and expedience, he accentuates his belligerence and diminishes his accountability. Yet he requires both to succeed as a symbol of manhood. He needs to be indomitable and deferential, relentless and well liked!

Hegel (who made discussions like this possible) was correct about the presence of a social contract in tragedy, but wrong in finding Athenian protagonists capable of honoring it, wrong in downgrading their exaltation of self. He did not notice the split of equally essential functions not only outside but also within tragic figures, whether they are sporadically aware of the inconsistency, as in Shakespearean tragedy at its best, or generally unaware, as in most Athenian tragedy. Prizing constancy among individuals at peace with some monolithic loyalty, Hegel could not imagine Greek characters repressing "social" goals or becoming deranged by ethical and emotional schism. Self-contradiction was no more admissible than self-worship: "For weakness in action consists only in a cleavage between the individual and his object, in which case character, will, and aim do not appear as having grown into an absolute unity. . . . From this swithering the Greek plastic figures are exempt; for them the bond between the subject and what he wills as his object remains indissoluble" (2: 1214).

Hegel overlooked the fact that "Greek figures" always undercut their jealously defended public standing: they could not abide negative judgment even though, according to the unwritten contract that defined them, they had to. The unsocialized Heraclean impetus persisted in fifth-century literature (and probably in politics too) alongside a contrary drive to integrate the strengths of all social levels, resulting in incompatible imperatives that unbalanced reputation-conscious but uncompromising aristocrats, neutralized their leadership, and developed far more theatrical energy than the duel between single-minded partisans proposed by Hegel. Casting aside internal as well as external restraints, motivated by self-centered ambitions even when courageously speaking out for a murdered father, daughter, or brother, and burying their intelligence beneath the obsession to be above reproach, heroic contenders embarked upon desperate, self-defeating maneuvers to forward their drive for priority—ego licensed to act as a god rejecting ego obligated to act as a subordinate.

Despite loss of face, they refused to accept what they felt were intrusions upon their right to realize a divine potential, and in doing so they sacrificed the "absolute unity" that should have ensured their triumph. In Hegel's theory, their motives were steered coherently by public purpose; in dramatic practice their uncoordinated intentions changed purposeful, socially bonded superstars into misfits, outcasts, and criminals. Such characters might still command the adoration of many citizens, but their struggle to redress insult or resist subordination turned every dispute into an encounter with annihilation. Vicious competitiveness made them incapable of constructive response, led them to pervert *both* parts of their value system, and forced them to widen beyond conciliation the divergence between their equally honorable demands for personal "inviolability" and social sanction.

There was no "resolution of the contradiction," no implied synthesis of duty to self and duty to authority. And there were no winners because for an Athenian audience the well-being of their state closely followed the integrity of its most distinguished citizens. Could the breakdown of a venerable concept that called for the popular acclamation of individual excellence possibly have been reassuring to an evolving democracy? Skepticism regarding the heroic standard provided cold comfort to choric types. Taking a broad view, Hegel maintained that an "obliteration of the opposition" between the whole truth and partial truths ensured a satisfying release from the spectator's sense of incompleteness, a happy introduction to the "supreme power over individual gods and men. . . . All distress and every misfortune has vanished, the subject is reconciled with the world, satisfied in it, and every opposition and contradiction is resolved" (1: 97). What the spectator usually sees onstage, however, is a shambles, the wreckage of both heroic and choric intentions, neither one viable without or compatible with the other.

Prometheus

Of the legendary characters brought to the stage during the century in which tragedy flourished in Athens, Aeschylus' Prometheus may seem to be the least likely candidate to illustrate the impotence of independence. He has so often been *praised* for his independence. As an immortal, not merely a godlike mortal, he portrays to many readers Hegel's "absolute unity," noble aspiration raised to a supernatural level—sublime courage, endurance, charity, loyalty, ethical purity. He is unselfish, having defied Zeus to rescue a backward species, conferring upon it life, hope, reason, fire, and the civilizing crafts. He stands out especially for his acuity: gifted with foreknowledge, he seems to understand his own constant nature, his adversarial relations in the past, present, and future, the upshot of his deeds. Not even Zeus knows all *that!*

And we can judge him favorably by his friends and enemies. Those who befriend him—Hephaestus, Oceanos and his daughters—are humane (so to speak), while his enemies—an ungrateful tyrant and some muscular lackeys—sound decidedly inhumane. In a word, his kindness to man and his pain, the punishment for his defiance of that tyrant, heighten our indignation and our empathy. Does this archetype of self-sacrifice and self-possession conform to the image of one incapacitated by inconsistency? Surely not.[5]

Yet the giant-sized temperament Aeschylus sculpted in *Prometheus Bound* is problematic as well as awesome, two-sided rather than one-track, endangered by its own stamina, the righteous resolve Hegel formulated as a universal solvent. Prometheus measures on a grand scale the might and the infirmity of willfulness exerted in the name of principle but centered on vanity. He registers gigantic egocentrism even when describing his generosity to humans, his speech revolving around himself: "I suffer," "I know," "I dared," "it was I and none other," "why should I fear," and so forth (trans. David Grene, *CGT* 1). "Marvel," he says, "at the crafts and resources I contrived." He can nurture his self-esteem by threatening revenge against Zeus, who will be challenged by a usurper identifiable only by Prometheus ("I alone know it and how"), but his imprisonment galls him since it closes down his exhibition of superlative talent for "thirteen generations." Worse than the torture and physical constraints, he has been fired as adviser to the king of gods, his will "bound" and his status devalued: "my enemies can laugh at what I suffer." Humiliation has polarized his need for public (divine) "recognition" and his need for self-respect.

As an immortal, Prometheus can afford to wait for deliverance; in the meantime, his angry fixation upon the injustice dealt him, along with huge self-pity, degrades his formidable competence. "My heart is eaten away when I am aware of myself, when I see myself insulted as I am," he complains, sounding like Homer's Achilles. His scorn of administrative interference, which may seem inspirational, has left him immobilized, pouting over his ignominy on a rock in the wilderness. Pursuing "some boundless, superhuman dream" (Euripides' words in *The Bacchae*), he has disqualified himself (for thirteen generations) from participation in the family of gods. "You are by nature better at advising others," a choric ally warns, "than yourself."

In contrast to a protagonist who becomes the victim of his own imperious "temper," Clytemnestra, an equally self-willed spirit re-created by Aeschylus, deals more constructively with a tyrannical opponent in the first part of the *Oresteia*. The contrast may help us recognize that the rigidity of Prometheus perpetuates his loss of prerogative. Aeschylus overturns gender roles in each play: he who is supposed to be strong turns out to be ineffective; she who is supposed to be weak turns out to be (in *Agamemnon*, at least) omnipotent. Where Prometheus withdraws into self-pity and denunciation, which only deepen disapproval by social authority, Clytemnestra summons a variety of resources—guile and ingenuity as well as force of will and indignation—to coerce and outwit her enemy, to confront her townsfolk without shame, and to enforce their acceptance. The "manlike" determination of each protagonist never wavers, but Clytemnestra does not wallow helplessly in emotion. Prometheus, on the other hand, disempowers himself with inflexible, mindless defiance: the patron of foreknowledge has stopped thinking. In *Agamemnon*, Aeschylus questions the conventional assumption of feminine frailty; in *Prometheus Bound*, he questions the utility of conventional masculine combativeness.

The reversals are temporary, of course, since each trilogy follows through with a second turnabout that normalizes our expectations. Clytemnestra will be assassinated by a revenging son dedicated to restoring male supremacy, and Prometheus (as best as can be surmised from fragments of the lost plays) is probably reinstated by Zeus.[6] Long before the reassuring outcome of the *Prometheia*, however, its author brings a skeptical viewpoint to his version of self-indulgent (Hegel's term), self-disabled masculinity. Prometheus sustains a manly bearing ("let it not cross your mind that I will turn / womanish-minded from my fixed decision") that reinforces his towering reputation among some observers but brings on trouble with others. Defiance prevents conciliation and deprives this heroic personality of an essential prop; his inability to cope constructively with negative judgment leads to dysfunction and immobility.

Io, another distressed target of a deity's displeasure, echoes his frustration, emotional indulgence, and helplessness. So does Cassandra in the *Oresteia*, who bears a striking resemblance to Prometheus in this respect. Both are victims of a god's revenge (like Io) and captives of domineering males. Both are endowed with prophetic vision that cannot forestall their incarceration; both endure their captors' taunts silently after their entrance, then protest against inequity in futile exclamations of anger and pain; and both find communication difficult with a chorus of well-wishers urging compliance. Eventually Prometheus will regain greater potency, and even at present his fortitude seems unconquerable, but at the same time his ignominious plight is uncomfortably similar to Cassandra's. This is not to deny the appeal of his pathos and self-vindication, yet admirable attributes can cause calamity. Dramatized suffering may be interpreted as pointless self-gratification; unflinching courage as immature "obstinacy"; resistence to oppression as rabid posturing; and dauntless self-reliance as antisocial withdrawal. It is true that adaptability can go only so far before compromising both honesty and usefulness, but the same also holds true for its opposite.

The friends of Prometheus refer explicitly to the malady of manliness, this impalement upon a "fixed" demand for unrestricted self-determination. In typical choric style, the minor female deities criticize "a mind that bends not":

> Leave your obstinacy and seek
> a wise good counsel. Hearken to [Zeus]. Shame
> it were for one so wise to fall in error. (1036–38)

Hephaestus too condemns a fanatic "disposition," and so does Oceanos, who speaks with knowledge of power:

> My poor friend, give up
> this angry mood of yours and look for means
> of getting yourself free of trouble. Maybe
> what I say seems to you both old and commonplace;
> but this is what you pay, Prometheus, for
> that tongue of yours which talked so high and haughty:
> you are not yet humble, still you do not yield
> to your misfortunes. (316–23)

And opponents like Hermes ("obstinacy standing alone is the weakest of all things") are harsher still.

We do not have to take all this choric censure as the final word: while extremism may produce psychological trauma and political stalemate, Prometheus struggles valiantly for poise and he makes a positive impression on his censorious allies. He elicits the respect of those who criticize him while provoking their dismay; the cautious chorus even decides to join him in his resistance. His giant-sized vanity promotes a favorable reception within a segment of his community, but it prevents the cooperation with authority necessary to satisfy that vanity—a paradox neither Aeschylus nor his successors were able to resolve.

Philoctetes and Ajax

The major characters of Sophocles delineate more poignantly than those of Aeschylus the disqualifications of (to borrow a term applied to Italian nationalism during World War I) sacred egoism. Philoctetes and Odysseus, Ajax and Menelaus, Oedipus at Thebes and at Colonus, Creon, Haemon, and Antigone, and Heracles in *The Women of Trachis* extend the concept of heroic grace and vulnerability under pressure. The leading actors in *Ajax* and *Philoctetes* are outspoken on this theme. They respond to affronts from their military commanders with behavior that demonstrates a real gift for self-defeat. As in *Prometheus Bound,* conceit nurtures anger, aggression, and vengefulness, while shame nurtures sorrow, cynicism, and helplessness. With greater grief than Prometheus permits himself, Philoctetes and Ajax fix their attention upon the pathos of an isolation they themselves foster: the word *bound* could be attached to their names too.[7]

Philoctetes acts with gusto the part of a traumatized scapegoat; he celebrates his deprivation in despairing detail. "Dishonored and cast away" on an uninhabited island by Agamemnon, Menelaus, and Odysseus some nine years earlier, he lost his place in the conquering Homeric army, the grand expedition to Troy, and was thrown into a social void even more remote than Prometheus' rock. Abandonment by his warrior chiefs poisoned his prestige, just as the snakebite that punished him for illicitly approaching a sacred area corrupted his body. Now he is devastated by his festering wound, clothed in rags, and barely able to subsist with the help of Heracles' bow. Transformed into a nonentity, "one that is dead, / a kind of vaporous shadow, a mere wraith," Philoctetes has been doubly discredited by his peers' disgust and neglect. Obscurity, he concludes, may be worse than ignominy:

> You never heard my name then? Never a rumor
> of all the wrongs I suffered, even to death? . . .
> Surely I must be vile! God must have hated me
> that never a word of me, of how I live here,
> should have come home through all the land of Greece. (251–52, 254–56)

He is, like Prometheus, "a man wounded" in pride.

Compensating for the crippling effect of ostracism, fortifying jolts of "outrage" keep his self-regard alive; like Prometheus and Achilles, he draws upon wrath to maintain his identity as a principal soloist (principle soloist, Hegel would call him). He praises his martial "spirit that did not break" ("no yielding to suffering"), symbolized by the bow of Heracles required by the Greek army to defeat Troy. Unrelenting enmity toward one's foes, however, if entirely appropriate to the masculine code of honor, again becomes self-destructive: the bow is potentially as dangerous to him as the wound. As Prometheus does, he damages his cause by adamantly closing his mind to an overlord's overtures; as Achilles does, he jeopardizes his rehabilitation by threatening to withdraw his arms from the war.

A chorus of sailors scolds him for refusing to rejoin the expedition. The sailors, who voice the doctrine of survival in a forthright manner similar to that of Oceanos and his daughters in *Prometheus Bound*, describe his plight as self-administered ("with better opportunity before you, / you chose the worse"). Riveted to revenge, he holds to his "fixed purpose" even though he admits that "a man crazy with storms of sorrow / speaks against his better judgment." A description by the chorus of *Prometheus Bound* pertains equally well to Philoctetes: "What you have suffered is indeed terrible. You are all astray and bewildered in your mind, . . . you are cast down and cannot find what sort of drugs would cure your ailment" (472–76).

Philoctetes explains his position in debate with his ethical opposite. But Odysseus is no pure-minded Hegelian antagonist. A counterfeit hero and also a mimic of choric attitudes ludicrously straddling both camps, Odysseus adulterates self-celebration with dishonesty, the ultra-adaptable man outwitting the would-be constant man. Philoctetes sees him as a "shabby, slit-eyed soul . . . clever in mischief," specializing in treachery, deception, and theft, one who has "never had a healthy thought / nor noble." For his part, Odysseus confesses that he uses "clever" words to disarm strong but stupid rivals: "everywhere among the race of men," he states, "it is the tongue that wins and not the deed." His "prudent" speech permits him to shift with no hesitation between service and selfishness, covering his shiftiness with a sleazy translation of the communal involvement, common sense, and pragmatic morality advocated by the sailors. The credo of Odysseus, "as the occasion / demands, such a one am I," undoubtedly sounds ignoble compared to the self-determination praised by Philoctetes, yet from their dialogue a truth emerges more comprehensive than either incomplete value (as Hegel would say). *Both* characters are outrageous egoists (as Hegel would not say), one mean-minded and efficient, the other sincere and impractical.

Synthesis of these polar values is almost impossible to come by in tragic drama, but young Neoptolemus labors to unify them. Son of Achilles, the most illustrious Greek fighter at Troy, he favors unyielding honesty and feels a "terrible compassion" for the castaway. "I have a natural antipathy / to get my ends by tricks and stratagems," he tells Odysseus; "I would prefer even to fail with honor / than win by cheating." However, while Philoctetes plays upon the youth's aversion to trickery and concern for unblemished reputation ("If you [rescue] me, men will say their best of you"), Odysseus pulls in the other direction with "clever" talk of allegiance to leaders and material "gain." Neoptolemus gets trapped between the two petitions—the heroic quandary. "I shall be shown to be dishonorable," he objects, flinching from Odysseus' sneaky plan to kidnap Philoctetes; at the same time, "justice and [self-]interest / make me obedient to those in authority."

He handles his dilemma by embracing both contestants. First he promises the fallen hero safe passage to his homeland, a promise that protects his own reputation and his petitioner's pride. Then he attempts to correct Philoctetes' irrationality. His criticism repeats the standard choric wisdom:

> Men that cling wilfully to their sufferings
> as you do, no one may forgive nor pity.
> Your anger has made a savage of you. (1319–21)

His remedy, reconciliation with the generals, could heal in two ways. At Troy, medical experts will tend the snakebite, and more important, a decision to return "of your own will" would interrupt the preoccupation with injustice that has almost unhinged Philoctetes' mind. Neoptolemus brilliantly connects the two kinds of healing:

> yield and be gracious.
> It is a glorious heightening of gain.
> First, to come into hands that can heal you,
> and then be judged pre-eminent among the Greeks,
> winning the highest renown among them, taking
> Troy that has cost infinity of tears. (1342–47)

For better or (more usually) worse, however, an offended man of honor cannot "yield and be gracious," cannot condescend to "be judged," cannot accept the indignity of surrendering to a hurtful superior even to attain preeminence. Self-regard has come to work against "renown," and Philoctetes is ready to convert a reparable separation into an irrevocable divorce. In such circumstances only mediation by a prototype of masculine perfection can keep the protagonist from destroying himself in childish pique. Just as Heracles, image of irresistible virility, will one day liberate Prometheus, so the spirit of this same "all-conquering" overachiever, whose bow had already ensured Philoctetes' survival, intercedes to save Philoctetes' face. Heracles knows a formula that evaded Neoptolemus; rather than link "winning" with "yielding," as Neoptolemus does in his paradoxical solution, he addresses his case exclusively to "the winning of deathless merit, . . . the winning of a life to an end in glory." This warlike gambit, coming from so distinguished a warrior, propels Philoctetes past his emotional blockage, as Prometheus may be propelled in the lost *Prometheus Unbound*. But although Heracles' intervention salvages dignity, it does not address the contradiction between self-sufficiency and conformity. The unsolved puzzle Sophocles inherited from Aeschylus persisted: does the quest for excellence produce a weapon or a wound?

"Your anger has made a savage of you"—the words apply to most tragic figures. In *Prometheus Bound* male "obstinacy" is at once laudable and questionable, in *Philoctetes* laudable but suicidal, and in *Ajax* laudable, suicidal, murderous, and insane. When his commanders award Achilles' armor to Odysseus, Ajax answers the slight by carrying to their limit the three tendencies that distinguish frustrated supermen. Again Agamemnon, Menelaus, and Odysseus compose an unholy trinity in the disturbed mind of a protagonist who reiterates his claim to "pre-eminence" and resists lesser recognition. But this time a god worsens the crisis instead of ameliorating it. Under Athena's malign influence, Ajax turns his "obsessive notions" to the killing of sheep and cattle he mistakes for his abusers, a ludicrous and crazy deed that makes him lose face for a *second* time, inhibits him from looking "to any of the race of gods for help, . . . nor yet to humankind," and thus permanently alienates him from his world.

Was his madness caused by Athena, or did she just bring to view an inherent instability? Ajax suggests the latter by insisting on the former. To protect self-esteem after his second public humiliation, he repeatedly denies any responsibility whatsoever. He grants that he was "distraught and frenzied" when he slaughtered the animals, but blames Athena, Odysseus, and Agamemnon. "An outcast / shamed by the Greeks" like Philoctetes, he declares his innocence even to his infant son! Immense conceit and self-pity cement his unflagging unawareness:

> Such a man (let me now speak my boast)
> As Troy ne'er saw the like of, not in all
> The warlike host that hither came from Greece.
> But now in dishonor
> I lie abject. (422–26)

He fails to understand his own contribution to his ruin, the impropriety of his murderous mission. His obtuseness and arrogance had antagonized Athena earlier, when during a skirmish at Troy he told her to "go stand beside the other Greeks; help them. / For where I bide, no enemy will break through." Such "graceless words," the prophet Calchas commented, "won for him / The goddess' wrath; they kept no human measure." Athena directs her revenge against this naïveté, this one-sided approach (to use Hegel's word) to a two-sided ideal. "Know that the gods," the chorus teaches, "love men of steady sense and hate the proud."

Following his double disgrace, Ajax elects that sanctified last resort, suicide ("let a man nobly live or nobly die"). Begged by his wife and friends to act reasonably, which he equates (following Prometheus) with being "womanish," he pretends to agree, but the sarcasm in his fake retraction underlines his stubbornness:

Strong oath and iron intent come crashing down.
My mood, which just before was strong and rigid,
No dipped sword more so, now has lost its edge—
My speech is womanish for this woman's sake.
. . . .
From now on this will be my rule: Give way
To Heaven, and bow before the sons of Atreus.
They are our rulers, they must be obeyed.
I must give way, as all dread strengths give way,
In turn and deference. . . . Shall not I
Learn place and wisdom? (649–52, 666–69, 676–77)

While he deceives Tecmessa and the chorus ("his heart is changed, and bends to bear the yoke / Of a changed purpose"), Ajax—like Prometheus and Philoctetes—cannot possibly "learn place and wisdom" without some stellar tutoring, but in this play no Heraclean negotiator supplies the instruction. So he dies alone, affirming his innocence, commanding the Furies to avenge his dishonor by spilling "the whole army's blood."

The debate on burial rights does little to exonerate the unworkable code Ajax dies to uphold. Defending his half-brother, Teucer assumes the same narrow-minded, egocentric stance. He too frets about his reputation ("in the end I'll be / Cast into exile and denied my country"); he too refuses to take responsibility for his difficulties ("this was the gods' contrivance"); he too looks to violence for a remedy. And those he debates with are equally unwilling to make peace. Behind their front as defenders of public order, Menelaus and Agamemnon are as "unyielding," self-indulgent, and insulting as Teucer, and even more brutal, disguising their will to sovereignty with specious appeals to society's needs.[8] When Menelaus mentions his duty to preserve law and order, it is really revenge ("he hated me, as I did him") that animates his attack. Agamemnon (like Creon in *Antigone*) argues for "precedence"—appropriate ranking—as a political end by boosting his own importance and demeaning his adversary. The brothers are obviously dictatorial and self-serving; Hegel misread the nature of promoters like these because he was taken in by the pretexts they used to make their motives appear respectable. But the chorus, another bunch of weary sailors, does not get deceived by politicians trying to have it both ways. It advises *all* parties to "learn a moderate mind!"

Odysseus makes a stronger case for choric moderation. Totally different from the scheming, unscrupulous Odysseus of *Philoctetes*, this character introduces the compassion expressed in that play by Neoptolemus:

> Yet I pity
> His wretchedness, though he is my enemy,
> For the terrible yoke of blindness that is on him.
> I think of him, yet also of myself;
> For I see the true state of all us that live—
> We are dim shapes, no more, and weightless shadow. (121–26)

Sympathetic with a rival who has blotted his "perfect excellence," Odysseus tries to bring combative men together in charity, a rare finale for tragic drama. Naturally, Agamemnon rejects this option with his mindless defense of prerogative and his fear of critical evaluation.

> Agamemnon: Do you intend pity to a corpse you hate?
>
> Odysseus: His greatness weighs more than my hate with me.
>
> Agamemnon: Men who act so are changeable and unsteady.
>
> Odysseus: Men's minds are given to change in hate and friendship.
>
> Agamemnon: Do you, then, recommend such changeable friends?
>
> Odysseus: I cannot recommend a rigid spirit.
>
> Agamemnon: You'll make me look a coward in this transaction.
>
> Odysseus: Generous, though, as all the Greeks will say. (1356–63)

No Heracles proclaiming victory over foes, Odysseus goes beyond the usual masculine belligerence and the usual choric conformity with a message about generosity.

Sophocles, like Aeschylus, neither worshipped nor dismissed the male stereotype, instead acknowledged its power and its perversity. After all, self-confidence, courage, decisiveness, and moral constancy deserve our praise; as Teucer states in his judgment of Ajax, "no nobler one has ever been." Teucer may lack the breadth of Odysseus, but he makes a valid point. Yet the qualities he praises can become distorted, precluding balance with vital qualities like adaptability, awareness of limits, and accurate judgment. To quote the sailors in *Ajax* again on this subject,

> Humble men without their princes
> Are a frail prop for a fortress. They
> Should be dependent upon the great,
> And the great be upheld by lesser ones. (159–62)

This reciprocity may well be unattainable, a wishful thought perhaps nurtured by Sophocles' hopes for the cohesion of the Athenian empire.[9]

Whether or not Sophocles had contemporary politicians in mind, such harmony certainly eludes his characters. Although Ajax finally manifests a degree of piety when he dedicates his suicide to Helios, to the avenging Furies, and to the "God of Death," he proves that temperance and reverence do not "come easily to a prince." "It is a painful thing," Tecmessa observes, "to look at your own trouble and know / That you yourself and no one else has made it." Ajax never glimpses her truth.

Pentheus

Euripides sharpens the critique: he satirizes the inadequacies of princely males more grotesquely than his colleague Sophocles or his predecessor Aeschylus. Pentheus, the young king in *The Bacchae*, Jason in *Medea*, Hippolytus, and Orestes in *Electra*, among others, pass into parody. These characters are often self-divided to a far greater extent than characters presented by Aeschylus, swinging madly between stiff juvenile narcissism and ludicrous-pathetic anxiety regarding censure. Euripides adapts the basic story line employed by Aeschylus and Sophocles in order to mock, not commiserate with, the heroic double duty, the devotion to divergent "obsessive notions."[10]

That story remains intact in broad outline: the legendary protagonist of *The Bacchae*, for instance, reacts impetuously to those who would restrict his jurisdiction. "We are disgraced," Pentheus mourns, "humiliated in the eyes / of Hellas" (trans. William Arrowsmith, *CGT* 4). Appeasement being unthinkable, his urgent protests ensure separation from family, friends, and city. Euripides filled in this outline with his distinctive coloration by intensifying Pentheus' chief symptom, mental imbalance, to a pathological condition more contorted than the contortions of Ajax and Philoctetes, more deranged than the frenzy of Io and Cassandra. A monarch formerly considered to be Thebes' most reliable citizen reacts insanely to the threat of "disgrace" and plunges himself and his kingdom into chaos. "What was most expected," the chorus announces, spelling out the irony, "has not been accomplished, / but god has found his way / for what no man expected."

Asian devotees of Dionysus set the theme, equating arrogance with madness. Their conservative counsel, enlisted for a radical new religion, recalls the counsel of Ecclesiastes as well as that of all Athenian choruses and many secondary characters like Oceanos in *Prometheus Bound* and Calchas in *Ajax*. They bow to social norms and superior force, to "the wisdom that accepts . . . the law tradition makes." Old Cadmus, blind Teiresias, and the messenger agree on this point; together they make up a choric alliance similar to those assembled by Aeschylus and Sophocles.

Anyone who ridicules their credo must be "mad." "Do not mistake / for wisdom the fantasies of your sick mind," Teiresias tells Pentheus, who by refusing to worship the new divinity has "presumed to wage a war with god" in order to "win / a glory towering to heaven." Cadmus too declares the young king to be spiritually sick when he forsakes the security of community standards and seeks the illusory haven of self-determination. "Your home is here / with us," Cadmus explains,

> with our customs and traditions, not
> outside, alone. Your mind is distracted now,
> and what you think is sheer delirium. (330–33)

Pentheus counterattacks by accusing *them* of insanity ("do not wipe your madness off on me"), but soon loses his composure.[11] In his "delirium," he changes in Euripidean fashion from wise to "blind," from manly to "womanish," and from human to bestial. First his vision comes into question. Experiencing hallucinations brought on by Dionysus, he confuses the god with a bull, just as Ajax (misled by Athena) took sheep and cattle for his enemies. Imperfect sight signifies imperfect insight, a connection that Sophocles had previously developed in *Oedipus Rex* and *Ajax:* Euripides and Sophocles both explored ironies raised by Teiresias, the celebrated prophet of legend who saw even though he could not see. The issue connects self-knowledge to the perception of social realities, any vision focused entirely on one's self amounting to a kind of blindness. "Your blasphemies have made you blind," Dionysus warns Pentheus:

> You do not know
> the limits of your strength. You do not know
> what you do. You do not know who you are. (505–7)

In the eyes of Dionysus, Pentheus becomes a weak girl as well as a sightless madman. To Pentheus, of course, it is the god, his "long yellow curls smelling of perfumes," who seems weak, marked by stereotypical feminine traits of fragility, promiscuity, and deceit. Pentheus treats the "effeminate" god, the chorus of Asian women, and the female Theban converts with sexist disdain. "Affairs are out of hand," he says, "when we tamely endure such conduct in our women." Yet he and his male servants are "shamefully defeated" in combat with women. Later he indicates his confusion by putting on a dress, by imitating feminine mannerisms, and by spying on the Bacchic rites from a treetop. These bizarre activities reflect the collapse of that unshakable will and "brute strength" supposedly available to aggressive males for resolving all problems. "Do not be so certain that power / is what matters in the life of man," Teiresias had warned him. In *Prometheus Bound* a jailer's chain symbolizes the protagonist's immobilization; in *Philoctetes* it is a festering wound; in *Ajax*, a slaughtered herd of animals. In *The Bacchae* the woman's gown Pentheus substitutes for his armor signals a reversal of gender roles, the ultimate degradation of masculine militance.[12]

Agave, herself maddened and flaunting the bloody head of her son, also illustrates the reversal without comprehending it:

> men of Thebes, behold the trophy of your women's
> hunting! *This* is the quarry of our chase, taken
> not with nets nor spears of bronze but by the white
> and delicate hands of women. (1203–6)

His mother unknowingly spares Pentheus the shame of being "paraded through the streets, a woman, . . . the laughingstock of Thebes." Agave's gory triumph as a huntress brings to a climax another result, besides blindness and effeminacy, of the loss of integrity—bestiality. Animals or animal behavior associated with Pentheus tends to be cruel and murderous, unnatural and repulsive. The Asian women, for example, refer pejoratively to his father, Echion, reputedly "born of the dragon seed," raising Pentheus as "a rabid beast," a "beast of blood." His grandfather Cadmus will be turned into a serpent caged "among barbarian peoples," and his mother (according to the chorus) must have been "one of the Libyan gorgons!" Consistent with the gorgon reference, Agave as monstrous destroyer takes her "trophy" to be "some mountain lion's head." This image fits Pentheus, for the rash king had intended to "hunt down" the Bacchae "like the animals they are." But Cadmus anticipated a change from hunter to hunted when he urged Pentheus to avoid the fate of his cousin Actaeon, who also defied a god (Artemis) and was also torn apart by those he trusted ("hounds he had raised himself").[13]

A less savage animal imagery—dogs, doves, and goats, mare with colt, cows with calves, fawns, and wolf cubs—configures the nurturing side of Dionysian vitality. But the vicious side of the "bull-horned god" makes a stronger impression. Divine justice can be as harsh, as illogical, and as self-serving as heroic justice. Although Dionysus calls himself "most terrible, and yet most gentle, to mankind," his dealings with Pentheus, Cadmus, Agave, and others do not bear out the second promise or his earlier pledge that "I shall not be touched to rage. / Wise men know constraint: our passions are controlled." Cadmus and Agave do adopt the new religion; they too are punished severely. "Gods should be exempt from human passions," Cadmus cries in his well-known complaint. Supernatural figures in Athenian tragedy, except for an occasional benevolent adviser like Heracles or Oceanos, can be as covetous of respect, as sensitive to insult, and as vengeful as any king or warlord.

Euripides joined Aeschylus and Sophocles in distrusting both human and divine willfulness clothed in noble words glorifying individual merit. Tragedy resulted from the collision not of public-spirited altruists fighting for family, community, and religious principles, as Hegel thought, but of self-important personalities who, intent upon precedence, intolerant of judgment, and disposed to violence when offended, committed antisocial blunders in the name of their obsession with personal elevation and thus blocked their own road to success. They wanted to be two things—socially-esteemed and self-esteemed—but those aims quickly became alternatives rather than complements, tearing apart the man caught in the middle (literally torn apart, in the case of Pentheus). The prideful paragon resisted peer evaluation but internalized it as shame; he ignored choric insecurity but internalized it as self-pity; he spurned divine wrath but internalized it as uncontrollable anger; and he despised feminine weakness but internalized it as fear of frailty.

Needless to say, he is given a distinctive personality in each play, and the male characters who surround him add further variety—Neoptolemus the fledgling and Teucer the loyal sidekick; Odysseus in *Philoctetes* the caricature of nobility, Odysseus in *Ajax* the consummation; the ultimate warrior, Heracles in *Philoctetes*, and the ultimate tyrant, Dionysus in *The Bacchae* or the unseen Zeus in *Prometheus Bound*. Despite the variations, however, they all share a common heritage (they are often former allies). The antagonist is especially close to the chief actor in his desire to assert prerogative. He exhibits the same polarity, usually with a firmer grip on political power or practicality and a weaker grip on honesty, but with the same unflagging devotion to the power of self. He too is a sacred egoist: although he can slant his campaign appeal to satisfy group interests, he does not genuinely represent the choric standpoint. His quarrel with the protagonist issues from the double imperative they share, tempting wellborn males into uninhibited self-advertisement while requiring them to operate within a rational order based upon corporate welfare as well as lineage, wealth, merit, and achievement.

It is ironic that the rivals, as in the interaction between hero and chorus, at once excluded and depended upon each other. Without Prometheus' help Zeus might not have been enthroned, and without it he will be dethroned; without Philoctetes the Greek generals cannot defeat Troy; when Ajax dies those same officers lose an outstanding warrior; and when Pentheus goes berserk, Dionysus inherits a demoralized kingdom. Civil and military leaders had to work together both for their own benefit and for the welfare of their state, and yet they came to treat their relationship as a perpetual struggle for status and respect. Evil was not a foreign commodity; it was the consequence of Greek males pursuing virtue. In its appraisal of contrasting instructions dictated by the code of masculine honor, tragedy lamented that profitless combat, that continual breakdown of value.

3
Women

Sexism Can Be Explosive!

The collapse of order occurs during duels not only between male stereotypes but also between male and female stereotypes. Hegel pays little attention to gender, but the characters in Athenian tragedy are very vocal on the subject: they are not neuters. Just as they believe in an ideal (or fantasy) of masculine superiority that promotes selected men to an outlandish potency, so do they also believe in a notion (or fantasy) of feminine inferiority that demotes almost all women to an outlandish fragility. Their typecasting calls for women to be segregated, suppressed, and silent, yet some females, impelled by motives as relentless as those of some males, refuse a subordinate position. Their refusal only confirms the fears or offends the pride of men, often arousing virulent condemnation. Polymestor makes this statement in Euripides' *Hecuba* after some ghastly byplay with the outraged heroine:

> On behalf of all those dead
> who learned their hatred of women long ago,
> for those who hate them now, for those unborn
> who shall live to hate them yet, I now declare
> my firm conviction:
> neither earth nor ocean
> produces a creature as savage and monstrous
> as woman. (1177–83)

Polymestor's judgment outlines in extreme form an attitude toward women regularly reported in Athenian tragedy, an attitude prominent in Western countries for the last twenty-five centuries or more.[1] This common derogation, like the adulation of super manhood, was challenged by the dramatists, who responded to the entrenched gender prejudice of their time with a startling question: does the stereotype foster rather than describe irresponsibility, passivity, and related failings? What might be the consequences when defiant women, instead of conceding, assume a masculine stance (no noncomic alternative being readily conceivable in fifth-century Athens) and burst through the negative habits expected of them? Aeschylus, Euripides, and Sophocles depicted ladies of aristocratic caste modeling ambition and intelligence ordinarily held to be the prerogative of noble men, demanding parity or even priority, throwing over their obligation to play at subservience and silence. Unhappily, their departure from the norm, like the male's departure from a more esteemed standard, could forfeit social approval and lead to self-division. Their talents frustrated by *both* traditional roles, female rebels complained as bitterly as their male counterparts on discovering that the model they adopted caused as much pain as the one they rejected.

In the tragedies, generalized accounts detailing the nature of woman (accounts delivered by female characters as well as by males) are simple, consistent, and numerous, describing her the same way Hegel described the Shakespearean hero—morally inconsequential or perfidious, moved solely by private initiatives, never by public concerns. Behaving like a child, a servant, a demon, or a freak, she deviates in every property of body, mind, will, and heart from the godlike male image celebrated in legend and epic. For one thing, she is thought to possess no manual skill, strength, or endurance except in the domestic area, an area of less importance than masculine enterprises such as governance, athletics, seamanship, and (most important) war. Because of her physical incompetence, she spends her time absorbed in the trifles of dress, grooming, and other cosmetic comforts.

Her mental incapacity is even more crippling. She lacks the ability to master logic and rhetoric, the practical tools for dealing with ethical or political issues. Her thinking tends to be naive, without coherence or depth, inclined to gossip and rumor, typically exerted on superficial subjects. Like a child, she needs to be sheltered from substantive matters to safeguard her peace of mind. At the same time, men need to be insulated from her irrationality.

As for willpower, courage, assertiveness, or force of personality, women in Athenian tragedy (as in Athenian society) would again be found deficient in the forum that counted most to men—public affairs. They can muster no tough aggressiveness, no directness, self-confidence, honesty, presence, leadership. They could be declarative enough in family matters, but even there they act contrary to the manly mode, becoming devious, petty, nagging, lazy, and insecure.

Finally, and worst of all, the stereotype trumpets the primacy of emotion. Females are inconstant, undisciplined, self-indulgent, changeable as the moon (a favorite metaphor). They incline toward sentiment, treachery, spite, fear, immoderation or immodesty, jealousy, and (unforgivably) promiscuity. Their unruly feelings frequently make them run amok. They must be carefully supervised.

In short, woman is seen in the tragedies to be helpless, unreasonable, passive, and unpredictable—pathetically, if not grotesquely, inadequate for leadership. As opposed to the socially dynamic yet self-reliant male, she is family oriented and completely dependent. All sorts of witnesses testify to the accuracy of this generalization—major and minor characters, young and old, male and female, aristocrat and commoner. "Lord, what a plaintive creature / womankind is!" Ajax exclaims (580–81). "Women!" Euripides' Hippolytus concludes, "this coin which men find counterfeit! . . . How great a curse is woman" (616, 627). Hippolytus and Ajax are biased observers, but Euripides' Medea, hardly a weakling or a counterfeit, repeats the almost universal aphorism, "a woman is a frail thing, prone to crying" (928); "women, though most helpless in doing good deeds, / are of every evil the cleverest of contrivers" (408–9). Clytemnestra in *The Libation Bearers* of Aeschylus refers to the secondary position of women when she welcomes male visitors: "if / you have some higher business, more a matter of state, / that is the men's concern, and I will tell them of it (trans. David Grene, *CGT* 1: 671–72). Medea and Clytemnestra spurn that simplification, but they acknowledge it to be a common sentiment.

Other female characters routinely defer to it, particularly in plays by Euripides:

It is proper for women, if they are wise,
Always to get things done by men.

—Aethra, *The Suppliant Women* (trans. Frank William Jones, *CGT* 4: 41–2)

I hope you won't
Think it was brazen of me to come out.
I know a woman should be quiet and
Discreet, and that her place is in the home.

—Macaria, *The Heracleidae* (trans. Ralph Gladstone, 3: 474–77)

A wife should give way to her husband in all things
if her mind is sound.

—female chorus, *Electra* (trans. Emily Townsend Vermeule, 4: 1052–53)

If a man die, a house, a name, is lost.
But if a woman die, what does it matter?

—Iphigenia, *Iphigenia in Tauris* (trans. Witter Bynner, 3: 1005–6)

For trouble is very easy
When women deal with men. Since good and bad
Are not distinguished, all of us are hated.
To this misfortune we are born.

—Creusa, *Ion* (trans. Ronald Frederick Willetts, 4: 398–400)

O women's love,
So full of trouble,
How many evils have you caused already?

—female chorus, *Medea* (1290–92)

"O what perversion," Euripides' Electra repeats, "when the woman in the house / stands out as master, not the man" (932–33). And the female chorus leader in Euripides' *Orestes* offers this overview: "Women by nature, it seems, were born to be / a great impediment and bitterness / in the lives of men" (trans. William Arrowsmith, 4: 605–6). Euripides may be more outspoken on the subject than Aeschylus or Sophocles, but he renders fairly the popular opinion heard in all Athenian tragedies. With so many liabilities, women are ordered to "stay within doors" (Aeschylus), obliged "to submit" (Sophocles), and led to believe that their "honor lies in silence" (Euripides). The female chorus in Aeschylus' *Suppliant Maidens* summarizes the point: "women are nothing alone; no Ares is in them" (trans. Seth G. Benardete, 1: 749).

There was, of course, dissent to the majority opinion. Prompted by their mythological sources, the tragic dramatists explored stories of untypical females acting like males. Assertive noblewomen, activated by despair, anger, and a powerful sense of their worth, reach beyond the foreordained limits. In varying styles they perform as hard-willed, practical, intelligent fighters. Their deeds may be denounced by discreet or frightened characters who find them immoral, antisocial, impious, and unnatural, but a few hardier souls praise their acts as legitimate avenues to celebrity and independence. "Consider that in women too / there lives a warlike spirit," Orestes maintains in Sophocles' *Electra* (trans. David Grene, 2: 1242–43). To the extent that they displace proverbial feminine defects with proverbial masculine strengths, such women disprove the premise that the latter belong only to men. To the same extent, however, they prove the liability of those strengths. Conditioned by a male-centered culture, the authors of tragedy could visualize no other way to discredit longstanding ideas about gender inferiority and superiority.[2]

Three works encompass the range of behavior displayed by radical females—Aeschylus' *Agamemnon*, the *Electra* of Sophocles, and Euripides' *Medea*. At one extreme, Clytemnestra operates with little reliance on traditional womanly attributes. In contrast, Electra brings a feminine style to her militancy. And Medea, whose outrage blasts through deeply held maternal emotions, grapples with both styles. The three have in common a powerful desire to justify themselves that scandalizes female choruses and minor characters—Cassandra in *Agamemnon*, Chrysothemis and the chorus in *Electra*, the nurse and chorus in *Medea*. But women of lower station or orthodox outlook sometimes cherish and even follow exceptional individuals of their sex. For them and for the audiences attending the theater, Clytemnestra, Medea, and Electra presented a dangerous, inspired option.

Clytemnestra

Clytemnestra, in the first play of the *Oresteia*, may be the most Hegelian of Aeschylus' chief characters: like Prometheus, she never vacillates. More stalwart than most male protagonists in Athenian tragedy, she not only refuses to admit the *validity* of an uncongenial social standard (as they do too), but also withstands the *emotional impact* of that standard (as they do not). When her monolithic resolve to revenge her daughter Iphigenia brings her into contention with regulations defending a husband's rights—rules upheld by her choric countrymen and later by Apollo, Orestes, and Athena—she, unlike the adamant but suffering Prometheus, does not allow her adversaries' criticism to shame or humiliate her. In the trilogy, it is Orestes, torn between the ego-centered duty of manly revenge and a social taboo against matricide, who endures tragic self-division. Clytemnestra, in contrast, conforms to Hegel's requirement of unambivalent allegiance to a noble cause.

Inconsistent with Hegel's dictum, however, her noble cause is centered upon self-assertion. The justification supplied by her altruistic wish to avenge Iphigenia turns out to be much less evident than her scandalous desire to dominate others with her "manlike" courage, intellectual clarity, and discipline—the sterling qualities deified in the male model. Although she eventually loses her claim to legitimacy, she wins the game of manly daring, contradicting all the clichés about women's cowardly, muddled, or hysterical conduct. Female defeats male as in *The Bacchae*, but Clytemnestra, totally different from Agave and the chorus of Asian Bacchants, overturns gender expectations with a calm, clear-eyed deliberateness.

The watchman forecasts this outcome: his "long weary" service ("Dog-like I lie here") to a queen "in whose woman's heart / a man's will nurses hope" introduces the idea of a strong woman controlling men.[3] Then the chorus of Argive elders takes up the idea. Too old to have joined the armada invading Troy ten years earlier ("in strength not men / but children"), the elders now respond dutifully to their queen's summons ("we come obedient to your bidding"). Impressed by her bearing, it is they who shift between indecision and trust ("Madame, your words are like a man's"). But when she broadcasts the Greek victory, they cannot keep from voicing the familiar misgiving that females are brainless victims of gossip and rumor. "Surely you feed yourself on unconfirmed report," they taunt. They hang onto masculine self-respect by explaining that the queen may be subject to feminine unreliability:

Women all are hasty-headed:
Beacons blaze—belief rejoices;
All too easily persuaded.
Rumour fired by women's voices,
As we know, is quickly spread;
—As we know, is quickly dead! (483–87)

The queen addresses her rebuttal straight to their prejudice: "you choose to criticize me as an ignorant girl!" To resolve their uncertainty, she awes her listeners with a detailed description of the ingenious telegraph scheme she instituted to relay news of the Greek victory. Once proof arrives confirming her report, she ridicules their skepticism, throwing back at them their sexist accusation: "someone took me to task: / 'Beacons! So you believe them? Troy, you think, is taken? / Typical female hopefulness!'" The city elders thus face a woman flaunting her advance knowledge of the central event in Mycenaean history—knowledge that was inaccessible to those who normally provide their state with essential information. Overruling their wisdom with hers, Clytemnestra demolishes the image of an "ignorant girl."

She does not embrace a male role completely. She feels a mother's grief for Iphigenia, a wife's jealousy toward Cassandra. Moreover, she disguises her intentions, deceiving Agamemnon and the elders with a momentary pose of submission. But she calls the spectator's attention to her contempt for such submission by overstating it, just as Ajax does before his suicide: any woman deprived of her husband, she points out with heavy irony in her effusive welcoming speech, would fall prey to "Rumour" and become desolate if not suicidal.

And at the moment of crisis she does not rely on feminine wiles to overcome the king's resistance to walking on tapestry dyed in a sacred color. In their short, intense debate she overrides the will of Agamemnon, who enacts not arrogance toward the gods so much as public capitulation to his wife. Although he resists such coercion, her persistence ("yield! You are victor: give me too my victory") and her agile, persuasive logic ("you are no kind of beggary!"; "why humble your heart to men's censorious tongue?"; "unenvied is unenviable") push him to commit a fatal error, perhaps the chief sign of weakness in his masculine world—changing one's mind. His last words indicate his surrender: "I have been subdued to obedience." After prosecuting an arduous ten-year war, the conqueror of Troy gives in to a woman, one of those "unexpected" outcomes in tragedy. Agamemnon walks on a carpet colored to symbolize divine status, but it is *she* who publicly promotes herself, over his head, to the highest rank.

If Agamemnon's manly image suffers in front of the town elders, Aegisthus never rises above subordinate standing. He does not enter into the proceedings until everything, including the assassination, has been accomplished by his lover, and then his bravado verges on the comic. He cannot impress the chorus, which vilifies him with the supreme insult:

You woman! While he went to fight, you stayed at home;
. . . .
Are we to see *you* king of Argos—you,
Who, after plotting the king's murder, did not dare
To lift the sword yourself? (1625, 1633–35)

Aegisthus answers, lamely, "to lure him to the trap / was plainly woman's work." Scorning his empty boasting, the townsmen show considerable courage: in fact, they take on the part of antagonist, a rare posture for a chorus (the chorus of Furies in the third play of the trilogy does the same). They mount a formidable attack, once they get over their initial disarray, though like Agamemnon they are soon mastered by the queen.

They criticize Clytemnestra again with their sexist vocabulary: "vile woman! What . . . transformed you?"; "spirit of hate, . . . / your power it is engenders thus / in woman's brain such evil art"; "sad, silent king! . . . caught by a ruthless falsehood of a wife." Again she mocks their misconception: "you speak as to some thoughtless woman: you are wrong. / My pulse beats firm." The queen does not merely confess her responsibility, she exults in it:

> A great while I have pondered on this trial of strength.
> At long last the pitched battle came, and victory:
> Here where I struck I stand and see my task achieved.
> Yes, this is my work, and I claim it. (1377–80)

And for her closing shot at the pretensions of men, she orders a truce between the chorus and Aegisthus.

The playwright brings into high relief one female's invincibility by offsetting it with another's helplessness. Cassandra's prophetic seizures may seem to a modern audience to be interruptions of the main action, but these melodramatic exclamations expressing fear, outrage, and pain serve as a foil to Clytemnestra's control of men and her own feelings. Cassandra consummates the gender model that the queen transcends, oscillating between passivity (after her entrance she exemplifies the Greek woman's greatest virtue by remaining silent for almost three hundred lines) and unrestraint ("she has the look of some wild creature newly trapped," the chorus says). To emphasize her pitiable position, Aeschylus takes up the legend concerning her defective ability to communicate, so that she acts out her destiny as an imperfect prophet as well as a feeble female. The chorus dismisses her "wild" outcries as irrelevant to the political situation ("the girl needs an interpreter"), and in a way they are. She perceives the reversal in Argos but fails to recognize the moral challenge in Clytemnestra's revolutionary daring. For her there is only a detestable crime against nature. "Will cow gore bull?" she asks; "female shall murder male: what kind of brazenness / is that?"

Cassandra's queries would occur to the Athenian audience too. Should Clytemnestra be applauded or condemned? If the best human qualities are in truth masculine, then she can be judged a vicious mutant, a monstrous criminal, as Cassandra judges her, no matter how remarkable the watchman and the chorus find her metamorphosis. If, on the other hand, women—at any rate, extraordinary women—can be as determined and intelligent as extraordinary men are supposed to be, as competent in public affairs, then she may be making a statement with world-shaking implications.

But even if conventional gender relations are shown to be questionable, her victory will come to a bitter end so long as the community's moral order remains endangered. Having established her force of will, therefore, Aeschylus must go on to discover whether a *new* legitimate order can emerge from the old rules of masculine competition, or whether the traditional rules will persist and bring on still another personal and social disaster. After Clytemnestra's assassination by a vengeful son reclaiming male sovereignty, the trial of Orestes permits supernatural antagonists to reassess commonplace beliefs on relations between the sexes.

In *The Eumenides,* Apollo, a male supremacist ("the parent is he who mounts"), argues with the Furies, ancient goddesses defending a mother's rights. Athena arbitrates between patriarchal and matriarchal orientations, and unsurprisingly—she is a virgin warrior-goddess borne by a male god—votes for Orestes to uphold "the father's claim / and male supremacy in all things." She placates the Furies by promising them a spurious kind of authority; they will donate an old-fashioned feminine principle—"unwearied fruitfulness," health, and domestic harmony—to a glorious renaissance in Athens.[4] Despite the promise of a Hegelian synthesis, however, this conclusion sounds like business as usual. While the warrior-goddess sanctions nurturance (fertility, growth, conciliation) as a necessity for social stability, men will still preside over political activities. Athena supposedly dignifies women's interests by redefining the responsibilities and rights of the Furies, but she does not really integrate those interests with the leadership abilities Clytemnestra personified so dynamically.

Her verdict favoring Orestes leaves difficult problems unanswered, especially for an audience of today. Was Clytemnestra, however powerful, wrong to imitate the masculine mode? How may we imagine the female other than as a negative version of the male or as his negation, usurping his distinctive strengths and faults? Can the sexes interact "fruitfully" to regulate their society together, avoiding the extremes inherent in the stereotypes, or is justice basically men's territory, for better or (inevitably) worse? Voting for "male supremacy" will not end the recurring sequence in which respect is demanded, challenged, and compromised; praising feminine nurturance, peace-making, and similar desirable ends may be only employing tactful words to dress up a perennial pejorative expectation. The trilogy closes with an optimistic program for change that does not address deep-seated human (not exclusively masculine) drives for vindication and authority. Aeschylus set a precedent by challenging male and female stereotypes, but his examination of gender relations, especially in regard to heroic ambition, stalled when fundamental innovation became essential. We needn't censure him for this: our culture's ineptitude in installing feasible new models still persists 2,500 years after he won first prize with the *Oresteia.*

Electra

In his four other surviving works, Aeschylus found a different dramatic use for collective wisdom on women's limitations. Concentrating upon the torment his female characters experience in a male-centered culture, he paid more attention to the anguish of a Cassandra than to the toughness and pragmatism of a Clytemnestra. A generation later, Euripides and Sophocles revisited both that turmoil and that toughness, but in their works one individual often enacts both, alternating between passive suffering and compulsive activity, playing victim and vindicator, a dual role anticipated by Prometheus. Hegel's opinion notwithstanding, Sophocles created male and female personalities who by cutting across gender boundaries accent their inconsistencies with as much flamboyance as characters created by his contemporary, the master of caricature, Euripides.

Sophocles' Electra is introverted, uncoordinated, and sad. On one hand, she caters to the feminine image, floundering in self-pity like an emasculated Ajax or Philoctetes, spending her energy on "wild" words of woe instead of incisive deeds that would address her complaints.[5] At other times, she manages (like a resolute Ajax or Philoctetes) to speak and act decisively in her own behalf as well as her father's, choosing a militant course that transforms her from mourner into warrior. In her dominant feminine role she bewails injustice; in her sporadic masculine role she attempts to channel indignation into disciplined retaliation. She differs from Aeschylus' Electra, whose early reunion with her brother allows her to push forward single-mindedly with a healthy athletic confidence. She differs also from Aeschylus' Clytemnestra by continually revolving between anger and sorrow. In *Agamemnon*, a woman acts primarily like a man, assisted by a man acting like a woman (Aegisthus). *Electra* reverts to a more traditional partnership: a woman acts primarily like a woman, cooperating with a man acting like a man! Electra turns into a formidable adversary, but during her evolution she spends much time loquaciously venting grief and hesitation (Eugene O'Neill exploited her mournful side). "I shall cry out my sorrow for all the world to hear," she moans; "suffer me my madness."

When she spins out her sullen despondency in lengthy "dirges," she focuses on the injustice done to herself rather than to Agamemnon. "Wet with tears," she indicts Clytemnestra not just for the murder but also for depriving a helpless daughter of the amenities that typically strengthen a woman's self-esteem:

I am one wasted in childlessness,
With no loving husband for champion.
Like some dishonored foreigner,
I tenant my father's house in these ugly rags
and stand at a scanty table. (187–91)

After several arias of frenzied, futile "lament," Electra switches to warfare. She enlarges her capability for fighting back by castigating her sister as a "traitor to [her] dead father." This choric sister counsels obedience and moderation in sorrow. "Yield to authority," Chrysothemis advises; "You are a woman—no man. . . . Learn to give in to those that have the strength." Electra will not give in, and her true grit comes out in the debate with Clytemnestra, when she finally matches her mother's combativeness. (She fails, however, to convert the chorus of prudent Mycenaean ladies: "I see she is angry," they remark, "but whether it is in justice, / I no longer see how I shall think of that.")

Yet she continues to swing between belligerence and pathos. She returns to extravagant grieving on hearing a false report of her brother's death ("I will abandon myself to waste away / this life of mine, unloved"); her mother wryly belittles the "never ceasing clamor." Then she goes against this habit and decides to kill Aegisthus by herself: "life on base terms, for the nobly born, is base," she decides. She also strains to invigorate her submissive sister, who doggedly cultivates the female stereotype despite their common antipathy toward their father's assassin. Scorning sexist guidelines, Electra begins to sound as "confident" as Clytemnestra in *Agamemnon*, but after a look at what she takes to be Orestes' funeral urn she surrenders to lamentation so sustained that she is criticized by the cautious chorus ("do not sorrow too much"), by Orestes following their reunion ("do not choose to talk too much"), and by the tutor ("have done once and for all / with your long speeches"). In feminine fashion she stands aside during the killings, which are carried out by Orestes and his quiet friend Pylades. As she says, deferring to proper etiquette, "dear ladies, now is the moment that the men / are finishing their work. Wait in silence." Still, she does spur her brother on with compact comments that reverse (once again) her penchant for doleful "lengthy speeches." At the critical moment she reveals an affinity with her mother by acting out the truth that, in Orestes' words, "in women too / there lives a warlike spirit."

In contrast to Aeschylus' Clytemnestra, then, Electra habitually behaves in a feminine manner, and her "redemption from / all past sufferings" depends upon a man. Because of her orthodox infirmities she escapes condemnation as an unnatural woman (manlike or demonic), her "sufferings" calling attention to her deficiency. And yet "warlike" outrage compels her to confront the one who has depressed her self-esteem and to mobilize for murder. She is an emotional chameleon, sometimes as hysterical as Cassandra, sometimes as implacable as Clytemnestra, jumping between the passivity or hysteria dictated by one traditional gender image and the strength ordained by the other. If Clytemnestra explodes truisms on the exclusiveness of gender characteristics with a domineering flair, Electra achieves the same result with her performance as a fallible female.

Medea

However vacillating she may be (Hegel's term), Electra, like most Athenian protagonists, has no doubts regarding the justice of her ego-centered claim to fame; Sophocles' interest lies in her difficult birth as a heroic avenger, not in the issue of matricide. But the horrendous deed that draws out her courage puts her (and Orestes) squarely into the tragic predicament, separated from social acceptability by the fanatical desire to perform an outstanding act of self-definition, an act both righteous and heinous, exemplary and monstrous. That paradox afflicts Euripides' females to an even greater degree: greater hostility between gender types complicates the propriety of their cause. Almost all Euripides' eighteen extant tragedies involve a plot or subplot highlighting agitated women who, believing themselves persecuted by men and feeling terror, outrage, or grief, attack and destroy their persecutors. As the messenger reports in *The Bacchae*, "the men ran, routed by women!" When these women justify their actions, however, some are so far from being guiltless that one cannot easily tell whether they are victims searching for fair treatment or criminals, just as one cannot easily tell that in regard to most male protagonists.

Medea reflects this ambiguity with mordant clarity. A sorceress, a murderess, and worst of all a foreigner ("no Greek woman would have dared such deeds"), she carries a discordant history to present time. She betrayed her father to consummate her lust for Jason, then caused the deaths of her brother and her lover's uncle. Now she kills King Creon, his daughter, and her own two sons, again apparently motivated by uncontrollable passion. Yet she insists that these later crimes only redress her mistreatment and the restrictive rules governing women generally. She makes her case not just as a deserted wife but more significantly as an aristocrat whose public stature has been unfairly diminished.[6]

Like Aeschylus' Clytemnestra and Sophocles' Electra, Medea transgresses both legal and psychological norms by refusing to accept silence as her response to insult. But her recourse is more radical than theirs, lacking the eye-for-an-eye plausibility cited by the queen (revenge for a daughter's death) and by Electra (revenge for a father's death). Agreeing with her society's censure of infanticide, she raises doubts unknown to those characters on the legitimacy of her remedy; she attains a consciousness of the negative consequences of heroic action that is foreign to most other protagonists in Athenian tragedy. Before Orestes ends her reign in *The Libation Bearers,* Clytemnestra never falters in her resolution to attain masculine goals—political eminence, destruction of an opponent—primarily through masculine means: "my pulse beats firm," "here where I struck I stand." Similarly, Sophocles' Electra nurses no uncertainty on the correctness of kin murder while she vacillates between fortitude and its opposite. Medea experiences neither emotional *nor* ethical equanimity: not at all deficient in fortitude but horrified at her moral originality, pulled in one direction by a mother's concern for her children, in a contrary direction by a warrior's concern for respect, she stretches to its limit a question comparable to one the playwrights ask about males: does woman-as-fighter equal woman-as-beast?

Jason, the unfaithful husband and political opportunist, myopically writes off her outbursts as the ranting of a female "wronged in the matter of love." To him a woman's judgment is piloted wholly by sexual urgency. "You women," he declares,

> If your life at night is good, you think you have
> Everything; but, if in that quarter things go wrong,
> You will consider your best and truest interests
> Most hateful. (570–73)

For Medea the issue goes far beyond sexual matters. She appeals to reason in a long (fifty-line) speech that examines not only her particular case but also the grievances of all women, grievances that include the dowry system and arranged marriages, domestic bondage, and the double standard of fidelity. These degrade the female. The chorus of Corinthian women, though appalled at the solution she devises, concurs with the logic of her plea for equity and her condemnation of the stereotype:

> Flow backward to your sources, sacred rivers,
> And let the world's great order be reversed.
> It is the thoughts of *men* that are deceitful,
> *Their* pledges that are loose. (410–15)

Reversing the world's great order, however, was not easy to envision in fifth-century Athens. Medea cannot completely dispense with woman's weapons—secrecy, deception, and poison. As do Clytemnestra and Ajax, she conceals her intention with a façade of compliance, imitating the stock second-rate female:

> We women are what we are—perhaps a little
> Worthless; and you men must not be like us in this,
> Nor be foolish in return when we are foolish.
> Now, I give in, and admit that then I was wrong. (889–92)

Her revenge, of course, will refute these ploys. Killing her sons will tell the story of her importance, her "courage, / skill of hand and heart."

> Let no one think me a weak one, feeble-spirited,
> A stay-at-home, but rather just the opposite,
> One who can hurt my enemies and help my friends;
> For the lives of such persons are most remembered. (807–10)

But she sways between pride and accountability as though between masculine strength and feminine weakness, tension increasing until it pushes her toward madness, a common reward for radical daring. She is fully aware, unlike most protagonists created by Sophocles and Aeschylus, of both sides of the heroic equation: "friends," she admits, "when I saw that bright look in the children's eyes. / I cannot bear to do it." And yet,

> Ah, what is wrong with me? Do I want to let go
> My enemies unhurt and be laughed at for it?
> I must face this thing. Oh, but what a weak woman
> Even to admit to my mind these soft arguments. (1049–52)

Medea's cry for recognition—normally the male's response—thrusts aside pity and feminine duty, violates natural and social law, and turns her in Jason's eyes into a "monster, not a woman." Does murdering the children, then, confirm men's conclusions on the excesses and deficiencies of females, rather than prove her worth in men's terms, or does it exemplify the horrors brought on by manly aspirations? Euripides goes beyond Sophocles in complicating the puzzle Aeschylus proposed. As in *Agamemnon* and *Electra*, gender roles become mutually invalidating: a destructive masculine attitude (rabid vengefulness in the name of honor) offers the only alternative to what would be for Medea a contemptible feminine attitude (resignation, self-effacement). When she crosses the boundary between these norms, she reveals the limitations of each as a sufficient basis for behavior. But in contrast to Clytemnestra and Electra, she is morally self-divided, retaining her compassion as a mother while knowingly inflicting a horrible wound upon herself as she discredits the customary separation of gender functions.

For her deed violates all customary truisms. It requires commitment to a concept of merit that joins "self-willed thought," "hand," and "heart" in a way universally held to be inappropriate for a woman *or* a man. Criminal and unbalanced, it gets to the core of ancient imperatives dictating how each sex should live nobly, imperatives formerly trusted and now seen to be explosive. The dramatist rehearses a no-win situation: strength in either sex can become a sickness when it turns into an absolute (and obsolete) commandment. "Great people's tempers are terrible," the nurse protests to Medea,

> always
> Having their own way, seldom checked,
> Dangerous they shift from mood to mood. (119–21)

If Medea and Clytemnestra are monsters, they were shaped by men, or by the male model, which denies them equal prominence in society, suppresses their "tempers" as unnatural and unfeminine, and dictates subservience in place of the maddening competition among men. Athenian dramatists called upon legends portraying female victimization and resistance in order to demonstrate the illogic of both gender models, a negative lesson since in their tragedies a program relating the sexes more profitably was not available. Among the enemies of pride they described, "womanish" flux and frailty offered a threat that most of their protagonists, male or female, internalized along with the threats presented by divine interference, peer judgment, and choric disapproval.

4

The Sequence of Athenian Tragedy

Twenty-five centuries ago the originators of tragedy advanced the incredible thesis that inherited beliefs about manly excellence and female inferiority were combustible, that they interacted like the ingredients of a bomb. Rather than ensure harmony, gender polarities could provoke murder, suicide, and insanity in society's leaders. To project this process on the stage, the Athenian playwrights developed a narrative rhythm, a predictable progression of events, that recurred in their best-known works, including the nine already discussed here and at least an additional six: *Oedipus Rex*, *Oedipus at Colonus*, and *Antigone* by Sophocles, and *Electra*, *Hippolytus*, and *Hecuba* by Euripides (most of the other surviving tragedies could be included also). An antagonist or his agent provided the impetus to that rhythm when (to rephrase Hegel's insight) he interfered with the leading actor's vision of executive prerogative. To borrow the terms Arnold Toynbee applied to whole civilizations, the framework story common to these fifteen diverse works is structured by the concept of challenge and response.[1]

First, an individual capable of exerting sizable political or religious leverage presents the chief character with some command, act, or evaluation taken by the latter as contrary to his desire and therefore insulting. Zeus ordains that humans, Prometheus' favorite clients, must be destroyed; Odysseus and his colleagues in the expedition against Troy maroon the wounded Philoctetes on an uninhabited island; Agamemnon and Menelaus pass over Ajax as a candidate for Achilles' armor; Dionysus orders that he and King Pentheus are to share sovereignty over Thebes. Although the catalytic act may not be intended to injure the protagonist, he views it as a diminution of his rights, reputation, and security, a humiliation.

His response, the next phase of the dramatic plan, marked by defiance, self-pity, apprehension over status, and a thirst for revenge, tends to alienate friends along with foes. Because his devotion to both reputation and autonomy has made him intolerant of disapproval or restriction, he cannot compromise: he becomes stuck in a truculent, self-justifying posture. So Prometheus thwarts Zeus, Philoctetes refuses to rejoin the army, Ajax aims to kill Agamemnon and Menelaus, Pentheus imprisons Dionysus.

In turn, this rebuttal (which along with the initial insult may be reported, not enacted, as in *Prometheus Bound* and *Ajax*) brings on a second assault—condemnation, punishment, or the *threat* of further humiliation and isolation—that moves the play to its climax. The protagonist now suffers more serious risk of detraction than before: Prometheus is bound and tortured for his insubordination; Philoctetes is pressured by Odysseus and Neoptolemus to return to Troy; Ajax, led by Athena to slaughter cattle and sheep instead of his superiors; Pentheus, led by Dionysus to assume a degrading role that advertises his blindness, irresponsibility, and brutality. In this chain of events, the second injury (or its anticipation) aggravates the initial insult, deepens the protagonist's outrage and grief, and instigates another counterattack—a last, often violent exertion to salvage pride. Prometheus bolsters his defiance and anticipates revenge, Philoctetes blocks his would-be abductors, Ajax commits suicide, Pentheus pursues the Theban Bacchae.

The other eleven works mentioned here conform to this double-jeopardy design quite closely. The heroine of Sophocles' *Electra,* after resisting her mother's harassment, resolves to take revenge despite the reported death of Orestes (her other problem). Oedipus at Thebes first answers the gods' challenge, made concrete in a blight on the city and interpreted through a prophet, by searching for the killer of Laius, then answers the imagined menace of Teiresias, Creon, and Jocasta by searching for his parents, his reputation at stake in both cases. Oedipus at Colonus successively resists the bids of Creon and Polyneices to use him in their cause; his justifiable anger at the latter, unlike his earlier, unreasonable outbursts, purges shame instead of increasing it. Antigone's (and Haemon's) suicide, the response to Creon's condemnation, follows Antigone's ritual burial of a brother, the response to Creon's ban.[2] The pain Hippolytus feels at the attack from his father supersedes the resentment he felt at the false confession (reported by an intermediary) of his stepmother. Double jeopardy in *Hecuba* occurs in two disconnected incidents, Hecuba's bid to avert her daughter's death being somewhat detached from her bid to avenge her son. In the *Oresteia* taken as a whole, Orestes, the protagonist of the second and third plays, responds to his father's murder by killing Clytemnestra, the antagonist of *The Libation Bearers;* when the Furies, antagonists in *The Eumenides,* try to avenge the matricide, he reacts to *that* danger by entrusting his case to Apollo and by seeking purification, a more constructive reaction than typically found in tragedy. Euripides' *Electra* reduces the narrative pattern to a single challenge and response (Clytemnestra's crime and its punishment by Orestes and Electra), as does *Medea* (Jason divorces Medea, who retaliates by murdering their sons and his bride); otherwise, two sets of injury and counterattack—detraction and rebuttal—determine the format of Athenian tragedy.

The antagonists, usually victimized by the same dichotomy of elitist values that frustrates the protagonist, may be as disruptive to social stability but do not always suffer the same injury to reputation or the same emotional deflation. They command enough prestige to avoid detraction while endangering (or seeming to endanger) their opponents through demotion in rank, loss of face, or physical harm. They command that prestige by virtue of office (six works) or rank and family tie, as in *Agamemnon*, the three *Electras, Antigone, Oedipus Rex, Oedipus at Colonus, Hippolytus,* and *Medea* (over half the conflicts involve family members). Their initial judgment often has to do with legal policies (laws on burial rights, patricide, adultery, incest, and so forth) that promptly become gateways to issues of political power. Antagonists seldom begin by threatening physical harm, as Odysseus does when he threatens Hecuba's young daughter with execution at the outset of *Hecuba*, but they or their allies almost always come up with that kind of menace eventually—desecration of a corpse, exile, imprisonment, torture, death, and similar punishments. Yet neither their violence nor their social authority can win over their rivals.

Since the warring parties remain inflexible, the sequence comes to an impasse epitomized by a debate that nobody wins.[3] In a more or less formally organized discussion, each debater (who may be represented by an aggressive friend) protects his or her reputation and abuses an opponent: Prometheus argues with Hermes (working for Zeus), Philoctetes with Neoptolemus (speaking for Odysseus), Teucer (defending Ajax) with Menelaus and then Agamemnon. *The Bacchae* brings together three debaters (Teiresias and Cadmus explain Dionysian religion to Pentheus). Clytemnestra, the protagonist of *Agamemnon*, disputes with the chorus (standing in for Agamemnon), and the chorus of *The Eumenides* (standing in for Clytemnestra) vies with Orestes and his patron Apollo.

Among the fifteen plays only one, *The Libation Bearers*, has no debate (among all the extant tragedies only eight have none); seven have a single debate; and in seven the argument falls into two parts or is supplemented by a second or even a third formal dispute. Sometimes, in a second debate, the chief actor disagrees with an *ally:* Oceanos offers friendly advice that Prometheus rejects; Tecmessa, advice that Ajax rejects; Chrysothemis, advice that Sophocles' Electra rejects. A verbal contest ordinarily follows the physical hostilities attending the second challenge, but occasionally precedes them as in *Hippolytus, The Bacchae, Medea,* and *Oedipus Rex*; for instance, Euripides' Hippolytus contends with Theseus just before his violent death.

These arguments, some twenty-four in the fifteen works, deal with one subject—honor. Eight entail the redress of insult; ten, revenge for a murdered relative; six, efforts to *prevent* disgrace. All feature the speakers' self-justification, but the "war of words" does not ensure success in preserving celebrity. For one thing, it occurs most often after distress has generated radical standpoints that preclude negotiation. With the exceptions of Neoptolemus, who gives in to Philoctetes, and the Furies in *The Eumenides,* who go along with Athena, neither party reevaluates his or her conclusions, and in no instance does either one listen with the objective of learning or compromising. The principal character staunchly maintains a compulsion to be constant to a fixed image; even though morbidly concerned about the opinions of peers, he or she stays pledged to an "inviolable" egocentric standard. Normally, therefore, the debate is spirited but inconclusive, further evidence of disunity between personal and social concepts of justice.

In addition, the debates are not only fruitless in result but also suspect in procedure: a distrust of "clever" words runs through many of the tragedies. A man of integrity can lose face when dealing with a manipulative adversary; as Achilles complains in the *Iliad,* "I, the best man in all the Achaean force, the best in battle, defeated only in the war of words." In the same vein, Oedipus at Colonus condemns Creon's "fraudulent speech": "what repartee! I know no honest man / able to speak so well under all conditions!" Medea condemns *Jason's* fraudulent speech:

> the plausible speaker
> Who is a villain deserves the greatest punishment.
> Confident in his tongue's power to adorn evil,
> He stops at nothing. Yet he is not really wise. (627–31)

And Hippolytus debates Theseus with reluctance:

> I am
> no man to speak with vapid, precious skill
> before a mob, although among my equals
> and in a narrow circle I am held
> not unaccomplished in the eloquent art.
> That is as it should be. The demagogue
> who charms a crowd is scorned by cultured experts. (986–89)

Neoptolemus in *Philoctetes* says of words, "if they are just, they are better than clever," a retort to shifty Odysseus who announces that "everywhere among the race of men / it is the tongue that wins and not the deed." Hecuba distrusts the "science of persuasion, / glozing evil with the slick of loveliness," although in her desperation she praises its utility ("the only art whose power / is absolute, worth any price we pay"). In *The Bacchae*, it is the protagonist who stands accused (by Teiresias) of dishonest speech:

> You are glib; your phrases come rolling out
> smoothly on the tongue, as though your words were wise
> instead of foolish. The man whose glibness flows
> from his conceit of speech declares the thing he is:
> a worthless and stupid citizen. (267–71)

Theseus in *Oedipus at Colonus* sums up the idea: "it is not in words / that I should wish my life to be distinguished, / but rather in things done." The honorable individual rarely descends to policies like that expediently adopted by Orestes in Sophocles' *Electra*, for whom "no word is base when spoken with profit."

Because quarreling with "base" characters might demean his central characters, Aeschylus—who does not devalue the male model as severely as Sophocles and (especially) Euripides—attaches less importance to the debate form. When present at all—none appears in four of his seven surviving tragedies—it is shorter than those conducted by his successors, averaging about 125 lines compared to 130 for Sophocles and 155 for Euripides. Aeschylus prefers brief contrapuntal dialogue (one to four lines per speaker); even his longer set speeches average only nineteen lines, compared to Sophocles' thirty-four and Euripides' forty. The statements of Prometheus, Clytemnestra, Electra, and Orestes are forceful but usually concise claims to equity.

Moreover, Aeschylus denies the antagonist equal time. The Furies questioning Orestes during the trial in *The Eumenides*, for instance, produce indictments that contain no speech longer than ten lines. Euripides and Sophocles, in contrast, make both sides in a debate deliver sizable tirades (between ten and sixty lines) of about the same length, and when imbalances do occur they frequently favor the antagonist, notably in *Oedipus at Colonus*— Polyneices pleads for a total of one hundred lines in his longer debate speeches, Oedipus responds with forty-seven—and *The Bacchae*, in which Cadmus and Teiresias overwhelm Pentheus ninety to sixty-three.

Whatever its prominence or balance, the debate represents a deadlock, not a reasoned exchange of views. That deadlock is terminated in the last stage of the action, the mediation, a conclusion not to be mistaken for the reconciliation of abstract values that Hegel thought the spectator would contemplate. About half the plays bring in some human or supernatural figure who contributes advice, assistance, or solace, and releases tension by implementing a more practical conclusion than the contenders were able to reach. In a lost sequel, Heracles will rescue Prometheus; Odysseus obtains permission from Agamemnon for a ceremonial burial of Ajax; Heracles persuades Philoctetes to return to Troy; King Aegeus (and a brace of dragons) befriends Medea; Athena votes for Orestes; Agamemnon intercedes for Hecuba; and the divinities receive Oedipus at Colonus. Or endings may be facilitated by prophecies in place of direct intervention, as in *Prometheus Bound, Hecuba, Antigone,* and *Oedipus Rex* (Oedipus receives oracular messages as an infant, young man, king, and exile). Only the endings of Aeschylus' *Agamemnon* and Sophocles' *Electra* lack intercession of any kind, human or divine.

But the prophecies or mediators arrange, at best, only a truce, extricating stubborn personalities from a predicament impossible to rationalize. And prophecy or intervention, especially from supernatural agents, does not always guarantee well-being, as Oedipus at Thebes, Orestes, and Hippolytus discover. The Furies harry Orestes at the end of *The Libation Bearers,* and the antagonist in *The Bacchae,* playing god and man, shatters his adversary. Like many humans, divine powers stress negation, not predication, failing to resolve the tragic contradiction between propriety and priority, and hardly attesting to a comprehensive spiritual wholeness.[4]

The progression outlined here does not take into account differing dramatic emphases. In some plays, interest centers on the consequences of shame; in others, including all those by Aeschylus, on resistance to shame. For example, an undeviating movement toward emotional and moral erosion in *The Bacchae* and *Oedipus Rex* runs counter to a tortuous movement toward reconstruction in *The Eumenides, Oedipus at Colonus,* and (presumably) the *Prometheia.* Yet one narrative plan shapes these works, and its recurrence suggests a simple conclusion. It suggests that individuals striving to consummate the model of manhood embodied in the tragedies fall naturally, like most young male animals, into a conflict mode. While this mode could conceivably provide them with a strenuous, wholesome opportunity to verify their worth and reputation, it actually evokes limitless insecurity, sorrow, and fury, their major motive in social relations becoming a crusade for revenge. Their obsession to defend and attack leads them to dissension, pain, isolation, and waste of talent. In a contest between dignity and disgrace, competitive noblemen brutalize each other, noblewomen reproduce the delusions of masculine vanity, choric types ineffectually decry the savagery, and mediators intercede after the debaters, estranged from kin or colleagues, have terminated sensible communication.

Madness comes to be associated with the tragic sequence as its cause or result. Among the secondary figures of Aeschylus, Io (*Prometheus Bound*) and Cassandra (*Agamemnon*) are subject to seizures arbitrarily brought on by a god, but in his principal characters the first tragedian often associates emotional imbalance with ethical extravagance.[5] "Your words declare you mad," Hermes tells Prometheus. In *The Eumenides* Orestes barely escapes the Furies, who appropriately punish with insanity not only certain crimes but also the presumption (itself a kind of insanity) that activates those crimes. Sophocles too shows us madness brought on by and signifying immoderate indignation and fear of disgrace. Philoctetes, prone to fits, refers to himself as "a man crazy with storms of sorrow / [who] speaks against his better judgment." Oedipus at Thebes vividly describes his state once he learns that Laius was killed at a certain crossroads by an impetuous stranger: "there comes upon me / a wandering of the soul—I could run mad" (trans. David Grene, *CGT* 2). And on identifying his parents he experiences "madness and stabbing pain and memory / of evil deeds I have done!" But even before that, his unfounded belligerence toward Jocasta, Teiresias, Creon, and others betrays a lack of balance. The intemperance and rashness he parades mark him as one who "could run mad."

Similarly, Creon in *Antigone* reports Ismene as "maddened, no longer mistress of herself"; following his own misfortune, he says, "I am mad with fear. . . . It was a god who . . . drove me to wild strange ways" (trans. Elizabeth Wyckoff, *CGT* 2). Creon may be dodging his own responsibility by blaming the supernatural, for even when a god does intercede it is usually to call attention to human arrogance. The sight of Ajax sitting among the animals he has butchered occasions these comments by his wife and comrades:

Tecmessa: Madness has seized our noble Ajax;
   He has come to ignominy in the night. . . .
Chorus: Insanity stands here revealed indeed!
   . . . .
   Better if he
   Were hidden in Hades, now his mind is gone:
   For though his proud lineage
   Excelled his warlike peers,
   He keeps no more the steady heart we knew,
   But ranges in extravagant madness. (216–17, 634–40)

Euripides can be said to specialize in associating arrogance with irrationality. Over and over he links the "chaos of our lives" to aristocratic "insolence" and "conceit." *The Bacchae* has already been discussed in this connection; a chain of reckless acts in *Hecuba* illustrates the point just as well. During his debate with Hecuba, Odysseus—an even more odious variant of this character than the one in *Philoctetes*—touts the sanctity of reputation:

> Tell me, what conduct could be worse
> than to give your friend a lifetime of honor and respect
> but neglect him when he dies? (311–13)

His words (quoted previously to define the heroic outlook) may seem sound, but he submits his pious query to exonerate himself for the murder of Hecuba's daughter Polyxena, a barbarous sacrifice intended to placate a dead warrior's spirit. He thus unwittingly underscores the viciousness of his creed, compounding its lunacy with specious arguments about "a lifetime of honor." Polyxena heightens the irony by interrupting the discussion, accepting her death, and disclosing a tighter grasp on "true nobility" than any of the highborn males whose idiotic persecution of innocents destabilizes their social order.

The persecution of Hecuba continues during another pair of attack-response actions accompanied by another formal argument that emphasizes the same confusion between "enduring excellence" and insane masculine egoism. Polymestor murders the son Hecuba entrusted to his care; she responds to this second challenge by blinding him and killing *his* sons. Incredibly, Agamemnon, the would-be mediator, calls upon the combatants, crazed by grief and hatred ("shrieking madness"), to carry on a debate!

> No more of this inhuman savagery now.
> Each of you will give his version of the case
> and I shall try to judge you both impartially. (1129–31)

Naturally, the case Polymestor makes to acquit himself is as specious as Odysseus' case in the first debate. Deprived of vision in a metaphorical as well as literal sense, he does not see that his bestiality begot Hecuba's; he blames his suffering, as many tragic figures do, on "the inconsistent gods" rather than on his own intemperance. In the resolution, his prophecy condemns Hecuba, then Agamemnon condemns *him*. These bizarre events bare the craziness of "heroic" ambition, not simply as practiced by particularly demented characters but as authorized by their rationale. Hecuba, untypically for a protagonist in Greek tragedy, spells out the message of disenchantment:

> We boast, are proud, we plume our confidence—
> the rich man in his insolence of wealth,
> the public man's conceit of office or success—
> and we are nothing; our ambition, greatness, pride,
> all vanity. (623–26)

"Random careless chance and change," Talthybius speculates, in a distinctly non-Hegelian frame of mind, "alone control the world."

Despite the world's commotion, Hecuba, heartened by the courage of her daughter, reaches beyond pain and pessimism to reassert a touching commitment to "uncorrupted, . . . enduring excellence" that answers the anarchic selfishness of both Polymestor and the good Greek soldiers. Sophocles and Aeschylus furnish similar reassurance. Oedipus, who at Thebes knew "madness and stabbing pain and memory of evil deeds," acquires this wisdom at Colonus:

> For every nation that lives peaceably,
> There will be many others to grow hard
> And push their arrogance to extremes: the gods
> Attend to these things slowly. But they [do] attend
> To those who put off God and turn to madness! (1533–37)

These enlightened characters, however, do not need to count on supernatural force to define justice, ensure safety, and cure mankind's "turn to madness." It is unnecessary for them to articulate their sense of decorum in hopeful, touching, even inspired statements predicting that those who desire unlimited rights will be, or should be, punished by a god or king. Retribution and the preservation of decorum are assured without such interventions: justice is already built into a storytelling scheme in which "fanatical" men and women invalidate themselves, dishonoring their convictions and deforming their personalities. To compensate for the denial of status, they suppress the supposedly inferior side of polarities like strong/weak, constant/changeable, self-sufficient/dependent, and they exalt the supposedly superior side out of sensible proportion. But in doing so they warp the basis of their social prominence while trying to preserve it; their emergency measures wreck the tenuous integration that produced their solidity. Desperation ends their tenure, a sad ending demonstrated through the logic of a sequence that transmits the irony of their glorious, doomed enterprise. Euripides, Sophocles, and Aeschylus uncovered chaos and rendered judgment through carefully structured collisions of talented, intolerant, self-negating personalities.

And the door to understanding this process was opened by Hegel! We stand indebted to him for the realization that the clash of opposing principles results in narrative inevitability. His error lay in overstating the rule of rationality. He did not appreciate the harsh, volatile egocentrism of the idealists in Greek drama, or the instability of their *two-sided* aim, or the anarchic result of their radical acts. He did not comprehend the cleavage—the mutual cancellation, to use his words—between pride and propriety, just as *they* did not. The defense of principle may bring about self-contradiction as well as factional strife, and that fact makes it difficult for us to visualize the spiritual harmony Hegel proposed. But he did perceive the basic pattern of actions that gave moral defeat an artistic form. He perceived the design of tragedy in the challenge to and calamitous response of impassioned characters battling for problematic values. He made us "sensitive to ruptures in a social order whose consistency is brought to a serious straining point, where justice collides with justice" (Gellrich, *Tragedy and Theory* 72).

5

Shakespeare's Fatal Female

A Dangerous Companion

Contrary to Hegel's observations on Renaissance drama, Shakespeare's tragic characters derive their careers from the same aristocratic cult or class that Athenian protagonists belong to, they subscribe to the same masculine objective of infinite excellence, and they fall into the same predicament that such an objective had brought about earlier. Their standards of outstanding performance and universal recognition are socially defined and socially oriented, at least initially, not arbitrarily set by each individual. Like their classical forebears, they require acceptance by their peers to be properly measured as magnificent beings, and when deprived of that fellowship they suffer similar disorientation. Their dedication to a stereotype of manly superiority is no less maniacal, their reversal no less unexpected, their need to defend the ego no more urgent and counterproductive, their confusion of gender roles no more pronounced, their solitude no more complete. "Princes are / A model which heaven makes like to itself," Simonides says in Shakespeare's *Pericles,* a work set in fifth-century Greece; "As jewels lose their glory if neglected, / So princes their renowns if not respected."[1]

But there is a different focus. In delivering his own critique of aristocratic values, Shakespeare retained the challenge delivered by one status-monger to another, then superimposed upon it a new kind of attack that diminished its importance. Like his predecessors, he saw tragedy as a tale in which a person of "renown" forfeits "respect," but he chose to relocate the chief source of respect. The attachment of his protagonist to a loved one is as absolute as the Athenian's concern for approval by military or civic leaders, and the breach of that attachment is as demoralizing. When Shakespeare revised the sequence dramatizing dissension and madness, he shifted his attention from a brittle communal interdependence to a brittle domestic interdependence.

Classical authors had, of course, extensively explored the family as well as public context of heroic behavior, so Elizabethan dramatists had a wealth of precedents to draw upon in addition to the gender stereotypes that family relations were usually based upon. Male-female alliances existed plentifully in many genres, including epic, drama, and mythological tale (Odysseus and Athena or Penelope, Electra and Orestes, Antigone and Haemon, Clytemnestra and Aegisthus, Tecmessa and Ajax, and so on). A man's reputation or welfare might hang on a woman's allegiance (Agamemnon and Electra, Oedipus or Polyneices and Antigone, for example). And quite often a relationship fell apart (Clytemnestra and Agamemnon, Medea and Jason, Jocasta and Oedipus, Agave and Pentheus, Phaedra and Hippolytus), especially during emergencies when the male insisted on his own judgment as the authority of last resort.

Combining these situations, Shakespeare devised a unique dialogue between traditional gender types. He did not feature female protagonists and therefore subordinated the themes of feminine protest and transformation; he presented the female as a crucial influence upon the male rather than an opponent or usurper. Shakespeare had the two share certain laudable traits like moral purity or indomitable will, contrary to the ancient emphasis on mutually exclusive gender functioning, then went on to destroy that mutuality. Having bonded with the hero by personifying qualities he worships, his dangerous companion abuses or appears to abuse their bond and in so doing alters the antagonism passed down by the earlier drama. Shakespeare's male characters face the threat that a trusted woman will weaken them, not that a strong woman will supplant them, as in *Agamemnon, Medea, Antigone,* and other works, or that a strong male will force them to "turn womanish" (*Prometheus Bound, Ajax, The Bacchae,* etc.) When the Athenian hero lapses in judgment, he does so in disagreement with others; Shakespeare's chief characters lapse through their *consonance* with another, taken in by bad counsel or bad example. Since there are few choric or supernatural advisers to supply the counsel or example, it is betrayal by an intimate that nearly obliterates their self-confidence. To harbor a traitor within one's inner circle is not new. The novelty occurs when a *soul mate* does great harm while wishing to help.[2]

Shakespeare's innovation probably took its distinctive features from the medieval doctrine that a pernicious, deceptive serpent acted as a false counselor in conjunction with a naive or misguided woman and brought about Adam's fall. Both serpent and woman are present in the major tragedies, only the female in *Coriolanus* and *Antony and Cleopatra*. *Julius Caesar* exhibits just the snake, with no Eve figure except for the well-meaning wife in a minor role who advises Caesar to forgo his "constancy." *Romeo and Juliet*, an exception to this practice, will be excluded from our discussion because Juliet stimulates Romeo to consummate, not savage, his honor during the classic standoff between a protagonist's personal and political desires.

The fatal female propels Shakespeare's tragic figures toward dishonor, but far from becoming amoral, those figures owe their dramatic lives to an untenable but tenacious double duty similar, though not identical, to what we see in Athenian drama, a failed commitment to integrate unqualified self-love (a solo act) with unqualified trust (a partnership). Hegel, of course, judged the failed partnerships in Shakespearean tragedy to be unenlightened by universal law:

> Subjective honour, love, and fidelity are not strictly ethical qualities and virtues, but only forms of the romantic self-filled inwardness of the subject.... Even if the subject has a noble will and deep soul, still what enters into his actions and their relations and existence is only capriciousness and contingency ... which, so far as an ethical content goes, is still without substance.... Romantic love also has its limitation. What its content lacks, that is to say, is absolute *universality*. It is only the *personal* feeling of the individual subject, and it is obviously not filled with the eternal interests and objective content of human existence, with family, political ends, country, duties arising from one's calling or class, with freedom and religious feeling, but only with its own self. (*Aesthetics* 1: 553, 556, 566)

It is easy to see why Hegel concluded that Shakespeare's modification of previous dramatic practice lacked ethical substance and confined itself to personal feelings. The rage of most Greek heroes and heroines dominates their personalities and cements them into a stubborn, uncritical posture. However wild and lethal their emotional shiftings may be, however severely they tear their social bonds, they maintain a relatively firm grip on the portion of their double standard still intact, their unstoppable campaign to realize an ideal of self-determination (although half a loaf does not suffice). Shakespeare's major figures too relinquish their reliance upon significant others. But in addition, as a result of the disillusion generated by a ruinous family relationship, they come closer than their Greek ancestors, except for devastated characters like Hecuba, to relinquishing also their devotion to a godlike, independent "self." As in the earlier tragedy, their own treason fractures a composite imperative regulating conduct, treason triggered by real or supposed insult; their indignation, however, is more seriously eroded by regret, and shame is compounded more grossly with guilt. Their infidelity and the infidelity of their female ally contaminate their assurance as an example of sterling manhood and preclude arbitration or restoration—loss of faith, admitted in speeches of unbearable bereavement, not loss of face.

The contamination is deadly: before the protagonist, disenchanted after misjudging a critical relationship, reclaims the spirit of his former majesty, he leaps into a pit of misanthropy and self-recrimination rarely encountered in Greek tragedy. At those times, his confession to complicity or his admission of futility denotes an awareness, momentary as it may be, far more mortifying than that reached by his Athenian counterpart. It leaves him with a *less* intense egoism than that retained by the classical hero, contrary to Hegel's observation. This awareness, this profound cynicism, struck Hegel as antimoral. But while Shakespeare's protagonist may seem to have given up the traditional "heroic" standpoint, he never quite jettisons high principle; it survives to engage his newly acquired cynicism in an inward debate between moral assertion and abasement that in the major plays replaces the old-fashioned formal debates between rivals. Like his predecessors, he attests to the continuing relevance of a code he has all but demolished.

Three Roman Plays

Shakespeare follows the classical sequence most faithfully, as we would expect, in his plays about Roman statesmen. The three best known—*Julius Caesar, Coriolanus,* and *Antony and Cleopatra*— duplicate that pattern: two rounds of attack and counterattack bring to crisis the monomania of a personage whose place or fame has been jeopardized. Brutus reacts with predictable violence to Caesar's presumed longing for dictatorial sovereignty; later he responds to the danger forwarded by Antony. Coriolanus also engages in two political-military battles, one foreign and one local: once the Volscians fail to unseat him, the Roman commoners and tribunes mount opposition that ends with his exile. His outrage at the second challenge repeats that shown by Athenian characters when their authority is questioned or put in harm's way. In *Antony and Cleopatra*, enemies of the state (Labienus and Sextus) again launch the first assault, then Octavius, a colleague of Antony, launches the second. Antony's self-pity and exasperation at his humiliating defeats could have been taken from the *Iliad* or the Greek tragedies.

Typically, an associate rather than some foreign enemy administers the more telling blow; in classical tragedy, after all, the closer the tie, the greater potential for mischief. It is this potential that Shakespeare seizes upon to modify the format by extending the challenge to an intimate companion. He introduces a female (except in *Julius Caesar*) who supports the protagonist and so is not identified as a menace, a cherished individual who misleads her confidant or entices him to act in an uncharacteristic, self-destructive manner when he responds to the political attack. The chief character confers trust in a peer, parent, or lover—Brutus in Cassius, Coriolanus in Volumnia, Antony in Cleopatra—that is equivalent to the confidence he holds in himself, yet each confederate exploits that bond. Cassius persuades Brutus to commit treason to safeguard honor. Volumnia convinces Coriolanus to forgo revenge upon his fellow Romans even though, in this case, *refraining* from treason jeopardizes honor. Cleopatra distracts Antony with her sexual allure, twice leads her navy into retreat ("betrayed I am," he wails), and further undermines his self-possession by shamming suicide. In each play, a male paragon is inveigled into abandoning the protocols of martial bearing that had buttressed his status, especially the protocol dictating loyalty (accountability to others) and "constancy": Brutus reneges on his allegiance to Caesar; Coriolanus, his to Aufidius; Antony, his to Octavia and Octavius. "For who so firm," Cassius wryly remarks, "that cannot be seduced?"

Initially, not one of these protagonists recognizes (Aristotle's term) his seducer, who is taken instead to be a loyal ally. Neither Brutus nor Coriolanus *ever* fully comprehends the causal connection between the betrayal carried out by his companion and his own outrageous crime, or the fact that he is not the passive victim he sometimes imagines himself to be. This inability to evaluate character correctly and estimate consequences handicaps most tragic actors, and can be blamed on their tendency to conceive principles of behavior as absolute commandments (Hegel's term), which makes them blind to or intolerant of alternative behavior, unwilling to negotiate, and obsessive when opposed. Even though they cannot survive without "respect," they persistently justify the self-indulgent attitude that antagonizes their peers and shreds their reputation.

Thus Brutus stays fixed in staunch self-acquittal like a Prometheus or an Ajax, with no awareness whatsoever that his "hasty spark," the rashness clearly visible to others, has deranged the essential relationships to Caesar and Cassius. He cannot concede error or "frailty"; he upholds his righteousness (though with some loss of equanimity) to the grave. "I shall have glory by this losing day / More than Octavius and Mark Antony," he grandly decrees, reveling in the same "formal constancy" boasted of by the man he kills. He never realizes that his search for glory has compromised his "formal" commitment with *in*constancy. Cassius too, however sneaky his intrigues, proudly celebrates an immovable posture. They both take their cue from the model they mistrust, who professes to be as changeless as the "Northern Star," and they all lack the insight of Strato ("Brutus only overcame himself"). Strato understands the ironic end game that their delusions of permanency have led them to play out. He understands how an inflated ego can thrust a man, intent upon an unattainable ideal and misled by a deceptive friend, into disastrous errors of judgment and resistance to blame.

Similarly, Coriolanus continues to believe in his impeccable rectitude and inexhaustible virility after his plans have come to nothing, plans to govern Rome or conquer it. Imitating the classical style until his last decision, he (along with Caesar, Brutus, and Cassius) equates retraction with cowardice. Ordinary folk, the "common cry of curs," reveal their "unstable slightness"; he, in contrast, endures every trying circumstance without wavering—self-reliant and unchangeable. "I'll stand," he brags, "as if a man were author of himself / And knew no other kin." His definition of manhood earns the respect of his society. "He's the rock, the oak not to be wind-shaken," a soldier comments; he has "affected the fine strains of honor, / To imitate the graces of the gods" (Volumnia); "he wants nothing of a god but eternity, and a heaven to throne in" (Menenius).

In time, however, the commoners denounce the inspiring but rigid stance that has made him stand out, and Volumnia agrees ("you are too absolute"), or as Aufidius puts it, "strengths by strengths do fail." At the conclusion even Coriolanus notices his absurdity and therefore decides (without much explanation) to give up his "strength"—his unyielding will—in favor of a greater good, "compassion." Deferring to Volumnia in a hasty reversal ("Is't possible that so short a time can alter the condition of a man?"), he "bowed his nature, never known before / But to be rough, unswayable, and free." He does not gather that this new position, denying both his "nature" and his pact with Aufidius, might be as suicidal as the old one. No, instead he falls back on his habit of mindless self-congratulation (he proudly remembers being as murderous toward the Volscians as "an eagle in a dovecote"), refutes Aufidius' terrible insult ("thou boy of tears"), and never perceives that he had vacillated from the start or that his defection could possibly be something more serious than a favor to his mother.

In *Coriolanus* and *Julius Caesar,* Shakespeare took up the subject first examined by Homer and Aeschylus—the immaturity and instability of an "absolute" temper—and embellished it with a theme of poisonous intimacy. But in those works he did not plumb the depths of renunciation such a temperament could submerge itself in. Instead of investigating that metamorphosis fully, the dramatist orchestrated elaborate self-justifications in the Athenian-Roman debate mode, with balanced arguments and elegant rhetorical techniques. He went further in *Antony and Cleopatra*, the Roman play nearest in conception to his major tragedies. Antony repeats with greater awareness the irony that a military career founded on "constancy" can reverse its direction in "so short a time," a reversal prompted by a beloved woman.

Lust, not filial deference, unmans him. His fellow soldiers judge that he has violated "experience, manhood, honor" for "present pleasure," just as Aufidius condemns Coriolanus for sacrificing manhood in response to "a few drops of women's rheum." He is criticized for neglecting honor, not for overindulging it: "the triple pillar of the world," Philo mourns in the sexist terminology inherited from Athenian drama, "transformed / Into a strumpet's fool." "For shame! Transform us not to women," Enobarbus cautions. Enobarbus, Octavius, Canidius, and Scarus all vent the same fear of gender conversion felt by Greek characters from Prometheus to Pentheus. Antony replies bravely to insult, but he acknowledges his inconsistency with a clarity foreign to Coriolanus or Brutus:

> If I lose mine honor,
> I lose myself. (III.iv.22–23)
>
> Indeed I have lost command. (III.xi.23)
>
> I have offended reputation,
> A most unnoble swerving. (III.xi.49–50)
>
>   here I am Antony,
> Yet cannot hold this visible shape . . . .
> She has robbed me of my sword. (IV.xiv.13–14, 23)

Since Antony is unable to unite his functions as fighter and lover—an unclassical sort of combat between martial "honors" and sexual "taints"—and since mediation by third parties makes even less impact in Shakespearean than in Athenian tragedy, he atones with a warrior's last resort. And as his grasp upon "reputation" weakens, Cleopatra's becomes firmer, contrary to the stereotypical opinion of Antony's colleagues. She goes from capriciously seductive to "marble-constant": "My resolution's placed, and I have nothing / Of woman in me." At the end she copies an image Antony had almost given up, the double "transformation" pivoting on their altered reputations for predictability, the ultimate Hegelian asset. Hegel saw the transience of Shakespeare's characters and their aims, never their heart-rending confirmation of value after its loss.

The Major Tragedies

The shaky marriage Shakespeare put together between the uncertain reliability of an intrepid male and the uncertain reliability of a nurturing female produced the gyrations of Macbeth, Othello, Hamlet, and Lear. His introspective tragedies trace the psychological twists and turns of glorious "princes" who mix intense egocentrism with intense trust. His conclusion: the princes, once those they rely upon deceive them (now clearly the primary challenge), surrender both vanity and trust. When they belatedly come to grips with their own complicity in evil—an awareness that Brutus and Coriolanus, in common with most Greek protagonists, do not reach—they descend to a cynicism ("Othello's occupation's gone!") expressed in Greek drama most caustically by Euripides and in Roman drama by Seneca. They waver between self-reinforcement and self-belittlement in a cycle moving from innocence to loss, criminality, relinquishment, and then reassertion, a subjective cycle Hegel misunderstood. Their fluctuations relegate the *political* relevance of insane actions, but not the *ethical* relevance, to second place.[3]

In the four works, wars that in Athenian tragedy might bring about the major confrontation, and that in the Roman plays would still carry heavy dramatic weight, often shrink to prologues and epilogues. The impending invasion of Denmark by Norway, the rebellion against King Duncan, the Turkish fleet making for Cyprus—these military excursions provide a background for more personal strife, and even when wars take on greater importance, as in the uprising against Macbeth and the French attack upon ancient Britain, they are overshadowed by the treachery of an esteemed female. The moral influence of Lady Macbeth (along with the witches) is for Macbeth deadlier than the civil war initiated by Malcolm and Macduff; after the Turkish invasion miscarries, marital, not martial, warfare assumes central attention in *Othello;* and Hamlet's self-esteem receives a harder blow from Gertrude's adultery, which poisons belief in honorable activity ("How weary, stale, flat, and unprofitable"), than from Norway's invasion or Claudius' treachery, which when verified can be met with a conventional reply. In *King Lear*, social and natural turmoil amplify the multiple shocks sent out by Lear's "unkind" daughters. Gloucester reviews the two kinds of "division," one rending the larger community, the second—a more insidious calamity—tearing apart society's foundation, the family: "Love cools, friendship falls off, brothers divide. In cities, mutinies; in countries, discord; in palaces, treason; and the bond cracked 'twixt son and father.... Machinations, hollowness, treachery, and all ruinous disorders follow us disquietly to our graves" (I.ii. 104–7, 110–12).

The fatal female delivers a test of manhood (stage one) when she counsels or commits infidelity (or seems to). The snake figure (Shakespeare's drama crawls with vipers, asps, adders, and other serpents) has either seduced her (Claudius and Gertrude) or made her *appear* unfaithful (Iago and Desdemona) or eclipsed her goodness (Regan-Goneril and Cordelia) or augmented her pernicious influence (the witches and Lady Macbeth). Since she does not *intend* to degrade the hero, and since the malicious serpents are disguised as friends, it becomes very difficult to tell friend from foe.

Set into incoherent motion by these would-be allies, the four protagonists duplicate the crime done (or supposedly done) to them by violating their duty to a family member or in *Macbeth* a virtuous "kinsman" and political superior. In this second stage, Macbeth breaks faith with his king; Othello, with his wife; Hamlet, with his father; and Lear, with his faithful daughter. Their own treason in an intimate relationship becomes the origin of their failure as leaders.

Lady Macbeth and the witches "betray in deepest consequence" by appealing to the masculine instinct for recognition animating Macbeth. To inflame it they point out that Duncan (and later Banquo's descendants) will override his "sovereign sway and masterdom," just as Cassius points out that Caesar will circumscribe Brutus. In choosing this tack, Lady Macbeth misleads herself as well as her husband, since she gives up not only feminine soft-heartedness ("unsex me here") but also, eventually, the manly brutality she summons so effectively (her "undaunted mettle," Macbeth observed, "should compose / Nothing but males"). Her double sacrifice outdoes that of her husband, who though "cowed" dies with "harness on [his] back." Reduced to feminine helplessness and hysteria, she differs from the steadily courageous Volumnia and the increasingly courageous Cleopatra, but all three introduce their men to betrayal.

Macbeth belatedly discerns his wife's self-subversion ("a mind diseased"). He had already discerned his own. "I dare do all that may become a man," he had protested; "who dares do more is none." He knew the ground rules of "this even-handed justice," whereby murdering Duncan amounted to spiritual suicide, given their common subscription to the warrior's code. "To know my deed, 'twere best not know myself"; "I am afraid to think what I have done." Yet while he anticipated his demoralization, he dismissed it, switching at moments of decision to the stoic manner of Brutus, Coriolanus, Octavius, and their soldierly comrades. "I cannot taint with fear," he insisted: he could block guilt with manly control. So he condemns himself to an interminable argument, carried on largely in his fantasies, between "valor" and "fear" or guilt. The argument is more fully reported than Antony's debate between "honors" and "taints";

never-ending, useless self-laceration damns an invincible general to suffer the emotional vacillation Hegel had contempt for, a condition popularly associated with madmen, children, cowards—and women. Lady Macbeth knows the supreme insult: "Your constancy / Hath left you unattended."

After bad advice from a friend, or bad example, Shakespeare's major tragic characters suffer radical metamorphoses, commit an unpardonable breach of faith, and then ask Othello's question, "Why should honor outlive honesty?" In *Othello* a male traitor manufactures the *illusion* of a female traitor, "honest" Iago prodding the protagonist to worse disloyalty than his own. Despite his renown as "a constant, loving, noble nature"—or *because* of that nature—Othello is predisposed to extremes of behavior, to the same sea change that turns Macbeth and Brutus into murderers, Coriolanus into a "boy of tears," and Antony into a "strumpet's fool." "Perplexed in the extreme," he laments his disenchantment with a loved one quite analytically, in the all-or-nothing terminology of Ajax, Prometheus, Clytemnestra, and Medea:

> But there where I have garnered up my heart,
> Where either I must live or bear no life,
> The fountain from the which my current runs
> Or else dries up—to be discarded thence. (IV.ii.57–60)

"That's he that was Othello," he exclaims; "My lord is not my lord," Desdemona notes; and Lodovico mourns the transformation from model to maniac:

> Is this the noble Moor whom our full Senate
> Call all in all sufficient? Is this the nature
> Whom passion could not shake? whose solid virtue
> The shot of accident nor dart of chance
> Could neither graze nor pierce? (IV.i.257–61)

When Othello, Antony, and Macbeth injure innocent parties in response to challenge, and thereby pervert their "solid virtue" while trying to preserve it, they articulate (along with statements to the contrary) their consciousness of devaluation:

> Farewell the plumèd troop, and the big wars
> That make ambition virtue . . .
> Farewell! Othello's occupation's gone!
>
> —*Othello* (III.iii.349–50, 357)

> No more a soldier....
> I... condemn myself to lack
> The courage of a woman.
>
> —*Antony and Cleopatra* (IV.iv.42, 59–60)
>
> I have lived long enough. My way of life
> Is fall'n into the sear, the yellow leaf.
> . . . . .
> I 'gin to be aweary of the sun,
> And wish th' estate o'th'world were now undone.
>
> —*Macbeth* (V.iii.22–23, v.49–50)

"When I love thee not," Othello prophesied to his wife, "Chaos is come again."

"Chaos" is Hamlet's theme too. Commenting on his "transformation," Ophelia sounds like Desdemona: "Lord, we know what we are, but know not what we may be." Hamlet extends to men, beginning with himself, his contempt for the unfaithfulness of women:

> the power of beauty will sooner transform honesty from what it is to a bawd than the force of honesty can translate beauty into his likeness.... We are arrant knaves all; believe none of us. (III.i.111–13, 129)

> Rebellious hell,
> If thou canst mutine in a matron's bones,
> To flaming youth let virtue be as wax
> And melt in her own fire. (III.iv.83–86)

Disappointed by his mother and by Ophelia ("frailty, thy name is woman"), and shaken by the deceptions practiced by Claudius, Hamlet in turn disappoints someone who depends upon *him*, his mourning as a scandalized son (initial response to challenge) interfering with his obligation as a dutiful son (the second response). Since honor in Greek and Elizabethan tragedy so often dictates revenge, his guilt comes from *not* engaging in murder. His father's spirit must "whet" his "almost blunted purpose" before he can complete the violent course that confirms the stereotypical male: "my thoughts be bloody or be nothing worth!" He echoes Shakespeare's other confused blue-blooded activists when he claims "I am constant to my purposes" while deriding himself ("what a rogue and peasant slave am I!") for his deficiencies and the deficiencies of others.

Like Hamlet, Othello, Macbeth, and Antony, King Lear entertains misgivings regarding characters upon whose "honesty" his "authority" hangs. Hamlet doubts the credibility of the ghost, Gertrude, Ophelia, and Claudius; Othello doubts Desdemona; Macbeth, the witches; Antony, Cleopatra; and Lear, his three daughters. In a variation of the theme, Lear initiates the usual chain reaction by denouncing his youngest daughter for her insulting sincerity ("thy truth then be thy dower!") rather than for the serpentine guile usually attributed to the female challenger and practiced by Goneril and Regan. He too goes on to condemn all mankind for the sins of individuals, a repudiation that questions the social cohesion necessary for heroic existence. As he compulsively endeavors to "resume the shape which thou dost think / I have cast off for ever," his own unfaithfulness, to Cordelia and to humanity in general, pushes him into insanity and impotence—into abandoning his royal identity. He turns into a caricature of his former self, in the Euripidean and Senecan tradition. His cry, "Who is it that can tell me who I am?" voices the derangement of Medea and Pentheus as well as that of Othello, Hamlet, and Macbeth.

For these Shakespearean characters, feminine trickery or disloyalty supplants forthright masculine hostility; the voice of choric moderation and common sense fades away; and shame, intensified by guilt, sours into cynicism and surrender. Self-awareness deepens the classical metamorphosis almost to the point where, having dishonored their allegiances, they also give up the sacred notion of being "all in all sufficient." For Macbeth, "Life's but a walking shadow"; for Hamlet, "We are arrant knaves all"; for Othello, "'tis the plague of great ones; / Prerogatived are they less than the base"; and for Lear, all men (including himself) are fools or knaves, all women Centaurs "down from the waist."[4]

Yet pride in immaculate manhood manages to survive such profound debasement. These failed fanatics continually commute from negation to reassertion, although they learn too much about human fallibility to regain the purity of their original dedication. As their foes launch further assaults (stage three), they renew their spirit and perform a last act of military valor that concludes the defense of exceptional quality (stage four). Macbeth regains self-possession and fights bravely to his death; Hamlet begs blessing of his mother, then defeats Claudius and Laertes; Othello reclaims "honor" and lost love, wounds Iago, and escapes further shame by taking his own life; Lear, after devising a prescription for rational living, manages to kill Cordelia's executioner. Their oscillations between innocence and awareness, courage and despair, responsibility and a demented egoism generate the vibrancy of Shakespearean tragedy.

Shakespeare draws out these back-and-forth motions in great emotional detail; he shows his chief characters surrendering control over their behavior and experiencing indecision or bewilderment as well as cynicism, rage, and sorrow, just those feelings that Hegel found unsuitable for tragedy. Hegel condemned "modern" drama most of all for its "vacillation":

> the weakness of irresolution, the swithering of reflection, perplexity about the reasons that are to guide decision.... Such dithering figures generally appear by being themselves in the grip of a twofold passion which drives them from one decision or one deed to another simultaneously.... To put this discord into one and the same individual must always involve much awkwardness....
>
> But what is worst of all is to exhibit such indecision and vacillation of character, and of the whole man, as a sort of perverse and sophistical dialectic and then to make it the main theme of the entire drama, so that truth is supposed to consist precisely in showing that no character is inwardly firm and self-assured. (2: 1228–29)

Hegel did not sense the vitality of vacillation, the ongoing internal struggle between self-veneration and respect for others. He did not see that both the enemies and the champion of pride could reside in one stereotype, creating an insoluble conflict that bedeviled Athenian as well as later tragedy. And he remained indifferent to the tremendous power released by the decay of an intimate rather than adversarial relationship. But is it so strange that pity and terror could be roused by unimaginable betrayals among friends instead of competition among rivals, or by simultaneous victory and defeat instead of unwavering loyalty and strength?

The Flux of Metaphor

6

Nietzschean Dream Imagery in Aeschylus and Seneca

Nietzsche Recasts the Problem

Tragic playwrights expose a two-sided truth. Hegel exerted a far-reaching influence (for better and worse) on students of Greek and Shakespearean drama because he perceived how contrary values were embodied in a sequence of divisive acts. We have modified his idea by relocating the chief source of conflict in a self-contradiction that disrupts the protagonist's system of values, but we can go further by saying that polarization extends beyond a conflict of positive principles. The model proclaiming the egocentric goal of masculine conduct turns out to be unstable, and that instability leads to his disintegration. "What was great before," recites the chorus of *Prometheus Bound,* is brought to "nothingness." Hegel could not accept as morally meaningful the alternation of affirmation and negation, yet such flux creates the tragic double-sidedness, a constant inconstancy that results from the clash of admirable but incompatible aims within the exceptional individual as well as within his or her community. This violent oscillation between assertion and rejection is as common in classical protagonists as in Shakespeare's deranged heroes, their distortion of traditional obligations no less extreme. When Hegel accused Renaissance and modern dramatists of questioning, endangering, or disregarding traditional laws, he was describing—without intending to—Greek as well as Shakespearean and later theater. Neither Shakespeare nor the Athenian playwrights, however, should be called amoral: they witness not only the inconsistency, destructiveness, and impermanence but also the power, validity, and attraction of the ancient masculine stereotype.

And there may be value in impermanence too! Another nineteenth-century German philosopher, Friedrich Nietzsche, announced the blessings of transience fifty years after Hegel delivered his lectures on aesthetics. Nietzsche recast the rules organizing the theory of tragedy. He rediscovered the emptiness of ethical directives and took up what Hegel despised—illogic, fluidity, degeneration. His hero, or antihero, starts off in the condition that the Shakespearean and Athenian heroes descend to, deprived of customary expectations, coalitions, and principles, no longer "all in all sufficient" according to a hallowed substantive scheme. We may still find Hegel's notion of warring ideals useful, but since wars between noble causes often trigger fundamental changes, we must also take seriously Nietzsche's ideas on the metamorphosis, not merely the conflict, of values. Nietzsche's remarks on literature in *The Birth of Tragedy* (published in 1872)[1] and *The Will to Power* (written 1883–88, published 1901)[2] offer us a stimulating way of looking at transformations not attributable to ethical or logical causation and unfolding primarily in a succession of ambiguous metaphors instead of a succession of ironic actions. Uncertainty follows the challenge to morality, appropriately expressed in ever-changing, enigmatic images.

This approach to tragedy does not make Nietzsche an unalloyed cynic: his account of flux in our natural life cycle includes renewal as well as decay. Flux, or "eternal becoming" (in contrast to eternal being or permanent order), involves genesis along with destruction. It is animated by discontinuity ("dissonance," mutation) and repetition (recurrence or reinstatement). Mutation endlessly reverses the kaleidoscopic "appearances" that take the place of Hegel's well-defined, stable identities and principles, but then it inevitably repeats the original structures. The raw desire to stay alive breaks down all forms and continuously restores them, reiterating an infinite number of times discordant, ever-shifting contraries. Innumerable outbursts of energy follow innumerable closures: "Everything becomes and recurs eternally—escape is impossible! . . . The law of the conservation of energy demands *eternal recurrence:* . . . the world as a circular movement that has already repeated itself infinitely often and plays its game *in infinitum*" (*Will to Power* 545, 547, 549).[3]

The process of becoming is thus both degenerative and circular, anarchic and predictable. Surprisingly, Nietzsche's cycle of decay followed by restoration is analogous to Hegel's rhythm of collision (mutual cancellation) and reconciliation.[4] In each, "eternal" intelligence transcends one-sided logic, but for Nietzsche a chaotic "life force," not an unchanging spiritual "substance," constitutes that intelligence. When he speaks of "eternal contradiction," he conceives it affirmatively as a nonrational, disruptive-creative "begetter of all things" (*Birth of Tragedy* 33). "This is the profoundest conception of suffering: the form-giving forces are in painful collision. . . . [In a] tragic-Dionysian state . . . the highest degree of pain cannot be excluded" (*Will to Power* 365, 452–53).

Modernist (or Romantic or Darwinian) as this sounds, Nietzsche names Heraclitus as his mentor; German thinkers in the nineteenth century never strayed far from Greek poets and philosophers.[5] He credits the theory of flux to his "predecessor" in the sixth century B.C.: "The eternal and exclusive Becoming, the total instability of all reality and actuality, which continually works and becomes and never *is*, as Heraclitus teaches—is an awful and appalling conception" (*Early Greek Philosophy*, trans. Maximilian A. Mügge, *Works* 2: 100). "In so far as the senses show us a state of Becoming, of transiency, and of change, they do not lie. But in declaring [as well] that Being was an empty illusion, Heraclitus will remain eternally right" (*Twilight of the Idols* 18).

And from flux comes disintegration and reiteration. Heraclitus envisioned "polarity as the divergence of a force into two qualitatively different, opposite actions, striving after reunion. A quality is set continually at variance with itself and separates itself into its opposites: these opposites continually strive again one towards another" (*Early Greek Philosophy* 101). "The doctrine of the 'Eternal Recurrence'—that is to say, of the absolute and eternal repetition of all things in periodical cycles—this doctrine of Zarathustra's might, it is true, have been taught [by Heraclitus]" (*Ecce Homo*, trans. Anthony M. Ludovici, *Works* 17: 73).

From his Heraclitean-Dionysian affirmation, Nietzsche goes on to claim "art as the redemption of the sufferer—as the way to states in which suffering is willed, transfigured, deified, where suffering is a form of great delight" (*Will to Power* 452–53). The tragic poet translates his exaltation—his "orgiastic" sense of "vitality and strength"—into symbols that communicate it with serene detachment (*Twilight of the Idols* 119). "Apollonian" dream-pictures, changing and reforming, can be arranged to give an "illusion" of artistic order, suggesting yet distancing the terror and shock of cosmic might (or night). Stories about lusty heroes and ecstatic choric groups carefully recast the "terrifying and questionable" facts as a "dream" or fantasy, a "mere phantom." "What therefore is truth?" Nietzsche asks in *Early Greek Philosophy*: "a mobile army of metaphors, metonymies, anthropomorphisms. . . . Truths are illusions, . . . worn-out metaphors" (180). In the hands of Aeschylus or Sophocles (Euripides gets rejected as a rationalist by Nietzsche and as an irrationalist by Hegel), tragedy becomes "an Apollonian embodiment of Dionysian insights and powers" (*Birth of Tragedy* 56).

Aeschylus: Now You See It, Now You Don't!

Can we make Aeschylus a forerunner of Nietzsche and a follower of Heraclitus? Unlikely as it might seem, Aeschylus, in common with Sophocles and (despite disapproval by both Hegel and Nietzsche) Euripides, contrived equivocal "dream" symbols that bear out Nietzsche's ideas on the fluidity of form at the same time that he was executing a Hegelian narrative format. Despite Hegel's dislike of "vacillation," repetitive swings between something (something valuable) and nothing (denial of something valuable) have characterized tragic stories since the Athenians first produced them, and that duplexity has been regularly manifested in imagery. The process of metaphorical annihilation and rebirth, like the progression of divisive actions, reflects the fluidity of tragedy.

To illustrate, we can follow the course of Nietzschean mutation and reiteration expressed through light and darkness references in the *Oresteia*.[6] The first play of the trilogy presents an extraordinary contest between the two metaphors. Although conventional values associated with light are subverted, light maintains its traditional nature while taking on the properties of its opposite, so that it becomes both positive and negative, and darkness exhibits the same convertibility.

As preparation for this elaborate paradox, Aeschylus first installs the customary associations. *Agamemnon* opens with a mood of good cheer: before dawn, a beacon fire signals the fall of Troy, an event promising "redemption" to different citizens for different reasons—to Agamemnon, who had found it necessary to sacrifice his daughter to achieve victory; to Clytemnestra, deprived of husband and daughter during the war; to the Argive elders, troubled by these matters and by something not yet stated; and to the watchman, after his tedious vigil. "Now let there be again redemption from distress," the watchman prays, "the flare burning from the blackness in good augury" (lines 19–20).[7] Disturbed by a threat he dares not name, he hopes that the "blaze of the darkness" will dispel the miseries of night, that a "harbinger of day's / shining" (21) will be an auspicious "prelude" to great joy.[8] The distant flickering of the beacon anticipates the stronger light of dawn; in the same way, his hope may soon be magnified by all Argos.

The watchman treats the signal not just as a fortunate metaphor but as the appropriate vehicle of communication put into service by a forceful queen with "male strength of heart." Clytemnestra's thirty-five-line review of the beacon's progress (281–316) elaborates this notion.[9] The fires of the Achaeans overcame the Trojan nation, and her fires overcame the immense distance to Argos from Troy—the second victory epitomized the first. She imagines the flame-herald as a "flare in exultation" leaping across Aegean islands to telegraph the most glorious triumph of the age, and the vivid details of her description come across as *her* triumph. Her terminology extracts a climactic, almost sexual vision from the "bright message." "Timbers flaming into gold" were "like the sunrise." "Far-thrown" blazes grew "stronger" as they advanced, building a "stintless heaping force." She proclaims that transition from night to brightness as prelude to a corresponding renaissance in the kingdom. And when her sacrificial fires replace the beacons in the brilliance of day, they complete her prediction of peace and happiness by invoking divine favor with *their* light.

Then the herald articulates for a third time the idea of beneficent light emerging from the darkness and signaling victory (503–37, 551–81, 636–80). His narration of the army's disastrous return voyage dwells upon the dangers encountered during a terrible night storm at sea. The only light that fell upon the destruction and chaos was given off by burning ships. Yet deliverance came with the dawn of a "pale sky"; the "sun's gleam," though feeble, meant survival. The herald gives thanks for his safe arrival "in daylight," hails the "sunlight" of Argos, addresses "divinities that face the sun," and announces the imminent return of Agamemnon "bearing light in the gloom."

All these reassuring signs, of course, actually presage moral and emotional darkness: the Greek audience knew that the "stintless heaping force" of light would be exerted by Clytemnestra to bring about revenge, that the "bright message" of flames actually foreshadowed (so to speak) unhappy times for the kingdom. Warned by the beacon, the queen (with Aegisthus) slaughters Agamemnon and usurps his throne, instituting an oppressive regime lasting until Orestes and Electra avenge the murder years later. By the end of *Agamemnon*, the chorus has turned from dawn thoughts to thoughts of "our sunset . . . as in the hour of death" (1122–23).

The chorus, in fact, expresses from the beginning a subdued fearfulness that deflates to some extent the buoyant emotions emanating from the celebration of light.[10] While delighted by "sweet hope shining from the [sacrificial] fires," the town elders, aware that Clytemnestra has embarked on a questionable course by taking a lover, and aware also that several gruesome crimes had already been committed by family members in the past, adopts the skeptical attitude hinted at by the watchman ("The house . . . might speak / aloud and plain"). Dismayed by "perplexity / that grows now into darkness of thought" (99–100), but not in a position to confess their trepidation openly, they ascribe their uneasiness to the "darkness of my heart" (546).

They have learned to acquire certainty through experience and hardheaded logic; the fainter the illumination, the less clearly one sees, a guideline they make plain in doubting Clytemnestra's words reporting the Greek victory in Troy. "All will come clear in the next dawn's sunlight" (254): sunrise illuminates facts, not visions, whereas night carries with it dubious information, "dreams of dark fancy" (983). Darkness for them portends deceit, illusion, uncertainty, ignorance, in addition to destruction, fear, and evil. The old men respond to Clytemnestra's victory proclamation by wondering whether a mere dream produced it; anybody who acts without wisdom is like "a dream that falters in the daylight" (82). She rebuts the accusation (275), but they repeat their misgivings. The "beacon's bright message," the "interchange of flame and flame . . . may be real" (475, 490–91) or it may be illusory. "Bright and dreamwise ecstasy / in light's appearance might have charmed our hearts awry" (491–92). For the chorus, dreams are unreliable messengers; they can be double-dealing, half light and half shadow, like beacon fires and burning ships.

Along the same lines, Menelaus fancies his absent wife "shining in dreams," even though "it is vain to dream and to see splendours" (420, 423). Only the clairvoyant Cassandra, grasping truths in enigmatic visions, respects the dream state, for example by describing the murdered children of Thyestes, "imaged as in the shadow of dreams" (1218). But since no one can fathom her reports, she yearns for the day when her intelligence will be comprehensible, "bright and strong / as winds blow into morning and the sun's uprise" (1179–80). In the meantime, the chorus members, puzzled by her suspension between truth and nonsense, remain in "darkness." "We want no prophets," they reply. To them, her words are obscure, not ambiguous. These honest townsfolk, while they do not treat the dream seriously, can hardly tell fantasy or falsehood from reality.[11]

Agamemnon's return in daylight does not dispel their uneasiness. "Dreams of dark fancy" (983) persistently spoil their "good hope":

> I murmur deep in darkness
> sore at heart; my hope is gone now
> ever again to unwind some crucial good
> from the flames about my heart. (1030–34)

Here, as before in the herald's storm scene, flames reveal a dark side of confusion and distress in contrast to their earlier association with uplifted spirits. At the same time that Clytemnestra, the herald, and the watchman look to fire as the harbinger of new life, Cassandra and the chorus prepare the onset of danger, depression, and guilt with images that participate in both camps.

No single significance monopolizes either light or darkness. Just as light is never free of shadow and foreboding, darkness is never without constructive potential; it may join with light to achieve positive benefits. When the city's elders speak out against evil, they conceive justice in terms of darkness as well as light. They dare not name the evildoer until late in the play, so they must restrict their comments either to previous crimes involving Thyestes, Atreus, Paris, and others, or to the workings of morality in general. In those general terms they picture a network in which positive and negative values share properties while retaining their original potency. He who spurns goodness, they meditate, goes "down to darkness" (384), where his sin "burns to evil beauty" (389). In that flaming darkness, retribution waits "in the hooded night"; "the black Furies" hunt the unjust person in order to "drop him to darkness" (458, 463, 466). "Men's dark actions," incited by pride, are punished by "black visaged Disasters" (764, 770) or by a "dark angel" (1342).

Thus the sinner and his crimes, and also his judges and punishment, are all black. In contrast, "righteousness," veiled by deep shade, keeps on glowing as "a shining in / the smoke of mean houses" (773–74).[12] Good and evil interact ceaselessly and sometimes become almost indistinguishable, yet still do not lose their primary nature, as if they had to function simultaneously. Multifaceted light—salvation, peace, justified revenge, truth—disputes with and at the same time intermingles with darkness—death, suffering, sin, illusion. Life or happiness for one character may mean death or grief for another; one calls righteousness what another calls vice; insight to one is babble to the next. Light and darkness do not merely take turns evicting the other in perpetual strife; they each repetitiously *mutate into* the other, with flames, dreams, and prophecies conveying their mercurial nature. In *Agamemnon*, Aeschylus delineates the ambiguity of heroic endeavor not through a character's emotional contortions or ethical vacillations—melodramatic agonizing of the sort displayed by Prometheus and the long line of temperamental protagonists that followed him—but through the interaction of contradictory images.

Though immune to fluctuation herself, Clytemnestra causes insecurity in others; her questionable actions throw Argos into moral uncertainty that ends with her death and the defeat of her claim to justice. In the second and third works of the trilogy, when the dramatist moves toward a resolution of the issue raised so confidently by his bold heroine, he curtails his amazing orchestration of light and dark (blood images become more frequent), but his ingenuity on that subject still reflects his characters' involvement with a problematic enterprise. *The Libation Bearers* again arouses a positive expectation, as at the start of *Agamemnon*, this time an expectation that light will finally supersede the darkness of cruelty, cynicism, shame. The land has been haunted by memories of the killing: Clytemnestra, "shaken in the night," lights torches to relieve the "blind dark" of her fear (524, 536–37). The chorus of female servants laments the terror that arises as "a cry in night's suffering" (34). The servants dress in black to demonstrate their loyalty to Electra; they despise evil whether it strikes in "brightness" or "in gloom of half dark" or in "desperate night" (63–65). They bemoan the "sunless" ruin of their once-great court (51). And they pray to divine powers to deliver the injured parties from their "helm of darkness" (810). Darkness may give birth to light as certainly as light may spawn darkness.

Orestes, who will implement that delivery, vows to eliminate "madness and empty terror in the night" (287). He calls for "the dark arrow of the dead men underground" (285), although he plans to placate his father's shade with "light that will match your dark" (319). Vengeance will "kindle a flame / and light of liberty" (863–64), enabling him and his sister to "look on the shining of daylight" (808), for with the fulfillment of justice "light [will be] here to behold" (961). The chorus seconds his goal: it waits for a "light" of punishment to "fall on the man [Aegisthus] who killed" (328).

Despite this extensive preparation, darkness threatens to retain its ascendancy; in the third play, *The Eumenides*, revenge plunges Orestes into the shadow that had benighted his mother's "dark heart." Even though he acted in accordance with the "luminous evidence of Zeus" (797), the Furies, "daughters of the night," insist that a matricide cannot escape his sin:

> He falls, and does not know in the daze of his folly.
> Such in the dark of man is the mist of infection
> that hovers, and moaning rumor tells how his house lies
> under fog that glooms above. (377–80)

The Furies possess the double valence possessed by flames and dreams: underworld immortals personifying black terror, they are enforcers of primeval law protecting the mother. They draw Orestes, who has discharged a valid obligation to his father, toward their horrors of guilt and death. The deeds of *both* sides are at once just and damnable, enlightened and "under fog." Positive and negative, Nietzsche might say, have again become interchangeable or equivalent as well as competitive.

But irresolution and high tension, *Hegel* might remind us, are inappropriate for the ending of drama; so the inventor of tragedy, having scripted such an agitated dialogue between contraries, tries to impose an orderly conciliation. To settle the moral-metaphorical issue—to release his actors from the immense confusion at the intersection of light and dark— Aeschylus commemorates the mythical metamorphosis of the Furies. Their darkly repellent retribution for kin murder, he submits, is to be reformed and relocated in a different jurisdiction. Under their "gracious" guidance, Athenians will henceforth be endowed with good luck, prosperity, and peace. The Furies are going to "put to sleep the bitter strength in the black wave" (832) in renovated underground quarters, where they may "sit on shining chairs" (806) and act as sources of creativity that will "wash over the country in full sunlight" (906). Torchlight brightens the last scene with "sacred light" (1005) during a groundbreaking treaty between "the primeval dark of earth-hollows" (1036) and "the sun's bright magnificence" (924). The verdict declared by Athena at the trial of Orestes prophesies rapport, not conflict *or* flux, between light and dark.

Are these descriptions sufficient to realize the promised conciliation? Can the daughters of night be so easily reformed? The prophecy may be just a dream. Aeschylus falls short, as I argued earlier, of a definitive solution to the deadlock. In his patriotic enthusiasm to propose a change for the better, at least for Athens, he does not succeed in visualizing a final alteration that would resolve the agonizing Nietzschean assault upon established identities and values. The torchlight procession reportedly held in the theater at the conclusion of the trilogy must have been exciting and gratifying to the Athenian spectators, but to a distant reader in our own age the sudden invention of beneficent light-dark goddesses may seem less convincing. Athena's few remarks about "flaring torches," "sacred light," and "shining chairs" lack enough immediacy and complexity— enough full-bodied weight of imagery—to countermand the Furies' acrid function as rulers of "the evil darkness of the Pit below" (72). Nietzsche would have understood the symbolic transformation, and Hegel would have applauded the absorption of principled partisans into a higher spiritual administration. But Aeschylus, daring as he was, could not configure a stable union between these primeval male and female opponents. He could not enforce closure for either their antipathy or their convertibility. The poetic brilliance of the *Oresteia* shines in their complicated hostility, not in their simple harmony.[13]

Seneca: "The Murk of Hell"

Not all classical masters of drama possessed the talent or inclination to play so brilliantly with multiple meanings attached to polar images. Five hundred years after the *Oresteia* was staged, Seneca, the first-century Roman philosopher, statesman, and adapter of Athenian tragedy, took a more limited view in regard to the mutation of form and value. For him the heroic stereotype revealed by his predecessors to be grossly inadequate, despite its persistent popular appeal and longstanding claim to validity, was no longer visible even as a failed ideal.

Nietzsche's concept of eternal recurrence, therefore, which guarantees at least the temporary rehabilitation of each transformed identity, along with Hegel's concept of warring imperishable principles, loses its relevance. Seneca required neither the Hegelian sequence outlining a noble antagonism nor the Nietzschean ebb and flow of resurgent images: he is not concerned to show a continuing exchange between mighty opposites, whether in story or symbol. His drama—probably not intended for the stage—exemplifies an *un*ambiguous version of Heraclitean flux: after things change for the worst they stay changed. Instead of a dynamic interplay between discordant, shifting meanings, his metaphors project a steady permanence that could have satisfied Hegel if they did not focus so persistently on the dark side of each dualism. Seneca centered his adaptation of *Oedipus Rex*, for instance, on negative reactions to newly uncovered facts rather than on the contrasting reactions to those facts found in Sophocles' work. His cynicism was immutable, his dream-pictures consistently hellish.

We shall not belabor the Latin author for his simplicity; his control of images was impressive within its limits. But he would have been the first to credit the superiority of his Greek sources, and we can enlarge our understanding of how metaphor operates in tragedy by comparing the intricacy of the *Oresteia* with his monochromatic poetic strategy in *Oedipus*—a more convenient comparison than one with *Oedipus Rex* because the works by Seneca and Aeschylus both contain a large number of allusions to an imagery of light and dark.[14]

To fix his reference base at the outset of *Oedipus*, Seneca deals efficiently with ordinary connotations of darkness—sickness, insecurity, death, and evil (the chief association); a tight, straightforward connection between image and import contributes to an atmosphere of visual and moral obscurity. Night equals blight. Oedipus spells out the connection: "fog, dense, and black, / Broods over all the land.... The murk of hell / Has swallowed up the heavenly citadels."[15] The chorus of Theban elders, though unclear about the cause, agrees on the consequence. The darkness engulfing their kingdom originated in Hades as punishment for some unknown sin: "Black Death has opened his ravenous mouth to devour us." The allusions suggest corruption of the body and soul through conventional associations with blackness.

Allusions to light are not so conventional. Light normally relieves darkness with good health and emotional balance, honesty and justice, but Seneca has cleverly rescinded those affiliations. The life-nourishing sun was so severely infected by evil that it lost its usual connotations and rises in the murky dawn as an ambassador of darkness—a neat metamorphosis! Casting a "dull glow," Oedipus explains, the sun "is a torch / Of evil omen," illuminating with its "pale fire" the "havoc of night." Night, lacking stars to alleviate its blackness, had been absolute; now the day, "overcast with clouds," adds to the gloom. Light was not banished; it was recruited by its antithesis. It has forfeited its unique merits. Like darkness, it exerts only one influence, but one that goes against normal expectations.

Blind Tiresias expands the subject of darkness triumphant with a variation on the dark-evil association. This character usually, in legend and in Athenian drama, links light with knowledge, dark with ignorance; again, however, there is a departure from common usage. Ordered to interpret the Delphic oracle's diagnosis of the current spiritual malady, the prophet has no luck searching for information on how to get the "day once more [to] ride brightly in the sky." His sacrificial bull "seemed to fear the daylight, / And shied at the sun's rays." In addition, the sacred flame he kindles quickly goes out, *real* light being in such short supply. After "dying into blackness," it flares up again to give off "dense clouds of smoke enveloping the King, . . . the light of day / Lost in black fog." It is darkness, not light, that reveals facts: light and fog have conspired again to form an absurd alliance, this time hinting at the cause of evil (the unpunished killer of King Laius) rather than the consequence (Hell's persecution). Seneca replaces light's traditional job as emissary of truth with light's new job as partner of perversion—a partial anticipation of Nietzsche's theory on the unending reversal of values.

With blackness reigning over living and dead alike, truth and decency its subordinates, Tiresias decides to visit Hades, the heart of darkness, there to ask the ghost of Laius to name the murderer. The wise prophet keeps the irony intact by inaugurating his second search for light in a grove outside the city that "was dark as night" even before sunset. When he sets fire to several black oxen and black sheep—his passports to the underworld—a "black void opens" upon sordid "things / Created and concealed in the dark womb / Of everlasting night." From these shadows, the current setting for revelation, Tiresias emerges with the answer, designating Oedipus as the disseminator of blackness that properly belongs in Hell. Seneca completes light's reversal with a final irony once Oedipus locates in himself the evil oppressing Thebes. Having seen the same light that blind old Teiresias saw, the king puts out his eyes, the better to receive the darkness of such a sight:

> He tests his vision, holding up his head
> Against the light, scanning the breadth of sky
> With eyeless holes, to see if all is dark,
> Then tears away the last remaining shreds
> Left of the raggedly uprooted eyes.
> His victory was won; he cried aloud
> To all the gods: "Now spare my country, gods!
> Now justice has been done; my debt is paid.
> Here is the darkness that should fitly fall
> Upon my marriage-bed." (248)

Seneca is not willing to restore light to its rightful kingdom after Oedipus pays his debt. Light continues to serve as midwife to darkness; the two never do resume an antithetic relationship. Though satisfied that "there will be brighter skies when I am gone,"[16] Oedipus takes on the "blackness that enshrouds my head" as a memorial to his guilt. Since "daylight itself has run away" from him, he will forever comport with "all grim spectres of Disease, black Plague, / Corruption and intolerable Pain!" He will stumble along a "dark road" into exile, "feeling [his way] through the night." Even after revelation and retribution, the play ends almost as gloomily as it began; metaphor unwaveringly drifts toward a nightmarish shadowing of light. Seneca makes no attempt to show *cyclic* alteration of traditional moral qualities (invalidations that turn into revalidations and then back again, in the Nietzschean style), or an alternation of equally solid and consistent attributes (the Hegelian style)—both of which are evident in the *Oresteia*. If Hegel could not factor invalidation into his tragic equation, Seneca could not figure in revalidation. Oedipus begins and ends in darkness, a victim of entropy, his subversion as leader and sage intensified by the subversion of light. He can be called tragic in his sabotage of the social confirmation he requires, but he does not fluctuate between a positive and a negative outlook. He cannot be accused of ambivalence.

7

Nietzschean Dream Imagery in Strindberg and Kafka

Nietzsche Sets a Direction

Other tragic heroes *can* be accused of ambivalence. It would not be hard to illustrate this volatility of values with the kaleidoscopic imagery of Shakespeare. In his tragedies, virtue and sin are often indistinguishable; even honest confidantes appear to be weirdly malignant in association with disguised messengers of darkness ("juggling fiends") and ever-changing, self-denigrating noblemen. But we can find later characters and images that correspond more conspicuously to the principles announced in *The Birth of Tragedy* and *The Will to Power*.

Many novelists, poets, and playwrights in the twentieth century who demonstrated a profound affinity with Nietzsche emphasized, as foreshadowed by Seneca and foreseen by Hegel, the downward phase of the natural cycle. From their literary perspective, death due to inexplicable devaluation attained epidemic magnitude, overwhelming traditional artistic and ethical criteria. Although Hegel placed such radical devaluation as far back as the Renaissance, it did not transform tragic literature until after his time; in attributing amorality to Shakespeare, he accurately described the course some influential writers would take in the 150 years that followed the *Aesthetics*. For these writers an orderly sequence of challenges and responses conducted by a revered male stereotype could no longer channel intense longings for recognition and justice. No longer could authors ironically ascribe irrational behavior, as Shakespeare still could, to an elitist code and an awesome expectation. Their characters became tragically separated from social commitment, but in addition their sense of self, as well as their sense of moral principle, grew even more amorphous and illogical than that displayed by Shakespeare's disoriented heroes.

Following Shakespeare's lead, dramatists in the past century often avoided the trial of excellence held in a public arena, with its verdict of shame and guilt, opting to explore further the trial of trust conducted in a domestic arena, with the same verdict. They went beyond Shakespeare: their attention turned from discredited male models to choric nonentities, so-called common people, who had very limited resources available to sustain the prehistoric argument between security and independence, community and self-sufficiency, patient practicality and bloodthirsty idealism—a deficiency, not an overdose, of heroic aspiration. These characters desired both solidarity and self-respect but had no rationale capable of supporting either—no conservative political policy geared for group survival and no flamboyant guidance from born leaders, inadequate as that policy and those leaders may have been in the past. Thanks to the Nietzschean revolution they endured life's crises without help from gods or social alliances: they knew the disillusionment of defeat but could not carry off a grand gesture to defy it; they knew the anxiety of ordinary folks but lacked the religious consolations they once enjoyed. Once united in the chorus, they had lost its unanimity while retaining its anonymity. Each person was alone. Nietzsche had done his work. The ego was free at last!

Modern choric figures sometimes lapsed into an incoherent dreamworld: pointless iterations and changes confused their efforts to shape meaningful activities; a jumble of incomprehensible images blurred their perceptions, images as nightmarish as the dark scenes in Seneca's plays. They could not discover an internal cause, like arrogance or self-contradiction, for their misfortunes. Nor could they locate evil agents to blame, divine or human, although they criticized each other endlessly. Misfortune seemed to emanate from their universe without discernible logic: the enemies of pride, the sources of humiliation, seemed to be unknowable, their madness disconnected from specific motives.

According to Nietzsche, however, the chaotic events that confused and intimidated the reasonable mind (he called it the herd mentality), or that denuded the vainglorious mind of its pompous pretensions, invigorated the modern species of tragic superman—*nature's* aristocrat. Irrationality, Hegel's terrifying beast, could confer the greatest benefit. Liberated from ethical and religious programs, the strongest men gloried in "eternal becoming," the exhilarating rush of vitality. The truth can be depressing, depriving everyday ventures of point and consistency; yet it can also be satisfying when it releases us from preoccupation with purely personal concerns (Hegel would approve of *that*) and puts us in touch with primal power (Hegel would not approve) defined as "sensuality, intoxication, superabundant animality" (*Will to Power* 435). Discontinuity and recombination may either instill a maddening sense of futility or inspire incredible motivation because creativity cannot be separated from pain. Confronting "the terrors and horrors of existence" might result in alienation, resignation to injustice and loss; on the other hand, acquaintance with grief, our "terrifying and questionable" common experience, might make an individual (a male individual, in Nietzsche's view) resilient enough and self-conscious enough to accept the ecstatic "joy" of "complete oneness with the essence of the universe" and its "overflowing vitality" (*Birth of Tragedy* 23–41).

> For a brief moment we become, ourselves, the primal Being, and we experience its insatiable hunger for existence. Now we see the struggle, the pain, the destruction of appearances, as necessary, because of the constant proliferation of forms pushing into life, because of the extravagant fecundity of the world will. . . . Pity and terror notwithstanding, we realize our great good fortune in having life—not as individuals, but as part of the life force with whose procreative lust we have become one. (*Birth of Tragedy* 102–3)[1]

This notion of the strong man's "oneness with the essence of the universe" Nietzsche ascribed again to Heraclitus: "The yea-saying to the impermanence and annihilation of things, which is the decisive feature of a Dionysian philosophy; the yea-saying to contradiction and war, the postulation of Becoming, together with the radical rejection even of the concept *Being*—in all these things, at all events, I must recognize him who has come nearest to me in thought hitherto" (*Ecce Homo* 72). Nietzsche found in Heraclitus a message that human activity revolves between hell and heaven, insanity and vision, deterioration and rehabilitation, an endless cycle possessing only one certainty: some individuals will be sturdy enough to embrace the whole pulsing mess as it perpetuates its life-renewing, life-rending propensities.

Not all twentieth-century dramatists accepted Nietzsche's diagnosis. Few wished to visualize amoral supermen or analyze dictators like Mao, Stalin, or Hitler. Some writers tried to return to the relative intelligibility of earlier tragedies. They took up the persistent classical theme of the ignoble nobleman or its democratic adaptation, the commoner with noble aspirations; in *Death of a Salesman*, a "low man" pursues the ghost of aristocratic hopes. But other writers, in works such as Beckett's *Waiting for Godot*, Strindberg's *A Dream Play*, and O'Neill's *Long Day's Journey into Night*, concentrated on the choric man's perplexity as outlined by the theory of flux, patented by Heraclitus and reinvented by Nietzsche.

Strindberg: "Supreme Joy in the Greatest Suffering"

Rather than attempt an encyclopedic survey of the variations on this theme, we shall seek some depth of detail in two works whose surreal dream imagery orbits between Nietzsche's versions of heaven and hell. August Strindberg wrote *A Dream Play* (1902) soon after Nietzsche published his radical thought, and Strindberg was well acquainted with that thought. In 1888 the Swedish playwright attended lectures on Nietzsche delivered by Georg Brandes, a well-known Danish literary critic and historian; later that year he read several of Nietzsche's books in German; and just before the philosopher's breakdown in January 1889, the two authors exchanged lively letters filled with admiration for each other.[2] Strindberg was highly impressed: "everything could be read" in Nietzsche's writing, he declared to a friend. Even so, these facts do not necessarily indicate intellectual debt. An enthusiastic man of the theater may have only been expressing delight at finding his own hard-won innovations seconded by the renowned German genius—affinity, not influence.[3]

In either case, *A Dream Play* might have been designed by Apollo working closely with Dionysus. On one hand, "Dionysian" instability results in aimlessness and formlessness, moving individuals toward exuberant or dismaying freedom from substantive ends like honor and love. On the other hand, "Apollonian" integration generates new forms or returns old ones, moving individuals toward consummation of such ends. (The two Greek gods, of course, are themselves merely metaphors clarifying a concept that in reality supersedes intellectual dualisms.)

The principle of flux, Nietzsche believed, dictates that each value or image decompose and become transmuted into its negation, an obliteration or loss of identity rather than a conflict with its opposing quality. In Strindberg's play, every positive attitude, perception, emotion, or trait unaccountably changes into its opposite: for no reason, tolerance turns into cruelty, enthusiasm into disenchantment, affection into suspicion, beauty into shoddiness, innocence into corruption, wisdom into stupidity, authority into impotence, kindness into greed. Order turns into disorder without preparation or explanation. But the style is circular as well as discontinuous, consistent with Nietzsche's theory, because the principle of flux dictates also that each decomposed entity be resurrected to its virginal integrity before repeating its collapse. Solidity gives way to fluidity, then resumes its solid nature, in an infinite succession.

Strindberg's frustrated characters, disjointed episodes, and grotesque images reflect this alteration and alternation; they may look randomly composed, but they construct a "mad world" (Strindberg's term) on the

Nietzschean grounds of impermanence and regeneration. Any number of exclamations spell out this scheme:

How inconsistent people are!

What a strange world of contradictions!

People, struck with dizziness, live on the borderline of folly and insanity.

Life's riddle still remains unsolved. . . . Incomprehensible world!

Ah, this life! If you do something good, someone else is sure to think it bad; if you are kind to one person, you're sure to harm another.

Ah, now I know the whole of living's pain!
And so the human heart is split in two,
emotions by wild horses torn—
conflict, discord and uncertainty.

All that is most lovely will now be dragged down, down into the mud.

You have not experienced the worst thing of all. Repetitions, reiterations. Going back. Doing one's lessons again. . . . The whole of life is only repetition.

I seem to have lived through all this before.

Surely suffering is redemption.[4]

But it takes more than bald generalizations to communicate to a theater audience with "Apollonian" clarity what by definition cannot be articulated in abstract propositions. To give incongruity a concrete and "apparently logical form," Strindberg imitates the "form of a dream" (author's preface). "I have had faith many times," the Poet laments, "but after a while it drifted away, like a dream when one awakens." "This world, its life and its inhabitants," Indra's Daughter adds, "are only a mirage, a reflection, a dream image."

As befits a mirage, the characters act out their "discord and uncertainty" in short disconnected episodes that suit their sudden transformations and circularity, forsaking the full development (beginning, middle, and end) advised by Aristotle. When Dionysian turbulence disrupts their marital peace and professional pride, it fragments their stories; they can only produce undramatic, transient samples of a daily purgatory. They substitute momentary satisfactions for momentous ambitions, one-line whimpers for catastrophic complaints, and repetitious skirmishes for a climactic confrontation. The grand challenge-response pattern breaks down into poignant vignettes among figures usually lacking names, much less elevated social positions, their generic condensed histories outlining the ephemeral nature of their experience. Their discomfort seems interminable and sickeningly specific, but they suffer still more from dreamlike abbreviation and impersonality—from Nietzschean insubstantiality.

No less than eight abbreviated incidents repeat the "incomprehensible" strife in family life, strife between male and female that changes love to contempt or despair. Father and Mother, after a lifetime together, admit "we have both hurt each other. Why, we don't know. We could not do otherwise." Concerning *her* marriage, Lina laments that "beauty has perished, joy has vanished." "He and She" enjoy "perfect happiness, utter bliss, the ecstasy of young love" until "life's little discomforts," represented by the noxious fumes and sights of Foulstrand, beset them. The Doorkeeper mourns a lover who defected thirty years ago; brief contentment enjoyed by the Naval Officer and Alice brings grief to another; a newlywed Husband and Wife decide upon suicide before "happiness consumes itself like a flame"; and the Officer courts an opera star who never shows up. "Life together is a torment," the Lawyer complains: "one's pleasure is the other's pain." And Indra's Daughter adds, "the sweetest is also the bitterest—love!" As in Shakespeare's tragedies, each couple exemplifies a deterioration from trust to sorrow, but here mutuality deteriorates due to petty, not grandiose, grievances, and metamorphosis takes place without the instigation of a formidable, or even definable, antagonist.[5]

In addition to sketchy scenes of marital discord, even briefer vignettes iterate equally bleak, inconsequential, and irrational transitions in professional life. The Lawyer is condemned, not rewarded, for defending the poor or the falsely accused. The faculties of higher education—theology, philosophy, medicine, and law—twist the search for truth into a ludicrous, inconclusive debate about "nothing." After his debacle as a lover, the Officer begins a promising occupation as a teacher ("the whole of life is now mine!") but once again falls victim to the laws that govern chaos—mutability and duplication. After losing patience with the recurring inanities passing for wisdom, his own knowledge reverts to that of a schoolboy, and he must relearn everything.

The nameless figures of *A Dream Play*, then, are subject to puzzling regression, picayune hostility, and infuriating repetition; an unknown dominion twists their generic loyalties, pleasures, and animosities into unrecognizable, transient shapes. They seem to have lapsed into what Hegel called modern amorality. And yet (the two most important words in tragedy), and yet Strindberg like Nietzsche testifies to the possibility of personal fulfillment (revaluation or reconversion), not despite, but in terms of, these daunting facts. He attaches his somewhat quixotic hope to dream images consistent with Nietzsche's faith in natural resilience. Some symbolic objects, of course, remain darkly pessimistic and anticlimactic—the Billsticker's pathetic green fish box "that was my dream when I was little," a mysterious clover-leaf door that promises paradise but opens to reveal "nothing," the yoking of Foulstrand to Fairhaven. Apollonian illusion, however, may present Dionysian reality in a more optimistic light.

Cleansing the silk shawl, for example, renews its purpose. Originally a touching gift from Father to his dying wife, the shawl caused contention when she loaned it to a servant, prompting the refrain, "if you are kind to one person, you're sure to harm another." Someone suggests that the garment, soiled by thirty years of abuse, be burned with "all its griefs and miseries." But Indra's Daughter washes it clean and resumes her compassionate pilgrimage protected by its warmth and ready for new frustrations.

Strindberg's flower imagery—blossoms rising from "muck"—elaborates this Nietzschean concept of natural toughness tempering natural vulnerability. Plants provide an obvious analogy for the pitiable-joyous cycle that goes from growth and maturity to decline, then back to fertility and rebirth. A "small lime tree ... with a few pale green leaves" serves the Officer as a timepiece, marking with its buddings and sheddings the seasons of his untiring vigil for Victoria; in the poetic language of botany it connotes longevity and conjugal love, an ironic implication in this case.[6] The Officer also treasures "a giant monkshood," a beautiful poisonous plant that signifies hidden danger and also chivalry or knight errantry—an appropriate association for a military man engaged in perilous romantic service. He repeats the theme of disguised peril when he recalls seeing the poisonous plant as a boy; his attempt then to trap a bee inside its flower—an earlier fruitless, childish, and dangerous endeavor—anticipated his frustrating courtship. And grass growing around the lime tree and monkshood decorates the motif of his service and submission. Together, the grass, tree, and blue monkshood blossom mirror his cheerful, thwarted, unflagging innocence, a passive innocence entirely foreign to the demonic demand for justice motivating earlier tragic characters.

Similarly, a bouquet of roses reflects his "radiantly happy" countenance, his lovely expectations, and (when the roses fade) his perennial disappointment. The roses and monkshood wither, the grass turns brown, the lime tree loses its leaves, the Officer's hair goes gray, his clothing becomes shabby. Yet rejuvenation comes to both humans and plants: beauty relieves squalor; light, darkness; harmony, dissonance; pleasure, pain; purpose, pointlessness; union, isolation, and enlightenment replaces ignorance. Flux fertilizes fruition. Strindberg projects his hopefulness by means of the "growing castle" that rises from "heaps of straw and stable-muck" surrounded by "a forest of giant hollyhocks" (connoting fertility) and crowned at its summit with a chrysanthemum bud (connoting love and happiness). A glazier explains: plants "don't like the dirt, so they shoot up as fast as they can into the light—to blossom and to die." The castle, drawing its sustenance from the debris of worldly enterprise, rises from soil and manure to "freedom in the light." Light for Strindberg has come to symbolize growth rather than rectitude.

Plants and flowers, in particular the castle flower, encompass a journey of maturation undergone by almost every individual, including, in the central action, Indra's Daughter. On descending to earth she was "bathed in its mud" or choked by its dust and smoke ("poor little flower, without light, without air"). On returning to heaven, she sets fire to the growing castle: as a cavalry stable it produced gross animal waste; as a blossoming plant it portrayed botanical glory; and as a flaming pyre it gives off godlike energy. To transmute their lifelong strivings into purer form, several characters consign to the flames those objects, such as the roses and shawl, they have associated with the mixed blessing of their passage. Bedeviled, battered, and bewildered, they participate in a liberating finale presided over by the Daughter (female-fire-flower force), until a huge chrysanthemum takes her place.[7]

The notion of resolving baser elements such as earth into purer forms (fire) recalls Nietzsche's references to Heraclitus on the subject of metamorphosis in *Early Greek Philosophy* (104–10). Strindberg's fiery finale accommodates Nietzsche's belief in the potency of saying "yes" to the excruciating anomalies of existence. Indra's Daughter, consumed by flames, achieves Nietzsche's "highest state," an intimidating-enlivening union with the earth's volcanic "fecundity." "Now you understand what love is," she instructs the Poet, "supreme joy in the greatest suffering." And the Poet comments, "surely suffering is redemption."

Indra's Daughter, the Poet's mentor, bears and surmounts pain; possibly the spectator enjoys a similar release during the theatrical experience. In his preface, Strindberg mentions the relief one feels upon awakening from an agonizing dream: when "the sufferer awakes, [he or she] is thus reconciled with reality." By extension, a spectator attending the play becomes the "dreamer," immersed in, yet distanced from, the absurdity of daily life and thereby led to "compassion for all living things." This conciliatory outcome seems almost Hegelian! Improbable as it sounds, our two philosophers may complete each other. Nietzsche took heart in the obliteration of values or identities and yet insisted that they recur eternally. If order ends in turmoil, and if all things recur—characters who are compassionate, faithful, and honorable as well as those who are disloyal and cynical—must not turmoil end (temporarily) in order? Chaos may be governed by a kind of logic after all. In tragedy, inescapable attacks destabilize an idealistic stance, leading to metamorphosis but also to reclamation of integrity in some guise. Frightening and invigorating, tragic drama shelters both dissolution and resolution. Being provides infinite kindling, Becoming unstintingly lights the fire.

Kafka: An Open and Shut Case?

Strindberg may have been the first modern Nietzschean dramatist, but dramatists were not the only artists to trace the shape of flux. Many novels, stories, and poems, not to speak of painting, sculpture, music, and other arts, took the same direction, sometimes labeled "expressionism" in the first half of the twentieth century. Even before *The Birth of Tragedy*, Poe and Dostoyevsky had evoked dream sequences in which lost souls lived out the terror and sorrow of hideous change. But no writer of fiction did this more poignantly or more painfully than Franz Kafka. His long story, "The Metamorphosis" (written in 1912 and published in 1915), rather than spread its concern among a broad sampling of choric types and their stories, as Strindberg did in *A Dream Play*, concentrates upon one pedestrian personality, suspends him between communion and impotence like an old-fashioned Shakespearean or Athenian hero, but plagues him with a fatal Senecan conversion that as if imagined by Strindberg's dreamer appears to be incomprehensible, incontestable, and gross.[8]

The characters in Strindberg's drama endured this plague and were finally awarded a sort of natural-mystical higher consciousness. For Kafka's protagonist, a dozen years later, the "torment" remains incurable: circularity no longer leads to rebirth; transformation no longer allows him relief (his family gets the relief). As in the older forms of tragedy, voluntary death provides the only escape from distrust and shame, but now those conditions arise from an unknown origin. Gregor Samsa, a traveling salesman (like Willy Loman in *Death of a Salesman*), simply desires acceptance by his family, yet thoroughly demoralizes it with the common man's disease of causeless self-depreciation. His cry for recognition, though repeated twice, is as unintelligible to his family as the reason for his metamorphosis, his father's hostility as mysterious to him as his mother's defection. While he dies from the same condition that kills an Othello or a Lear—blockage of reciprocal trust—their eloquent request for respect has now turned into the indecipherable "horrible twittering" of an enormous, disgusting bug.

To transmit the tragic consequence of crippled virtue and disabled power in Heraclitean terms of transformation and repetition, Kafka devised a dream metaphor, nightmarish yet "apparently logical"—Gregor's monstrous change into an introspective insect. And to give his repellent yet thoughtful insect room to roam as it falters from tenacity to paralysis, from connection to isolation, the author brought into play *another* dream image, also made of contrary premises, this one not nearly so striking but in practice equally grotesque—a door. Open, a bedroom door admits one to intimacy; locked, it becomes an obstacle to intimacy. With almost one hundred references to the doors enclosing Gregor Samsa, doors that are continually opening and closing, the author supports his account of a character who fails to reach through the misunderstanding and resentment that transform him. Three times Gregor approaches his mother, sister, and (most importantly) his father; three times they waver between tolerance and revulsion, blocking him with that age-old menace, humiliation. Why? Both sides wish to establish rapport, but neither side ever comprehends the source of their frustration, the origin of the impassable barrier that repeatedly separates them.[9]

Door imagery in the three parts of the story reveals successive degrees of Gregor's withdrawal, each section at once duplicating and advancing the evolution from anticipation to antipathy, from open (responsive and determined) to shut (reclusive and resigned)—the last section ending in the rejuvenation not of Gregor but his antagonist. At the outset, rescue from the prisonlike locked bedroom looks likely; goodwill literally encircles Gregor. His worried mother, after a "cautious tap" at the door separating their bedrooms, speaks through it in a "gentle voice." From another side, his sister Grete comforts him through *her* bedroom door, whereupon the elder Samsa, at a third door to his son's centrally located bedroom (this one opening to the living room), introduces a mildly dissonant sound. Figuring that Gregor has malingered to skip a day at his job, which supplies their sole income, he knocks "gently, yet with his fist." All three overtures inviting Gregor to open his doors and rejoin the family miscarry: dismayed by his overnight reincarnation, fearing the "anxiety, if not terror" his presence might cause "behind all the doors," he refuses to "take the risk." "He was not thinking of opening the door, and felt thankful for the prudent habit he had acquired in traveling of locking all doors during the night, even at home" (23).

The pressure to resume his professional position increases with the entrance of his superior, the chief clerk, at the outer door to the apartment. As before, voices must pass through the locked doors surrounding Gregor. Eventually he resolves "to open the door" to his room, but by then his father has sent for two more outsiders, a doctor and a locksmith, who will minister to the malfunctions of man and door. Congruence between the two problems becomes clear when Gregor's physical seclusion is equated with his emotional removal: "He felt himself drawn once more into the human circle and hoped for great and remarkable results from both the doctor and the locksmith, without really distinguishing precisely between them" (33).

Outsiders, however, turn out to be even less helpful than family benefactors, so Gregor chooses to unlock his cell by himself ("I didn't need the locksmith"). The only one to spur him on during his slow, difficult key-turning is the chief clerk. "They should all have shouted encouragement to him," he mourns, "his father and mother too." His reemergence, as he feared, shocks everyone, especially his father, who clenches his fist again "as if he meant to knock Gregor back into his room." For a moment Gregor leans against his side of the door, looking out his window or through the open hall and front door. But neither the window nor the outside door serves as an exit from the confrontation he must survive within the apartment.

That confrontation will be primarily with his father.[10] His mother, deferring to her husband's stereotypical belligerence, plays a passive role, and his sister's sympathy and intelligence cannot cure his affliction. The sister "would have shut the door of the flat" against the intrusion of the chief clerk, he muses, "and in the hall talked him out of his horror." But she does not, his mother and the clerk draw back, and Gregor has to "handle the situation by himself." At a loss because his father "had merely the fixed idea of driving Gregor back into his room as quickly as possible," he rotates between his need for acceptance and his need for independence, like Philoctetes or Lear; his contortions while trying to reestablish connection, then escape it, are comic, pathetic, revolting. Wounded by those he loves, yet incapable of negotiating with them, he seeks sanctuary behind the three closed doors: "From behind his father gave him a strong push which was literally a deliverance and he flew far into the room, bleeding freely. The door was slammed behind him with the stick, and then at last there was silence" (41).

Section 2 ends in a similar way: the family's tentative tolerance turns to aversion, and for the second time a father who cannot accept this detestable vermin as a son wounds Gregor and "drives" him past the door, back into his room. At the beginning of the chapter there are no further overtures for him to come out, no further attempts to extricate him from his solitude and "silence," no further expectations, just a temporary, unproductive truce. "Gregor now stationed himself immediately before the living-room door, determined to persuade any hesitating visitor to come in or at least to discover who it might be; but the door was not opened again and he waited in vain. In the early morning, when the doors were locked, they had all wanted to come in; now that he had opened one door and the other had apparently been opened during the day, no one came in and even the keys were on the other side of the doors" (43). Grete, his ally, "jumped back as if in alarm and banged the [bedroom] door shut; . . . this made him realize how repulsive the sight of him still was to her" (53). Although Grete leaves food scraps, he requires a kind of nourishment not forthcoming from her. Even the servant "keeps the kitchen door locked." As his "horrible" body slowly dries up, he eavesdrops at the doors, and occasionally gazes out the window "obviously in some recollection of the sense of freedom that looking out of a window always used to give him." "If only the door were opened," he thinks, "he would disappear at once" (62).

But when his sister and mother remove his bedroom furniture ("everything he loved"), leaving him to "lord it all alone over empty walls," indignation shoves him past the doors in another effort to communicate. As usual, his intentions are misunderstood. While he does not comprehend his plight, he blames himself for it, "shame and guilt" at his detestable nature sharpened by awareness that he has let his family down as its only wage earner. Unexpectedly, the father compensates for Gregor's double failure as son and as income producer by growing in both dignity and earning power. He goes through a Nietzschean metamorphosis of his own, evolving from a feeble, aging dependent to a militant leader wearing a "smart blue uniform with gold buttons." At the chapter's end he recruits his wife and "in complete union" with her injures Gregor again, forcing him back into his room for the second time.

The last section, though analogous to the two preceding, bears witness more decisively to the death of hope, to the closing of a door that might have permitted Gregor to enter into acceptance and control. At first, as previously, the father feels some compunction. He reminds himself "that Gregor was a member of the family, despite his present unfortunate and repulsive shape, and ought not to be treated as an enemy, that, on the contrary, family duty required the suppression of disgust and the exercise of patience, nothing but patience" (65). He therefore allows the door between Gregor's bedroom and the living room to stand ajar for an hour or two each evening so the insect can observe from within its room their congenial activities. Watching from that distance, Gregor "was often haunted by the idea that next time the door opened he would take the family's affairs in hand again." Unfortunately, "his mother, pointing towards his room, said: 'Shut that door now, Grete,' and he was left again in darkness" (69).

Finally he finds *their* doings as noxious as they find his: "not one of them thought of shutting the door to spare him such a spectacle and so much noise" (71). When Grete enters his room he "stayed motionless where he was, as if the door had never been opened." The three weird lodgers leave him unaffected too, "reconciled . . . to the shutting of the door." He loses interest in the others, gives up his quest, and sinks into an immobilizing "indifference to everything" except Grete's violin practice, which briefly creates an illusion that "the way [was] opening before him to the unknown nourishment he craved." Since no way does open, both sides acknowledge their permanent estrangement; his sister "turned the key in the lock" at the close of his third foray from the bedroom. The door to the security he seeks is finally closed for good, and he terminates his "shame and guilt" by allowing death to pass the "bolted and locked" door.

His suicide, which in tragedy is often the only release from shame, is passively executed and elicits only relief, not regret, from the survivors. Once he dies, his window, the doors opening into his room, and the outside door are all thrown open with an air of celebration. His "disappearance" makes it possible for the other Samsas to cultivate satisfying interaction, a Nietzschean regeneration after the agony of shutting doors on a monster. The resurgent father completes his reformation to youthful, dominating vigor; Grete changes from a homebody into a blooming, outward-looking young lady. The lodgers, who like Gregor had disrupted the home, are ejected along with the corpse. And, after disposing of the quickly forgotten dried-up insect, the charlady departs also, "with a frightful slamming of doors." "Human beings can't live with such a creature," Samsa senior had commented, pronouncing Gregor's epitaph. His triumph reverses the usual father-son succession; older takes over from younger as one metamorphosis displaces another. A son's closure may be a father's opening.

Gregor's oscillations resemble the fluctuations experienced by Lear, Hamlet, Macbeth, and Othello, but this pathetic character claims no exceptional ability, challenges no law of social accommodation, makes no horrendous misjudgment, blames no evil adversary. He can invoke no compensating justification or discovery, as they do, no cleansing last act. He was not meant to be a Hamlet, questioning and affirming traditional standards of manhood. When Kafka, Strindberg, and other authors shifted their interest from heroic to choric fragility, they downplayed abstract goals and witnessed what Hegel disparaged, the undirected freedom and frustration of natural passions. In their works, fluidity of character, structure, and metaphor intrudes upon the defense of sacred principles to a greater degree than in earlier tragedy. Kafka's hybrid story structure combines Hegel's gentlemen's duel headed toward finality with Nietzsche's endless cyclic change, the progressive pattern of reaction to insult merged with the rotary pattern of repetitive, inexplicable deflation and revival. Gregor Samsa fertilizes the seeds of his family's growth with his poignant, pointless decline; the baffled lovers of *A Dream Play* endure the decay and evolution of botanic transmutation, not the clash of ethical beliefs. Social and family solidarity or division, individual dignity or disgrace—all survive as absurd dreamlike pictures.

But was it so much different in the Athenian or Shakespearean theater? From the beginning, flux has operated upon seemingly immutable expectations; the reversals in "The Metamorphosis" and *A Dream Play* continue the inversions of character and image inaugurated by Athenian tragedy. The first playwrights encompassed, in our "modern" mode, the *alternation* of value or identities (one against the other), together with an endless *alteration* (one turning into the other). They were concerned not only with conflict between fixed states of "being," where one polar extreme competes with its opposite, but also with a process of "becoming," where one pole changes into its contrary. These categories were not mutually exclusive: metamorphosis did not *replace* conflict (until Seneca); it *internalized* conflict, often resulting in self-contradiction and self-cancellation.

Aeschylus' Clytemnestra, it is true, does not internalize conflict, but though not self-divided she appears two-faced to others, the guide and corrupter of Argos, messenger of light and Queen of Night, selfless masculine avenger and self-centered "cow." Her scandalous attitude represents a transformation of the female stereotype that arouses social disapproval: she causes moral division that climaxes in an imperfectly resolved debate on justice. More obvious victims of polarization, Medea and Pentheus (among many others) jump back and forth between male and female roles—honorable warrior and madwoman—their defiant natures seeming to be both weak and strong, criminal and noble. In later drama, King Lear too (along with other Shakespearean protagonists) undergoes a personality conversion; although he promises to "resume the shape which thou dost think /I have cast off for ever," he maintains a questionable grasp on "authority" as he sinks into a pit of misanthropy and madness. Shakespeare and the Greek tragedians, like recent writers, imagined characters who splinter supposedly rock-firm imperatives, then juggle permanence and flux in their figurative language and narrative journeys. Most tragic figures, ancient and modern, are two things trying unsuccessfully to be only one thing; the more they stay the same, the more they change.

The Duplicity of Rhetoric

8

Plato's Distrust

Heraclitus may have preceded Nietzsche in claiming that the illusion of solidity could mask the reality of flux, but Plato turned that formula around when he stated that the illusion of flux could mask the reality of solidity. Plato is well known for condemning the inconstancy and shallowness of poetic language. He distrusted poets because they fictionalized events, defamed legendary heroes, and catered to emotion with embellished speech; their rhetorical techniques, he said, were as double-dealing as their misleading images and reconstituted narratives. He wanted words, important words like *justice,* to mean one thing and one thing only, as opposed to the multiple meanings poets gave them.

Rhetorical craftiness, of course, had been suspect long before Plato wrote his dialogues. "Everywhere," crafty Odysseus states in *Philoctetes,* "it is the tongue that wins and not the deed." Noble people, Plato added, perform noble deeds, and philosophers get at truths, but poets, orators, and popular politicians put words together cunningly to manipulate our feelings and thoughts. Even a storyteller's honest effort to describe human values could be crippled by the inherent deficiencies and deceptiveness of persuasive or narrative speech. Wouldn't our easily misled citizens be better off without the distractions not only of demagogues but also of poets? This question has dogged fiction writers and literary critics ever since Plato raised it in the *Republic* around 380 B.C. and answered "yes."

Although Plato could not abide the duplicitous medium of the poets, his criticism may be of use to us in our effort to understand tragedy. In the *Republic* he brought together two vital, if contrasting, ideas—the idea that literature was either immoral or amoral (the latter point was taken up by Nietzsche), and the idea that literature might serve as a moral messenger (a viewpoint taken by Hegel). Plato finally rejected the second notion because of the first, but we can deepen our sensitivity to contradiction in tragedy by appreciating the validity of both proposals.

The first writer to tackle this project was Plato's star student, Aristotle, who after absorbing crucial distinctions he borrowed from his teacher's analysis of the arts made a different evaluation. Aristotle illustrated his argument with lines from Homer, Aeschylus, Sophocles, and Euripides; much later, an English playwright illustrated Plato's view that poets merely contrive illusions ("imitations") and also Aristotle's rebuttal that such illusions could be truthful as well as stimulating. In dealing with the heroic stereotype, Shakespeare—crafty juggler that he was—played off faith against skepticism, certainty against ambiguity, something against nothing. His language was sincere, serious, and substantial, as Plato (and Hegel) wished, and at the same time it was manipulative and emotive, which Plato detested but Aristotle (and Nietzsche) commended. Words spoken in Shakespearean tragedy may sound momentous, definitive, pacifying; the same words may also be petty, dubious, and hurtful.

That such disparate impressions could be made by one character scandalized Plato, and his conservatism was shared by another English poet, Milton, who met Plato's objections by championing an honest ethical and religious purpose. Milton's sobriety and Shakespeare's trickiness (contrariness) mark the boundaries of rhetorical contrivance in tragedy, and we stand indebted to Plato for laying out those boundaries. His thoughts on ethical solidity and inconstancy anticipated the contrasting philosophical positions taken by Hegel and Nietzsche, and the contrasting rhetorical practices of Milton and Shakespeare.

Because in commenting on poetic art in the *Republic* Plato himself seems to be inconsistent despite his urgent concern for consistency, we need to sort out his reasoning. At first reading, *Republic* books 2 and 3, with their emphasis on literature as a possible transmitter of actions portraying manly and divine excellence, offer no problem. Plato's prescription for the poetic subject (lines 376–92) is clear: to be helpful in the education of the young, stories told by poets should be informed by standards of superior behavior.[1] Hegel (but not Nietzsche) would probably have agreed with Plato that heroes ought to serve as models of happy righteousness and self-control, never showing fear, cowardice, weakness, disobedience, irreverence, wrath, vengefulness, or self-abandon in regard to food, drink, sex, money, language, or laughter.

Gods too should always be represented as good, never causing evil, ill will, inequity, injury, or suffering, and they too should be shown as unchanging—constant in appearance and viewpoint, never ugly, unstable, dishonest, or deceptive. Subjects *not* appropriate are common men, slaves (especially when doing menial labor), and women (especially when bickering with husbands, defying gods, boasting, wailing, ailing, toiling, loving, or giving birth). Every detail of a story ought to contribute toward moral instruction: in poetry—as in music, painting, weaving, embroidery, architecture, and "the manufacture of household furnishings"—the aim is "to recognize the forms [standards, principles, essences] of soberness, courage, liberality, and high-mindedness" (402c). The subject of poetic art must be "the true nature [the admirable abstract qualities] of gods and heroes."

When Plato turns from subject "matter" to technical "manner," he asserts (3: 392–98) that there should be two sorts of narration—nonimitative, or "pure" (description of event, as in the dithyramb), and imitative (dialogue, as in drama). There may also be a mixture of imitative and nonimitative narration, as in the epic. We can illustrate Plato's three kinds of narration ("everything that is said by fabulists or poets" is narrative) with a biblical character:

Pure (descriptive): Then he rose and claimed to be Lazarus, come from the dead.

Imitative (dramatic): "I am Lazarus, come from the dead."

Mixture (epic or reportorial): Then he rose and said, "I am Lazarus, come from the dead."

This neat summary, however, hardly does justice to the examination of literary technique in books 2 and 3. For one thing, the classification according to "the matter and the manner" (3: 392c) can be misleading unless one realizes that narration involves a *third* factor that Plato leaves unlabeled. To give this third factor a name, narration also requires a *medium*, the medium of the poetic arts being "right speech" (the media of music are rhythm and melody). Secondly, Plato implies—he does not develop the idea until the tenth book—that the medium of poetic speech, which can be descriptive or dramatic or mixed in its manner, is not in fact capable of representing the essences or virtues he has prescribed as the proper subject. When the poet describes (nonimitative manner) or reproduces (imitative manner) the praiseworthy words and deeds of heroes or gods, he depicts just the activities of particular individuals, not the ideal "forms" of conduct those characters embody. Homer can easily reproduce, say, an honest speech recited by Odysseus, but only the real Odysseus can embody the essence of honesty by "doing the things themselves of which the [poetic] imitations are likenesses" (395b).

Thus (by implication) what literary craft ("poetry") takes for its immediate subject turns out to be merely the medium (concrete activities) of another art, the art of enlightened living evoked at second hand by characters in the poet's stories through their speech and actions. It is therefore incorrect to maintain, as we did earlier, that for Plato praiseworthy qualities make up the subject matter of poetry. A more accurate account would be this: the medium of the best poetry is speech that narrates, in an imitative or a nonimitative manner, words and deeds serving heroes or gods as *their* media for expressing definitive values (*their* subject). By limiting imaginative literature this special way, Plato prepares the ground for his later conclusion on the disability of imitative speech, which creates an unbridgeable gap between the poet's subjects (the heroic words and deeds reported) and truly significant subjects (values embodied in words and deeds actually performed).

Furthermore, he complicates the notion of "imitation" in books 2 and 3 by extending its usage. In addition to a manner of *speech* (a rhetorical application), the term may also be applied to a manner of *speech delivery* (an oratorical application) and of *mental conditioning* (a psychological application). After the poet reports a hero's words, an actor or speaker repeats those words in *his* medium, impersonation and mimicry, bringing to bear histrionic virtuosity in voice and gesture. In turn, the spectator may imitate the actor's impersonation through the medium of his "good disposition": "Imitations, if continued from youth far into life, settle down into habits and second nature in the body, the speech, and the thought" (3: 395d). "We must supervise and compel [the poets] to embody in their poems the semblance of the good character, . . . and so from earliest childhood insensibly guide [young men] to likeness, to friendship, to harmony with beautiful reason" (3: 401b, d). The spectator's reception completes an imitative chain that goes from heroic or godlike action to poetic tale to recitation or dramatic performance to psychological response. Representatives of each level imitate the medium of the next level, translating it into their subject. Only the gods and heroes do not imitate an intermediate medium; they translate directly into action (though with inevitable distortion) the forms of excellence—the supreme subject of and justification for the entire process.[2]

Poetry, then, may relate activities and words re-presenting (from a considerable distance) an exemplary standard. Does Plato consider this a worthy business? In the third book he does with qualifications; in the tenth book, with exceptions, he does not. In books 2 and 3, he only has doubts. Literature can serve a serious purpose in the hands of upright artisans, but he warns against mishandling the subject, the manner (there should be "a small portion of imitation in a long discourse"), or the delivery.[3] Base motives can do great harm during an imitative succession: when aspiration to reach the good and the true falters, when the poets lie or actors exaggerate, the literary work can become an instrument employed to titillate the appetites, encourage selfish diversions, and dissipate one's energies. Plato warns against dispersing talent among a multiplicity of interests; everyone should cultivate, as much as possible, genuine knowledge through expertise in a specialized occupation.[4]

In *Republic* 10: 595–608, Plato repeats these strictures and in addition advances a more damning charge based upon further examination of the imitative sequence he had outlined earlier. Even with the best intention we cannot bridge the gap between spiritual attributes and artistic representations. Each transposition into another medium additionally distorts the original nonmaterial essence until the last receiver in line, the spectator, gains only the vaguest impression of a source that really should be experienced at first hand, not vicariously. It is much more profitable for individuals not fortunate enough to be gods or heroes to approach truth by "doing the things themselves" under the guidance of the best kind of intermediary, a philosopher with *his* unique medium, the rational dialectic. Poetic creations, Plato concludes (to summarize his two principal objections), "are inferior in respect of reality," and their "appeal is to the inferior part of the soul" (10: 605b). The poet *may* lose his desire for goodness; he will *always* be too benighted to know truth. Imitation might or might not corrupt the spectator, but it undoubtedly will misinform him.[5]

This conclusion has fired up passionate scholarly controversy: how could Plato reject the poets in book 10 after, in books 2 and 3, he had awarded them (including the imitative kind) an educative role in the state, so long as they were carefully monitored and restricted? He undeniably does put forward, in the earlier chapters, a positive role for imitative narration:

> A man of the right sort, I think, when he comes in the course of his narrative to some word or act of a good man will be willing to impersonate the other in reporting it, and will feel no shame at that kind of mimicry, by preference imitating the good man when he acts steadfastly and sensibly . . . .
>
> Then the narrative that he will employ will be of the kind that we just now illustrated by the verses of Homer, and his diction will be one that partakes of both, of imitation and simple narration, but there will be a small portion of imitation in a long discourse. (3: 396c, e)

But then Plato begins book 10 by "refusing to admit at all so much of [poetry] as is imitative" (595a). The "mimetic poet" traffics exclusively in appearances, illusions, "semblances," "phantoms," and he caters to feeling, not thought:

> And so we may at last say that we should be justified in not admitting him into a well-ordered state, because he stimulates and fosters [the inferior part of] the soul, and by strengthening it tends to destroy the rational part . . . . (10: 605b)

> We must know the truth, we can admit no poetry into our city save only hymns to the gods and the praises of good men. For if you grant admission to the honeyed Muse in lyric or epic, pleasure and pain will be lords of your city instead of law. (10: 607a)

These comments entail some kind of semantic shift or jump in logic, yet all sorts of ingenious explanations have been volunteered to acquit Plato of self-contradiction. It would probably be better to pass over in silence the contention that he was just joking (always an ironist, that Greek);[6] that he could not have condemned poets since he was one himself;[7] that he banished only "bad" poets;[8] that he was merely angry at Homer, or at illusionist schools of acting and painting in contemporary Athens;[9] that the hymns and praises he does permit encompass almost all the genres, including drama;[10] and that he found poetry permissible for children in book 3 but not for adults in book 10.[11]

Somewhat more plausibly, it has been submitted that in book 10, after reappraising the pernicious effects of imitation, Plato vetoes *imitative* narration—he is indeed inconsistent on this point—but continues to enjoy recitation that is not "honeyed" and "embellished" with dramatic dialogue. His approval of "pure" narration in "hymns to the gods and praises of good men" allows plenty of room for choral (nondramatic) productions.[12] Another interesting interpretation finds Plato retaining his faith in the limited efficacy of properly contrived and prudently delivered poetic art, but losing his faith in the feasibility of ever realizing that art. *If* the poets could be persuaded to "bestow not only pleasure but benefit," then "we would gladly admit" them; however, they will *not* be persuaded, mainly because they are a pack of lazy crowd pleasers. In principle, poetry could be valuable; in everyday practice, Plato supposedly decides, it falls short of its potential contribution.[13]

Few of these theories take into account Plato's final use of "imitation" in the *Republic*. Plato in book 10 enlarges his original sense of the term denoting a particular narrative manner using dialogue to a broader sense denoting *all* narration, including nondramatic description.[14] By doing this, he permanently associates the poetic medium and subject with the imitative manner and with the limitations he now makes explicit. Except for one or two references,[15] the concept of a "pure" (nonimitative) narration disappears: "*all* the poetic tribe, beginning with Homer," Socrates says, "are imitators of images of excellence and of the other things that they 'create,' and do not lay hold on truth" (10: 600e); "the poet himself, *knowing nothing but how to imitate*, lays on with words and phrases" (601a); "those who attempt tragic poetry, whether in iambics [drama] or heroic [epic] verse, are *all altogether imitators*" (602b, emphasis added).

If then the poet knows "nothing but how to imitate," and if—as Plato announced previously—"everything that is said by fabulists or poets [is] a narration of past, present, or future things" (3: 392d), then the only (or certainly the chief) manner of poetic narration will be imitative. A healthy nonimitative kind, if it existed, probably could not balance the mimetic kind in a hypothetical "mixed" hybrid; but it does *not* exist except (possibly) for those blessed hymns and praises, so any management strategy to govern artists becomes irrelevant. Despite the declaration that his "chief accusation" against poetry is "its power to corrupt," Plato devotes about ten times more space in book 10 to his other objection, poetry's removal from truth—the discrepancy between true knowledge and imitation.

Actually, his two complaints come to the same thing: denied access to unchanging truth, the poets turn out multiple misleading approximations. Once Plato concludes that narration is primarily mimetic, his distrust turns into condemnation, and the poet's inability to escape the mimetic sequence—now identified with all (or most) narration—turns into an insoluble problem. The maker of narratives becomes reduced to a mere technician "knowing nothing but how to imitate" and lacking direct access to moral realities, his knowledge confined entirely to the literary mechanics effective in producing sensory and emotional stimulation. Since the incidents reproduced by drama and epic cannot faithfully transmit the "qualities" sought by the philosopher-moralist, a poet could never become even a satisfactory propagandist. His imitative manner, as defined in book ten, can never integrate speech and story with truth.

We may not find this conclusion palatable, but probably we can accept, after 2,400 years of Platonic influence, the simple observations it is based upon. Narratives do in fact employ the medium of language ("words and phrases") and an imitative manner to deliver an artificial construction, an "illusion," that differs radically from the speech and acts delivered by real-life individuals. Storytelling relies on poetic and oratorical expertise, on rhetorical, narrative, and metaphorical devices, among others, to organize a subject and bring about specific reactions in an audience. Artistic technique may therefore be considered the primary source of whatever meaning resides in a literary work.

But since poets, according to Plato, subordinate moral values and metaphysical considerations to technical virtuosity (when not deliberately obscuring them), their account of legendary heroes and gods will necessarily be slanted or limited by the tools of their trade. Poets say what their methods condition them to see or imagine instead of what they ought to say as judged by ethical, religious, and philosophical criteria. Their methods, not directed by those criteria but rather designed to "imitate" the manifold appearances and motives found in experience, present their version of reality in a biased way. The best-known tragic and epic authors mix scandalous information with admirable speech and deeds; they show their characters to be imperfect, *not* always virtuous, happy, self-controlled, and consistent. In fact, their characters are often fearful, weak, disobedient, impetuous, and irreverent. Gods too are seen to be inconstant and deceptive, causing evil, ill will, injury, and suffering. Plato concluded, and we must concur, that the poet often presents a mongrel version of humanity based upon multiplicity, ambiguity, and flux—attributes arising from the artistic process itself.

Plato assumed that these attributes were sufficient to disqualify poetic products. He deplored weaknesses in figures known for strengths; gods and heroes should be models of excellence—gold, not base metal or alloy. But even if we agree with Plato that such models can never be imitated by narratives without adulterating their purity with a show of imperfection, we can still recruit Plato's description of the poet's equipment and vision to accredit rather than discredit tragic drama. That is just what Aristotle did in the *Poetics*, his response (a generation later) to his tutor's rejection of the poets. For both Plato and Aristotle, the worth of a literary imitation depended upon the capacity of its mechanics to render significant activities. The question Aristotle faced was whether that capacity in fact existed, whether tragic plays could benefit a spectator even though they might not be guided by ethical directives, philosophical speculations, or historical reports. Going far beyond "a loyal working out of his teacher's real views,"[16] he decided in the affirmative.

As a preliminary, Aristotle accepts Plato's basic premises regarding imitation. He states at the beginning of the *Poetics* (chaps. 1–3) that all stories are imitative: imitation, far from being a dispensable rhetorical technique, is the distinctive mode of narration. He follows *Republic* books 2 and 3 by differentiating between poetic subject ("the doings of people"), media (in theatrical or choral productions, language collaborates with melody and rhythm), and manner (description, dialogue, or a mixture). But he does not limit imitation to a dialogue manner, as Plato did initially; instead, he follows *Republic* 10 by calling all poetic species imitations, whether tragedy, comedy, epic, or dithyramb. When Aristotle names the major genres "imitations" in his opening statement, he starts exactly at the point that Plato, after discarding the notion of a nonimitative narrative manner, ended. He draws upon Plato's insight when he treats the tragic tale as a whole, in its narrative, rhetorical, histrionic, and psychological aspects, as an imitation.

And he accepts the idea implied in *Republic* 2 and 3 that the subject of poetic imitation is the concrete activity of famous heroes and gods, not abstract attributes of excellence. The "soul" of tragedy, he contends, "is a certain kind of doing, not a personal quality" (chap. 6). His summary: "the poet must be a maker of fables rather than of verses, in that he is a poet by virtue of his imitation and what he imitates is doings" (chap. 9).[17] On these subjects Aristotle follows his mentor closely; it was Plato, not Aristotle, who first realized that the artist was restricted to a sensuous vocabulary and a technical grammar, that the poet was a craftsman, not an educator, a philosopher, or a historian.[18]

But what kind of craftsman? Plato gave poetry a sensuous medium, then condemned it; he awarded poetry a moral purpose, then withdrew it. His disciple, while concurring on the centrality of imitation, differed on its capability and usefulness. He realized that when models of excellence were revealed to be imperfect (or unlucky), the models were at fault rather than the artistic vehicle. If the subject of heroic delinquency or misfortune could be delineated truthfully and powerfully through the poet's medium and manner, then the poet might perform a worthwhile activity. Aristotle felt that such narratives served a legitimate social purpose when they maneuvered spectators toward an emotional crisis that ended in discharge, in contrast to Plato's plan to cultivate the spectator's rationality through a display of exemplary actions. The kind of "doings" he envisioned were precisely those Plato wished to avoid in poetic representations.

When Plato still assumed (books 2 and 3) that tragic drama could reinforce ethical dogma, he advised poets to avoid reference to ignoble or changeable characters and to fasten upon the praiseworthy; Aristotle declared both perfection *and* meanness inappropriate for a protagonist who, perhaps in innocence, could misperceive identities, make terrible mistakes, and suffer a fearful and pathetic fall. We benefit by empathizing with noble figures who excite us with their deadly errors. Both philosophers discussed the impact of well-made drama, but Plato despised the unstable or "base" feelings of pity, fear, and anger ("what we ought to do is dry them up"), whereas Aristotle argued that to discharge (release, relieve) these emotions, tragedy should first intensify them. Both found family conflict the most fearsome and lamentable circumstance in drama: Aristotle thought it therefore most suitable, Plato least suitable, to accomplish the differing missions each assigned to the theater. And both thinkers acknowledged Homer as the father of tragedy yet placed contrary judgments on his controversial presentation of legendary personalities.

For Plato, finally, involvement with sense media interfered with enlightenment; for Aristotle, the qualities sought by poets—qualities of probability, wholeness, amplitude, unity, complexity, and crisis—could inform the narrative medium when structured by plot formulas that traced a "certain kind of doing." In fact, Aristotle held poetry more valuable than history since it uncovers inherent probabilities of situation and character, as opposed to ideal portraits or historically accurate accounts of uncoordinated happenings. Poetry should be excused for not teaching proper behavior. Although artistic criteria need not clash with rules dictating laudable conduct and literal accuracy, the aim was different; drama impresses an audience with its technical command and emotional zest rather than with its educational correctness or historical precision. Characterization should be "appropriate" and "lifelike": "the standard of rightness is not the same in poetry as it is in social morality" (chap. 25).[19]

Aristotle's confidence in the worthwhile emotional effect of carefully designed plots refutes Plato's position on the emptiness of narration eternally estranged from "standards of rightness," and most discussions on tragedy, including this one, have assimilated the terms Aristotle used to advance his disagreement. Unfortunately, his work (probably recorded from lecture notes) was incomplete, especially in analyzing the heroic dilemma, as if he were trying to avoid his mentor's moralistic bent. Even if we do not consider the artwork to be an agent for ethical standards, the problematic characters and actions in tragedy raise certain issues. Aristotle did not explain, for example, how contradictory masculine values get expressed by literary mechanisms. How do great men use deceptive rhetoric when they suffer a fall? Aristotle pinpointed misperception of identity and reversal of status as story elements necessary to make the proper impression on an audience, but what beyond bad luck brings about those horrible misperceptions and misjudgments? Why does the protagonist experience such agonizing demoralization? And (an age-old question) how does an audience discharge pity and fear? Aristotle suggested a crucial adaptation of Plato's principal assumptions, but he left his work unfinished.[20]

Innumerable commentators have tried to provide further details, but not until the nineteenth century were important advances made in understanding the dynamics of tragedy. Nietzsche's views on flux enlarged Aristotle's idea about reversal of status to include transformation of personality, and Hegel's views on spiritual division enlarged Aristotle's idea about errors of perception to include moral one-sidedness (narrowness of commitment). For both German philosophers, as well as for Aristotle, witnessing the tragic spectacle could lead to awareness and emotional adjustment, differently as each thinker conceived those effects.

Their explanations turn out to be complementary! We can agree with Plato that the tragic form mirrors an unreliable rather than an unchanging and praiseworthy identity, but we can also agree with Nietzsche that there is a truth (perhaps an unpleasant truth) in unreliability and change, at the same time acknowledging Hegel's dictum that the clash of opposites confirms an enduring (as well as unreliable and changing) standard. If subjecting an elevated conception of behavior to stressful experience ("doings") results in a catastrophic outcome, we may need to explain that outcome, the death of integrity, not as a betrayal of Platonic-Hegelian ideality nor as a victory of Platonic-Nietzschean actuality, but as a perennial interaction between the two.

Which one is the "illusion"? Plato claimed that imperfection has no real existence; we could say with equal justice that *perfection* has no existence apart from visible signs and symbols of imperfection. What he called the crippling limitation of the literary medium becomes an advantage once we admit one thing: the model of virtue leads a double life. The mechanisms Plato disparaged—in particular, clever rhetorical devices—can appropriately and movingly communicate to an audience moral disaster and recovery because such mechanisms, when employed by skilled artisans, possess a double function: like the tragic hero, they can augment and subtract, posit and negate, sound weighty and empty.

Abstractions about perfection, then, might be impossible to translate convincingly into concrete acts without a simultaneous revelation of inadequacy or perversion. If so, then poetic artistry as Plato visualized it is uniquely suitable for the task of showing at once the inconsistency and authority of manly stereotypes. Tragic drama does not denigrate those stereotypes; it projects their oscillation between nobility and meanness (Plato would say between truth and untruth), each nullifying the other yet requiring the other to be fully defined. Plato was right about the duplicity of dramatic dialogue. He much preferred the conclusiveness of philosophical dialogue, but we are grateful to him for giving us this key to the door of tragedy.

9

Milton's Single-mindedness

Just as we compared light-dark images in the *Oresteia* and Seneca's *Oedipus* in order to measure their relative complexity, so can we compare rhetorical practice in Shakespeare's masterpiece, *King Lear,* and Milton's only tragic drama, *Samson Agonistes.* We shall focus on speech forms that bring out the "Dionysian" mutation and iteration ordained by male stereotypes who lose and reclaim their noble identity, a progression despised by Plato and later by Hegel. *Samson Agonistes* might seem to be another strange choice for a Nietzschean analysis since in his only play (published in 1671), John Milton worked hard to meet the requirement Plato formulates early in the *Republic* that a dramatist should treat spectators to deeds of high import. But he worked equally hard to meet Aristotle's requirement that a dramatist should bring about emotional discharge in spectators by skillfully orchestrating pitiful and terrible events. Milton labored to enlighten and to pacify (Hegel's aim too!), to prove that "just are the ways of God, / And justifiable to Men," and then leave an audience with "calm of mind, all passion spent."[1] Because he was rooted in the Christian tragic tradition as well as the Athenian, he wished also to demonstrate a cycle, previously exploited by Shakespeare, among many others, in which characters moved from faith to despair and back to reaffirmation.[2] So he produced a work with the incredibly difficult purpose of satisfying Plato's insistence on ethical predication and linguistic clarity, Aristotle's insistence on plot structured with errors of judgment and loss of status, and Shakespeare's insistence—one that was later paganized by Nietzsche—on cyclic alteration of personality.

Consistent with his deference to Plato, Milton sought precision in language. A cluster of words in his play (like a cluster of images in Seneca's play) will always be unified by a single connotation or concept. Polarities such as strength and weakness are never attached to the same object at the same time. Samson possesses a strong body and a weak mind, then the body becomes weak too, and finally they each regain stamina; his body and mind are either weak or strong, not both at once. Similarly, his confidence in fulfilling God's plan changes to confusion and depression, his sight to blindness, then back to the original condition. Such conditions do not coincide: the alterations alternate. If Aeschylus and Shakespeare enjoyed the concurrent operation of contraries, Milton, lawyerlike, stolidly stresses one point at a time. His single-minded rhetoric attests to a sober mission and a systematic, even legalistic, procedure. It attests to a Platonic—a monovalent, not ambivalent—mentality.

Even so, we cannot call John Milton a faultless disciple of Plato (the Plato of *Republic* 2 and 3) because heroes ought not lose their poise and become sorrowful, disobedient, angry, vengeful, intemperate in language, or reckless in sexual affairs, nor ought they do menial labor like slaves. They should perform (as Hegel also wished) without interruption as exemplars of "sobriety, courage, liberality, and high-mindedness," avoiding vacillation or shows of base emotions, shows of "pleasure and pain instead of law." And women are best kept out of sight, particularly when quarreling with their husbands. On top of his violations of these "ancient rules," Milton necessarily employed dialogue as his sole narrative manner. Nevertheless, he meant to do what Plato desired in the *Republic* before giving up in book 10—to imitate "profitable" behavior in right speech. "Tragedy, as it was anciently compos'd," the poet reminds us in his preface, "hath been ever held the gravest, moralest, and most profitable of all other Poems."

Trying to please dissenting masters, Milton was also an imperfect disciple of Aristotle. Contrary to the precept in the *Poetics* that fear will be aroused by "the misfortunes of normal people," not those far above or below the average in rectitude, Samson was quite "distinguished for excellence and virtue." Furthermore, although Samson commits a wrongful, painful act in ignorance when he betrays the secret of his God-given strength, an even better arrangement, according to Aristotle, would have him only *intending* to reveal his secret, then averting that error thanks to a timely disclosure or recognition of Dalila's true motive.

But he does misperceive a family member, and his downtrodden state—a "miserable change," as Manoa puts it, from high to low, leadership to helplessness, vision to sightlessness, security to uncertainty—does heighten our pity and apprehension even though it goes against *Plato's* guidelines. Actually, while a fall from high place occurs in almost all Greek tragedies, Samson's decline and subsequent recoup owe more to the pattern Milton derived from Christian allegory than to the reversals observed by Aristotle. Still, Milton tried to make his story probable, coherent, and properly complex, as Aristotle recommended. Reaching for the notorious three unities (which were not, of course, either omnipresent in Athenian tragedy or uniformly promoted by the *Poetics*), he simplified the biblical narrative, condensed the time, and restricted the location.

For further technical help with his multicultural undertaking, he looked to classical drama ("tragedy as it was anciently compos'd") and rhetoric. Aeschylus was his "best example" among dramatists: Milton set up an Aeschylean series of encounters between two actors in a challenge-response format (Samson versus Eve, Samson versus Harapha, Samson versus the Philistine officer), the series (as in most classical drama) preceded by introductory dialogue, followed by a messenger's speech, and punctuated by a chorus. He made extensive use of expository monologues, as Aeschylus did, to recite information (historical summaries, offstage actions, predictions), sentiment ("restless thoughts ... rush upon me thronging"), and choric commentary ("O mirror of our fickle state"). He copied (somewhat crudely) the transitional speech employed by Aeschylus, Sophocles, and Euripides to prepare the entrance of a character: "But who are these? for with joint pace I hear / The tread of many feet steering this way"; "But see here comes thy reverend Sire"; "But who is this, what thing of Sea or Land?"

And he conducted an Athenian debate in which Dalila's petition ("To light'n what thou suffer'st"), defense, emotional appeal ("Life yet hath many solaces"), and reply to the verdict mesh neatly with Samson's accusation, rebuttals, and judgment. Dalila obviously plays a part similar to one performed by Shakespeare's Eve-seductress, the biblical female betrayer of trust ("in argument with men," Dalila mutters as she storms off, "a woman ever / Goes by the worse, whatever be her cause"). But the debate takes a classical form, and the most relevant meaning of *agonistes* in this respect is "debater" or "contender."[3]

When playwrights in seventeenth-century England reached for rhetorical figures to carry out their educative, argumentative, or therapeutic intentions, they had available a nearly unlimited arsenal handed down by the Greek and Roman orators, especially Cicero, and dramatists, especially Seneca. Often they gravitated to a popular technique that drove the listener unrelentingly toward a single unambiguous significance—heaping up synonyms, near synonyms, or other closely related terms. That iterative technique supplied the linguistic cement for Milton's effort to combine Platonic clarity, Aristotelian catharsis, Christian doctrine, and Athenian construction.

Needless to say, figures of antithesis also enter into a work built upon the contrast between Samson's former glory, present disgrace, and impending victory.[4] During his long opening monologue (lines 1–114), for example, Samson bewails his humiliating transition between "what once I was, and what am now" ("O glorious strength / Put to the labour of a Beast, debas't / Lower than bondslave!"). The antitheses accumulate—beast of burden and hero, blindness and sight (that venerable coupling), slavery and freedom, toil and rest, dampness and fresh air, "impotence of mind, in body strong." But it is always the negative half that receives the rhetorical stress of repetition. Like a lawyer pleading a "cause" (or a professor teaching composition), Milton repeats certain depressing themes over and over to enhance their singularity of meaning (a Senecan meaning during most of the play) and to avoid the multiplicity Plato detested.

The point can be illustrated by this well-known passage:

O loss of sight, of thee I most complain!
Blind among enemies, O worse than chains,
Dungeon, or beggary, or decrepit age!
Light the prime work of God to me is extinct,
And all her various objects of delight
Annull'd, which might in part my grief have eas'd,
Inferiour to the vilest now become
Of man or worm; the vilest here excel me,
They creep, yet see, I dark in light expos'd
To daily fraud, contempt, abuse and wrong,
Within doors, or without, still as a fool,
In power of others, never in my own;
Scarce half I seem to live, dead more than half.
O dark, dark, dark, amid the blaze of noon,
Irrecoverably dark, total Eclipse
Without all hope of day! (67–82)

In putting together this verbal fugue, Milton sounds his motif ("O loss of sight, of thee I most complain!"), then restates it five times in the next fourteen lines, each restatement stuffed with synonymous words. The two sections of the line "Scarce half I seem to live, dead more than half" express one idea in synonymous ways by repeating a word ("half") at the beginning and end; rhetoricians in Milton's time, borrowing their nomenclature from the classical masters, called this technique *epanalepsis*. In the next line, "dark, dark, dark" illustrates *epizeuxis*, repeating a word with no words intervening, and it is followed by *ploce*, repeating a key word ("dark" again) with other words intervening. Even nonsynonymous terms are strung together to accent the theme: blindness is "worse than chains, / Dungeon, or beggary, or decrepit age!" and it "exposes" Samson to "daily fraud, contempt, abuse and wrong" (*brachylogia*).[5] These iterative figures, built on the duplication, similarity, or congruence of words and meanings, give a one-track immediacy and emphasis to the theme of blindness referred to in the initial comparison (*antitheton*). The passage is Platonic in its single-mindedness though not in its melancholy, since Plato thought that paying attention to frailty, error, and decline was unbecoming and unprofitable.[6]

Milton repeats the motif of Samson's downfall endlessly. "O miserable change!" Manoa cries, echoing Samson and also the protagonist of *Antony and Cleopatra* (IV.xv.51):

> Select, and Sacred, Glorious for a while, [*synonymia*]
> The miracle of men: then in an hour [*paradox*][7]
> Ensnar'd, assaulted, overcome, led bound [*brachylogia*]
> Thy Foes' derision, Captive, Poor, and Blind, [*brachylogia*]
> Into a Dungeon thrust, to work with Slaves. [*brachylogia*] (363–67)

Samson keeps remembering his weakness during the seduction by stringing like terms together:

> O *indignity*, O *blot* [*synonymia*]
> To Honour and Religion! *servile* mind
> Rewarded well with *servile* punishment! [*epanalepsis*]
> The *base degree* to which I now am fall'n, [*synonymia*]
> *These rags, this grinding*, is not yet so *base* [*brachylogia, ploce*]
> As was my former *servitude, ignoble* [*comparatio, traductio*][8]
> *Unmanly, ignominious, infamous,* [*synonymia, alliteration*]
> True *slavery*, and *that blindness* worse than this, [*synonymia, comparatio*]
> That *saw not how degenerately* I *serv'd*. [*synonymia, traductio*] (411–19, emphasis added)

The passage also exemplifies *epanodos*, expansion of a subject by repeating and amplifying key words. Its two comparisons constitute a logical scheme (*proportion*) based on analogy: present is to past servitude as present is to past blindness, Samson's earlier condition being worse in both cases.[9]

Synonymia and *brachylogia*, lists of words that signify more or less the same thing, cumulate pathos and hammer away at the author's "argument." In no other work, prose or verse, does Milton engage these figures to the same extent; even Harapha and the Philistine officer get off a few. Samson's laxity was not merely "ignoble," it was "Unmanly, ignominious, infamous, / True slavery." As a result, Dalila "turned me out ridiculous, despoil'd, / Shaven, and disarm'd among my enemies." Now, "effeminately vanquish't, . . . blind, disheart'n'd, sham'd, dishonour'd, quell'd," Samson sinks into unmitigated shame. He

> lies at random, carelessly diffus'd,
> With languish't head unpropt,
> As one past hope, abandon'd,
> And by himself given over. . . . (118–21)

He resigns himself, indeed, to becoming "bed-rid, not only idle, / Inglorious, unemploy'd, with age out-worn." But the "chief affliction, shame and sorrow, / The anguish of my Soul" is that

> . . . I
> God's counsel have not kept, his holy secret
> Presumptuously have publish'd, impiously,
> Weakly at least, and shamefully. (496–99)

His betrayal caused God to be "Disglorifi'd, blasphem'd, and had in scorn," not to speak of the "Dishonour, obloquy, . . . scandal / To Israel, diffidence of God, and doubt / In feeble hearts." The downcast Hebrew warrior summarizes his distress with a torrent of synonymous verbs:

> My griefs not only *pain* me
> As a ling'ring disease,
> But finding no redress, *ferment* and *rage*,
> Nor less than wounds immedicable
> *Rankle*, and *fester*, and *gangrene*,
> To black mortification.
> Thoughts my Tormentors arm'd with deadly stings
> *Mangle* my apprehensive tenderest parts,
> *Exasperate, exulcerate*, and *raise*
> *Dire inflammation* which no cooling herb
> Or med'cinal liquor can assuage,
> Nor breath of Vernal Air from snowy Alp. (617–28, emphasis added)

Here "mortification" (as defined by *OED*) catches the denotations of all ten verbs: death of part of the body, deadening of vital qualities, shame, self-inflicted pain. As in Seneca's monochromatic portrait of Oedipus, the near-synonyms build up varying shades of gloom.

But then the similarity to Seneca's invincibly dark protagonist ends; Milton has iterated the sorrowful facts of Samson's Aristotelian-biblical decline so abundantly in order to make the greatest possible contrast with the subsequent resurrection, a second coming, a revived dedication to God's plan, a reentry into light—reintegration rather than continued disintegration, as experienced also by Oedipus at Colonus and (eventually) Prometheus. Milton had enunciated this redemptive journey with the same dark-light and low-high pairings in *Paradise Lost:*

> What in me is dark
> Illumine, what is low raise and support;
> That to the highth of this great Argument
> I may assert Eternal Providence,
> And justifie the wayes of God to men. (1: 22–26)[10]

Samson's rehabilitation, completed in offstage revenge upon the Philistines, is prepared by the disputes with Dalila, whom Samson turns away ("lest fierce remembrance wake / My sudden rage to tear thee joint by joint"); with Harapha, whom he challenges to a duel; and with the Philistine officer, whose invitation to appear in public he accepts ("I begin to feel / Some rouzing motions"). These confrontations develop the classical split between prideful self-sufficiency and accommodation (to the Philistines), yet they also allow Samson to renew his original alliance with the Hebrew people. His choric reverence curbs the excesses of heroism. The challenges and his responses, Hegel might say, reinforce his merger of self-confidence with a social-religious cause. And Nietzsche might say that reinvigoration takes turns with demoralization.

Once preparations are complete, the transformation takes place rapidly, "fiery virtue rouzed / From under ashes into sudden flame." In revising Samson's outlook, Milton avoided the prolonged iterative treatment he gave to the earlier attitude. The chorus does employ repetition to argue the thesis that "vertue giv'n for lost, / Deprest, and overthrown," now "revives, reflourishes, . . . vigorous most / When most unactive deem'd." And Manoa certifies, in a similar vein,

> Nothing is here for tears, nothing to wail
> Or knock the breast, no weakness, no contempt,
> Dispraise, or blame, nothing but well and fair,
> And what may quiet us in a death so noble. (1721–24)

The rhetoric of faith, however, is not nearly so vociferous and elaborate as the rhetoric of defeat. Milton lavished his talent on the darker layers—physical, emotional, moral, intellectual, spiritual—of a change from prosperity to misfortune.

Samson's regeneration may receive less elaboration, but it is as univalent as Samson's humiliation. The upward journey proves as undeviating in its affirmation of "invincible might" as the downward journey was undeviating in its hopelessness. That downward route did not get relieved by much hope: before Samson rises again, like Jesus or the Phoenix, his misery almost never played off against references to retained or anticipated potency. He never countered all that repetitious lamentation with a voice speaking of indignation or inspiration. Until he "heroically . . . finishes / A life heroic," the wealth of rhetoric publicizing his debility went unchallenged. In contrast to one of Sophocles' most woeful figures, Philoctetes, who describes himself as "a sufferer, and angry," Samson reacted to injustice solely with indulgence in grief and self-abasement ("Surely I must be vile," "take pity on me"), not with anger as well as sorrow. His might was just a memory during the first half of the tragedy, a memory that emphasized his present woe.

Then as soon as the depleted warrior feels those rousing motions and finally stands up in "rage," his new outlook displays the same one-sidedness. He switches off the sound of self-pity and suffering, sheds his woebegone demeanor, and shifts the dramatic interest to "some great act." "O how comely it is, and how reviving / To the spirits of just men long oppressed," the chorus expounds, "when God into the hands of their deliverer / Puts invincible might." Milton does not duplicate the tension of opposites kept in constant motion by Aeschylus, his Greek model, or by Euripides and Sophocles, for whom predication and denial—the assertion of power and the counterassertion of limitation—were inseparable. The iterations and antitheses fortify a sense of succession, not simultaneity.

Milton arranged it this way deliberately: the style of *Samson Agonistes* limits its vision to nothing or all—pathetic impotence or invincible might, disaster or triumph, ignorance or insight—one acting as precursor for the other, never the two at once. Plato, when he still allowed some merit to poetry, might have pardoned Milton for those marching legions of doleful synonyms because they prepared an edifying recovery and because they sounded a single clear-cut note. We acknowledge that accomplishment, but we ask, without disrespect for the piety of Milton and Plato, whether their single track to truth arrived at the whole truth. A few tragic playwrights have articulated with greater rhetorical sophistication the problematic nature of strength and weakness.

10

Shakespeare's Trickery

Piling up Nothing

In his tragedies Shakespeare devised rhetoric that involved a continuing exchange between positive assertions and negations, the self-contradiction exposed by a great man's fall. For instance, negative grammatical forms ("never tell me!") continually erode affirmations throughout *Othello*, and equations between traits like courage and cowardice, manliness and femininity, uprightness and evil occupy the dialogue of *Antony and Cleopatra* and *Macbeth* ("Fair is foul, and foul is fair"). When he composed *King Lear* (1605), Shakespeare took an unusual tack by amassing likes (synonyms, near-synonyms, and related methods of repetition) to give emphasis and amplitude to unlikes, the exercise Milton repeated sixty years later in *Samson Agonistes*. But Shakespeare's linguistic method was far more enigmatic than Milton's. Speakers not only *followed* repetitive declarations with a contrary point, they also expressed a contrary point *during* their repetitions. Their iterations built up a base of supposedly constant meanings, in accordance with the arguments of Plato in the *Republic* books 2 and 3 (and Hegel's *Aesthetics*); and yet, bearing out Plato's misgivings in book 10 (and Nietzsche's declarations on the fluctuation of all meanings), they contradicted themselves.

If Samson seldom mingles affirmation with negation, characters in *King Lear* habitually do as they incessantly inflate their status and reduce the status of others. Often the standing they reduce is their own: the derisive constructions put together by Lear, urgently intending to sound magisterial, undercut themselves. His repetitions accumulate egoism, inconsistency, and insanity, bearing out Plato's fears about poetic dialogue. His redundant misanthropy signifies nothing legitimate, and his denials of orderly governance compromise his credibility, his stereotypical need for such governance. At the same time, he opposes his cynical iterations with iterations that affirm something valuable (as Plato wished). While self-pity and indignation urge him to denigrate moral law in general as well as certain individuals in particular, his pessimism comes accompanied by an upbeat counterpoint that replays the old song about the necessity for respect, authority, and social sanity!

Milton addressed Plato's thesis on the ephemeral nature of literature with a straightforward rhetorical bid to rediscover imperishable truth after its eclipse in darkness; Shakespeare, in contrast, drew his strength from a constant, unremitting dialogue between truth and falsity, awareness and blindness, light and darkness. Though he never studied the *Republic*, Shakespeare profited from the conflict Plato witnessed between poetry as conduit and mutilator of sacred canons. Commemorator of those canons in the Miltonic-Hegelian mode, he was nevertheless a book 10 poet in the Nietzschean mode, a master of deceptive, hollow speech, a juggler who invented a pliable procedure that permitted him to posit and deny simultaneously.

1

Before writing *King Lear*, Shakespeare had experimented extensively with the standard iterative figures. His narrative poems of the 1590s, *Venus and Adonis* and *The Rape of Lucrece*, were packed with such figures; one encyclopedic example of *brachylogia* has Venus explaining that she is not

> hard-favour'd, foul, or wrinkled-old,
> Ill nurtur'd, crooked, churlish, harsh in voice,
> O'erworn, despised, rheumatic, and cold,
> Thick-sighted, barren, lean, and lacking juice.

(*Venus and Adonis* 133–36)

And in Senecan fashion, the heroine of *The Rape of Lucrece* attaches a list of interchangeable names to the spirit of darkness:

> O comfort-killing Night, image of hell!
> Dim register and notary of shame!
> Black stage for tragedies and murders fell!
> Vast sin-concealing chaos! nurse of blame!
> Blind muffled bawd! dark harbour for defame!

Grim cave of death! whispering conspirator
With close-tongu'd treason and the ravisher!
O hateful, vaporous, and foggy Night!

(*The Rape of Lucrece* 764–71)[1]

Shakespeare, like Milton, borrowed heavily from the rhetorical catalogue for his plays too, his figures of restatement including, besides *synonymia* and *brachylogia*, (1) figures repeating single words, as in *epizeuxis* (repeating a word without other words between), *diacope* and *ploce* (repeating a word with other words between), and *anadiplosis* (ending a clause or line with a word that begins the next); (2) balanced or coordinate constructions, as in *polysyndeton* (phrases or clauses with conjunctions), *parison* (parallel phrases or clauses), and *climax* (parallel phrases or clauses of increasing weight); and (3) figures that amplify or extend an idea through comparison and example, division into parts, accumulation of data, and recapitulation, as in *enumeratio, distribution,* and *epanodos.*

By the time he wrote *King Lear,* Shakespeare had worked many of these Latin conventions into a unified scheme that we may label "addition" or "cumulation." Words can be said to make an addition when they are unified by grammatical coordination, by correspondence in meaning (equivalence), and by conjunctive linkage. Insofar as grammatical form, an addition may coordinate either single words (duplicating the part of speech) or syntax (duplicating the structure of phrases, clauses, or sentences). Insofar as equivalence—Milton learned this lesson quite well—additive terms may be identical, synonymous, or even unlike so long as they expand one connotation, whether spelled out or unintended by the speaker. And insofar as linkage, conjunctions and internal or end punctuation—especially the comma, semicolon, and dash—may join additions, or linkage can be implied simply by the adjacency of words and the correspondence of constructions or meanings. The coordinating conjunction *and,* when denoting "also," "added to," "associated with," "as well as," "thereupon," or "next," serves as Shakespeare's most useful bonding tool. From a rhetorical viewpoint, the most important word in *King Lear* is not *ripeness* or *love* or *authority* or *ingratitude;* the most important word is *and.* Sometimes other conjunctions, conjunctive adverbs, and a few prepositions build cumulations too—*or, for, but, yet, still, as, so, though, since, thus, therefore,* and so forth. Transitional words, of course, may also govern *non*cumulative constructions: for instance, *but* normally indicates contrast or exception, while *and* (the workhorse) can indicate contrast or causation as well as addition.[2]

These general rules scarcely suggest the variety, frequency, and flexibility of Shakespeare's usage. We may begin to do that by illustrating a half dozen additive techniques in the remarkable opening scene. In this preliminary survey, I shall introduce symbols to outline the structure of the examples, their versatility, and their diabolic participation in antithesis at the same time that they accumulate correspondences.

Many cumulations, needless to say, do *not* contribute to antithesis. The most elementary addition, repeating one word in a single sense with no other words between, may repeat a denotation without any implied or explicit contradiction. Lear's response to the apparent impertinence of his youngest daughter—"How, how, Cordelia?" (I.i.94)—exemplifies this usage, and can be designated by the notation 1+1, the "+" representing linkage. Here reiteration simply verbalizes exasperation—Lear's surprise, disbelief, and impatience.

Other categories of addition may be equally homogenous, in the Miltonic manner. Joined synonyms (1+1') are usually more malleable than repetition of identical terms because they allow the speaker, or at any rate the author, to project variations surrounding a central meaning. When Lear shouts to Kent, "Hence and avoid my sight!" (line 124), he fortifies his first imperative with another that stresses his unwillingness to confront anyone who displeases him (he echoes the thought in line 157: "Out of my sight!").[3] Nearly synonymous terms form variations on a theme in Kent's comment to Edmund (29), "I must love you, and sue to know you better; in Lear's proclamation (49–50), "now we will divest us both of rule, / Interest of territory, cares of state" (1+1'+1'); and in the warning to Kent (122), "Come not between the dragon and his wrath." The king's brusque offer to Burgundy (201), "She's there, and she is yours," distinguishes between the location and availability of Cordelia as it forwards one harsh intent. These examples are as unambivalent as any speech in *Samson Agonistes*.

Connected *non*synonymous words (1+2) may also contribute to an uncomplicated cumulative effect, as Milton discovered. In symmetrical predicates (96), Cordelia itemizes a debt to her father for having "begot me, bred me, loved me" (1+2+3); notation here refers to a temporal sequence that makes up a father's gifts to a child. Commas link the items in this sequence, but conjunctions too can announce the passage of time. Gloucester adds future to past to describe Edmund's transience (31–32): "He hath been out nine years, and away he shall again" (1+2).

Such constructs are modest enough; the capacity of a univalent addition to develop ideas and feelings enlarges as the coordinated units increase in number and intricacy. Any part of a cumulative construction may itself be devised of added terms, all of which merge to form a congruous whole, as 1+1'[a+a] or 1+2[a+a'] or 1+2[a+b]. By disinheriting Cordelia (113–14), Lear cuts off his "paternal care, / Propinquity and property of blood." The primary terms, *care* and *blood* (1+1'), would not be synonymous without their modifiers; "paternal care" is equivalent to close kinship ("propinquity") plus the obligations attendant upon that kinship ("property"). If these modifiers of "blood" are considered to make up a subordinate addition of nonsynonymous words in the second term, notation records the linguistic relationship as 1+1'[a+b].[4]

Shakespeare, then, often coordinates words, phrases, clauses, or sentences to clarify and emphasize emotional, factual (spatial and temporal), and ethical data that are tightly integrated and undisturbed by contrasting meanings. In passages where the coordination is formally balanced ("begot me, bred me, loved me"), notation can indicate parallel structure; Cordelia's three verbs would be referred to as //1+2+3. Similarly, Cordelia proclaims (101-2) that her husband "shall carry / Half my love with him, half my care and duty": //1+1'[a+a']. The symmetry (I take "care" and "duty" to be roughly synonymous) imparts a legalistic aura: devotion to her father, dictated by etiquette, will be impersonally reduced after marriage.

Lear more than Cordelia speaks as if he were celebrating symmetrically organized rituals conveying a single purpose. He appraises his domain (64–65) in these matched phrases: "With shadowy forests and with champains riched, / With plenteous rivers and wide-skirted meads": //1+2+3+4. Heaping together the diverse holdings so neatly may impress his listeners with the solemnity of the proceedings as well as the spaciousness of the grant, with the donor's sagacity as well as generosity. Lear's parallel constructions are usually more forceful: "She's there, and she is yours" can be compared to "I have sworn. I am firm" (245): //1+1'. In each statement close grammatical coordination stresses finality of judgment. In contrast to such peremptory phrasing, Burgundy's elegant diplomatic response to a dowerless bride lacks vigor (246–47). Its balanced dependent clauses are connected by a conjunction indicating causation, not cumulation: "I am sorry then you have so lost a father / That you must lose a husband": //1→2.[5]

Sometimes simple additions *collaborate* with the mode of causation, as in Gloucester's account of Edmund's nativity (12–14): "Sir, this young fellow's mother could [conceive]; whereupon she grew round-wombed, and had indeed, sir, a son for her cradle": 1→2+3. Gloucester concludes his description with a set of short prose clauses (20–23) that joins contrast, cumulation, and causation: "though this knave came something saucily to the world before he was sent for, yet was his mother fair, there was good sport at his making, and the whoreson must be acknowledged": 1/2+3→4. The linkages assemble his attitude toward Edmund's bastardy: his severity is moderated by the conjunction *though*, which subordinates the illegitimacy, by the conjunction *yet* and the coupling—so to speak—of two pleasant memories, which justify it, and by a periodic culmination after the conjunction *and* (in the sense of "therefore"), which regularizes it.

If Gloucester's comfortably prosaic summary of his pleasures and duties as a father reflects a cavalier but affectionate approach to responsibility, Cordelia's carefully quantified summary of her benefits and debts as a daughter reflects a correct but passionless approach. When she analyzes the behavior a child should properly show a father, Cordelia combines causation with addition in a parallel, not periodic, construction. A threefold obligation (the consequence) repays a threefold investment (the cause):

You have begot me, bred me, loved me. I	//1[a+b+c]
Return those duties back as are right fit,	→
Obey you, love you, and most honor you.	2[c'+c+c']

(I.i.96–98)

Though cause and consequence involve "love," to Lear this fastidious balancing of filial debits against receipts bespeaks cold courtesy.

These constructions would probably not have alienated Plato, Hegel, or Milton; though intricate sometimes, they make straightforward, unequivocal statements. That is often true also of Shakespeare's most elaborate additions, which amplify an idea according to an expansive logical plan in which a predication (A), usually abstract, precedes or follows details that explain or illustrate it. Cumulation occurs in the supporting information, or among revisions of the predication, or both, the added terms being approximately equivalent in meaning and coordinate in syntax: A:1+1'+2 or A+A':1+2:A' and so forth. In a specialized kind of amplification, appositives tie merits to a proper name. Kent enlarges upon the name and nature of his king (A) with this balanced salutation:

Royal Lear,	A:
Whom I have ever honored as my king,	//1
Loved as my father, as my master followed,	+1'+1'
As my great patron thought on in my prayers	+1'

(139–42)

The four verb phrases (the appositives) are parallel except that the order of verb and complement is reversed in the third and fourth pairs: this asymmetry alters but does not disturb the regularity. With great economy, the appositives allow the speaker to transform a commonplace list of complimentary titles into a dynamic testimony of allegiance. Kent attributes regal qualities to a glorified subject ("Royal Lear") by attributing reverential actions to himself; his commendation is as *self*-descriptive as his later obeisance to the "authority" he "would fain call master" (I.iv.27, 29).[6]

Defined narrowly, addition requires linkage or adjacency of words that are coordinate in form and equivalent in sense. This survey focuses on guidelines so restricted, but Shakespeare also repeats words more casually. Recurring key terms may still sound a single theme even though widely separated by many lines, even by whole scenes or acts. Iteration of the same word with different words intervening is heard during the conversation about Edmund's illegitimacy:

| Gloucester: Do you smell a fault? | 1 |
| Kent: I cannot wish the fault undone. | +1 |

(15–16)

In the same scene, Cordelia makes synonymous statements connected only by theme and without linkage or syntactic duplication. First (62) she addresses the deficiency of language in communicating love: "What shall Cordelia speak? Love, and be silent." Fourteen lines later she delivers a similar aside:

> Then poor Cordelia:
> And yet not so, since I am sure my love's
> More ponderous than my tongue. (76–78)

And thirteen lines further on (91–92), she advances the thought a third time: "Unhappy that I am, I cannot heave / My heart into my mouth." Neither welded by conjunctions nor identical in syntax, these variations compose a loose cumulation held together by a common purpose. The cumulation of nonadjoining words (sometimes called delayed restatement or incremental repetition) supplements tightly linked addition by laying down narrative and thematic continuity in larger segments of the play.

All these techniques duplicate single meanings. They stress one point at one time, as Milton did with such great perseverance. But Shakespeare wishes also to project contradiction or *dissimilar* meanings through repetition, and an obvious way to achieve this would be to have several characters interpret the same term in different senses, a *non*cumulative type of iteration. A word may carry so many unlike meanings that repetition enhances only an impression of diversity, dissonance, or incongruity—multivalence without a unifying idea. To take the most frequent example in the first scene, love is referred to no less than thirty-four times, not to mention allied words like *amorous, affection,* and *care.* Characters freely demand, donate, withhold, receive, confuse, or counterfeit that cryptic sentiment. The verbal fluidity drowns any single import, any certainty or constancy associated with the word.

Less obviously, Shakespeare features iterative methods that bring out congruence together with dissonance. Restatement in multiple senses can cooperate with single-sense restatement so that an addition put together by two speakers reflects both exception and conformity, antagonism and likeness. The emerging contest between Lear and Cordelia proceeds to an exchange featuring four repetitions of "nothing" that blends the modes of addition, contrast, and causation:

Lear: Speak.	
Cordelia: Nothing, my lord	1
Lear: Nothing?	+1
Cordelia: Nothing.	+1
Lear: Nothing will come of nothing.	/1←1

(86–90)

The repeated term carries two definitions: "no speech zealously verifying love" and, in Lear's second use, "no material benefit"; one will ensure the other. Typically, the king imparts a negative spin to imply punishment or revenge as Cordelia holds fast to a positive usage implying honest silence. "Nothing" thus gets repeated with the same meaning and also with a different meaning! In this quarrel, whose purpose is to signal a breakdown in communication, contrast controls the climax, not similarity. Dissimilarity overtakes a rhetorical form that requires correlation among meanings.[7]

Repeated words, then, can signify one thing and, at the same time, contrary things; a word spoken by two characters can maintain one denotation while indicating differences in connotation or usage. Another exchange between father and daughter again combines addition with contrast:

Lear: So young, and so untender?	//1[a/b]
Cordelia: So young, my lord, and true.	/2[a+c]

(106-7)

The addition in the second line rebuts the antithesis in the first (the initial *and* denotes "and yet"). *Young* means the same thing to the speakers as a time marker, but they differ on its meaning when qualified by the adjectives they attach to it. Or the passage could be construed another way. Because Lear attributes harshness (*untender*) to youth, Cordelia's answer represents to him a rephrasing of his own equation (*untender* equals *true*). From his perspective, the lines form an addition of two antitheses: //1[a/b]+1'[a/c]. In either case, the repeated sentence structure counterbalances a difference in connotation, underscoring the irony of the misunderstanding: just as the sentences are closely related, so are these warring characters, joined not only by blood but also by temperament, both being stubborn and self-righteous.

Similarly, when Kent is banished he communicates both disagreement and kinship. He does so with quick transitions that repeat a literal meaning yet change its usage. In a series of conciliatory responses to Lear's threats, he artfully links each of his rejoinders—with a repeated word, a synonym, or another variant—to a word ending the preceding repudiation by Lear. The passage imitates musical counterpoint, his vows of allegiance alternating with and intimately connected to Lear's rejections (here and following, only selected cumulative terms are notated or emphasized):

Lear: The bow is bent and drawn; make from the *shaft*	1
Kent: Let *it* fall rather, though the *fork* invade	/1'+1'
The region of my heart....	
Lear: Kent, on thy *life*, no more!	2
Kent: My *life* I never held but as a pawn	/2
To wage against thine enemies; ne'er fear to lose *it*,	+2'
Thy safety being motive.	
Lear: Out of my *sight*!	3
Kent: *See* better, Lear, and let me still remain	/3'
The true blank of thine *eye*.	+3'
Lear: *Now by Apollo*—	4
Kent: *Now by Apollo*, King,	/4
Thou *swear'st thy gods* in vain.	+4'
Lear: O vassal! Miscreant!	
[*Grasping his sword*]	[5]
Albany, Cornwall: Dear sir, forbear!	
Kent: *Kill* thy physician.	/5'

(143–45, 154–63)

These vicious attacks, unselfish replies, and the tight transitions between them (the word *kill* follows a corresponding *gesture*) buttress the idea, so prominent in act 1, of continued dedication among allies despite their disunion. The repetitions vary the relevance of constant terms, registering discord but at the same time revealing a verbal connectedness and a temperamental affinity, since Kent (like Cordelia) matches Lear's stubborn self-righteousness. Additions can testify to concurrent division and alliance; cumulative continuity, paradoxically, can give rhetorical substance to discontinuity.

So a word may be fortified by repetition and at the same time opposed by the same word taken in a different sense. Or instead of repeated single words, a string of synonyms or near-synonyms may contradict (rather than reinforce, as in *Samson Agonistes*) another set of synonyms. Shakespeare uses this method extensively: in his interview with Lear (120–87), Kent underlines his concern for the king's welfare by calling himself a "pawn," "true blank" (guide), and "physician"; to Lear, contrarily, he is a "vassal," "miscreant," and "recreant." Kent soon mingles his own negations with his affirmations: the "king," "father," "master," or "patron" becomes "old" and "mad," subject to "folly," "evil," "hideous rashness," and "foul disease."

These methods explicitly interweave likeness and disparity. Shakespeare discovered, in addition, that words repeated in a constant sense may accomplish the same mission when the contradiction is merely *implied*. For instance, disharmony may be suggested merely by ending reference to an addition that had connoted harmony. In the first scene, two recurring pairs of titles suggest courtly union. One pairing, "Cornwall and Albany," conventionally links names according to social position (they are brothers-in-law and dukes), like Rosencrantz and Guildenstern in *Hamlet* (they are classmates and spies). Reiterating the linkage calls attention to the peers' equality: when Kent's reference to Cornwall and Albany (1–2) hints at precedence favoring the first one named, Gloucester immediately corrects that evaluation (5–6), and Lear confirms their equal status with a commendation ("our no less loving son of Albany") as well as with the conjunction that coordinates their titles (41–42, 127). Until this coupling falls apart later in the play, the repeated conjunction sends a verbal signal of aristocratic concord and normalcy.

Playing off against this apparently harmonious alliance, the second recurrent pairing of titles, "France and Burgundy," again seems to betoken equivalence in position (they are suitors and foreign noblemen), but this one comes to a more immediate rupture. In this case, when Lear names France first (34, 45, 84, 188) he definitely is indicating a preference. When Cordelia displeases him he hints at precedence by summoning France first, to release him from the marriage negotiation ("Call France. Who stirs! / Call Burgundy," 126–27), then offers his disinherited daughter to the Duke of Burgundy while requesting France to "avert your liking a more worthier way" (211). After the King of France, contrary to Lear's desire, accepts Cordelia, Lear reverses his preference and ends the peaceful coexistence of the two suitors. In his last speech to them, his interjection of three lines between "Thou hast her, France" and "Come, noble Burgundy" (262–66) emphasizes their abrupt and irreparable separation, a point already made by the cessation of the formal *and* relationship. Just as other affiliations disintegrate in the first scene, the temporary bond between these noblemen, along with its rhetorical signature, disappears after some two hundred lines of "propinquity."

Shakespeare's repetitions mingle dissonance or exception with intimacy or likeness. Their linkages, grammatical correspondences, and semantic uniformity, in conjunction with shifts of meaning, dissimilarities, and ironies, indicate both congruence and discontinuity, integration and exclusion, constancy and fluidity. Plato knew that such linguistic "vacillation" could be subversive, as subversive as narrative and metaphorical reversals. He would not tolerate the interplay between consistency and contradiction, but Shakespeare found it entirely appropriate for his version of tragic uncertainty.

2

So far I have illustrated cumulative methods in the opening scene with little regard for their part in Shakespeare's "imitation" of the heroic quandary, yet by now the recurrence of two subjects prominent in Athenian tragedy, evaluation and precedence, must be evident. Lear judges his three daughters and Kent, and he is judged by them. Regan and Goneril are judged by Cordelia and Kent, Cordelia by France and Burgundy, Burgundy by France, and Edmund by Gloucester. These characters gauge the merit of their fellows in order to secure the privileges and discharge the obligations proper to their standing as they conceive it. They base all their evaluations, as the aristocratic characters in Greek tragedy do, upon the respect owed to them or owed by them.[8] But the opening of *King Lear* forecasts that many of them will isolate and devalue themselves rather than build a coherent hierarchy based on quality, and their habits of speech uncover that self-defeat.

Shakespeare's rhetorical interest, therefore, turns to satirical (ironic) cumulation. An addition, even though its terms are unified in meaning, tightly linked, and grammatically coordinated, may insinuate or predict or bring about the opposite of its stated intent. Redundant avowals (as Strindberg understood) can lie or instigate conflict; redundant disapproval (as Kafka understood) can compromise the disapprover. And a repeated demand for equity—the age-old compulsive drive to grasp prerogative—

can derail itself with blind judgment and an inclination to ride over social proprieties. When that demand for justification is wholly self-oriented it becomes suicidal, and repetitious attempts to promote something extraordinary come to "nothing." Balanced or amplified evaluations cumulate only violence, disunity, and disillusion; the congruence expressed in additive language systematically delineates an egoistic jungle.

Lear inaugurates this implicit irony by encouraging speech that professes harmony yet produces "division." He dispatches his wish to grade his heirs (and so ratify his own primacy) in nonadjacent requests for pledges of loyalty:

Tell me, my daughters	1
. . . .	
Goneril,	
Our eldest-born, *speak* first.	+1'
. . . .	
What says our second daughter,	+1'
Our dearest Regan, wife of Cornwall?	
. . . .	
Now, our joy,	
Although our last and least; . . .	
what can you say to draw	+1'
A third more opulent than your sisters? *Speak*.	+1'
. . . .	
Speak again.	+1'
. . . .	
Mend your speech a little.	+1'

(I.i.48, 53–54, 67–68, 82–83, 85–86, 90, 94)

These identical or synonymous imperatives urge his daughters to notarize his preeminent place, soliciting their devotion, compelling their obedience, and revealing his insecurity; their appraisal of *his* worth will decide his appraisal of *their* worth. His naïveté almost invites their "machinations." Furthermore, the additions in the titles of address betray a bias: the appositive referring to Cordelia is more affectionate than the other two. He hints at her greater importance ("our joy") even before he invites her to gain a "more opulent" portion by speaking in a more opulent manner.

When Cordelia declines his invitation, Goneril and Regan grab at the notion that inhibits their sister—the insufficiency of words vowing total loyalty. Goneril submits a short insincere amplification that extends its proposition (A) into four lines of clarification, each introduced by a comparative designed to prove the inadequacy of extravagant praise.

55 Sir, I love you more than word can wield the matter;   A:
56 Dearer than eyesight, space and liberty;   //1[a+b+c]
57 Beyond what can be valued, rich or rare;   +1'[d+e]
58 No less than life, with grace, health, beauty, honor;   +1'[f+g+h+i]
59 As much as child e'er loved, or father found   +1'[j+k]
60 A love that makes breath poor, and speech unable.   :A'[l+m]
61 Beyond all manner of so much I love you.   +A'

(55–61)

The kinds of coordination vary: linked nouns in two comparisons (56, 58) alternate with dependent clauses in the other two (57, 59), avoiding a monotonous repetition of syntax while preserving a balanced flow of adulation. After the clarifying details, Goneril twice reworks the thesis that no words can possibly define her feeling.

Cordelia will take this reasoning to its logical conclusion (therefore "love, and be silent"), but Regan cleverly follows Goneril's lead by claiming to surpass whatever degree of devotion Goneril may have managed to get across despite the failings of "speech." Although the three sisters agree on the difficulty of verbalizing love, only Cordelia chooses silence ("nothing") or formal accountability ("according to my bond"). Her "nothing" enforces something significant; their contrived additions, seeking profit from the duplicity of language, revoke honesty and duty while invoking them.[9]

In assembling additions to imply self-devaluation, Shakespeare concentrated rhetorical energy on forthright negations that rebound upon the negator rather than insincere validations that condemn the affirmer. Contending that the heart *can* be assessed by the tongue, Lear judges his judges as he goes about reevaluating worth ("her price is fallen"), reordering precedence, and reassigning prerogatives. Before descending into censure, he imitates Goneril's inventory of joined praise-words with a brief inventory (63–66) of joined reward-words ("forests," "champains," "rivers," "meads"), and later his award to Regan is even briefer. But brevity does not mark his sentence on Cordelia; he answers his "dear" daughter's challenge to respect with a quadruple disclaimer (secondary additions not noted):

Let it be so, thy truth then be thy dower!   1
. . . .
Here I disclaim all my paternal care,   +1'
Propinquity and property of blood,

Shakespeare's Trickery / 135

> And as a stranger to my heart and me +1'
> Hold thee from this for ever. The barbarous Scythian, +1'
> Or he that makes his generation messes
> To gorge his appetite, shall to my bosom
> Be as well neighbored, pitied, and relieved,
> As thou my sometime daughter.
>
> (108, 113–20)

He then musters six more remarks that give additional mass to the disinheritance and disposition of Cordelia's marriage-portion:

> So be my grave my peace as here I give +1'
> Her father's heart from her! Call France. Who stirs!
> Call Burgundy. Cornwall and Albany,
> With my two daughters' dowers digest the third; +1'
> Let pride, which she calls plainness, marry her. +1'
> I do invest you jointly with my power, +1'
> . . . .
> The sway, +1'
> Revenue, execution of the rest,
> Beloved sons, be yours; which to confirm
> This coronet part between you. +1'
>
> (125–30, 136–39)

To put the matter in still other ways (203-4), Cordelia stands "Unfriended, new adopted to our hate, / Dow'red with our curse, and strangered with our oath": +1'+1'+1'+1'. Lear concludes his series of dismissals by disowning her three *more* times:

> we
> Have no such daughter, nor shall ever see +1'+1'
> That face of hers again. Therefore be gone +1'
> Without our grace, our love, our benison.
>
> (262–65)

The causal adverb *therefore* may be taken as additive since denying Cordelia love and blessing is equivalent to disowning her.

The vehemence, number, and variety of these cumulations posit Lear's ignorance, intolerance, volatility, and narcissism: rejections deny but also disclose realities. Lear suspends love as Goneril and Regan profess love, in self-satirizing statements, theirs effusive, his explosive. His attacks, like the adoration conferred by Goneril and Regan, "speak" about the speaker. Later Lear turns ambivalent when he plays off one set of additions against another of opposite meaning; in the first act, however, his detailed indictments seldom incorporate contraries—a surprising omission if we consider the quantity of antitheses he proposes, antitheses like "young" and "untender," "merit" and "infirmities," "love" and "hate." Instead, his speech builds tremendous tension through a merciless accumulation of corresponding pronouncements as darkly monochromatic as Samson's strands of synonyms, though more energetic and unknowingly revealing.

In contrast, the King of France, like Samson, does not betray himself with unintentional irony; he consciously correlates positive and negative in his reply to Cordelia. First (214–16) he questions the "strange" reversal of attitude whereby Lear's "best object, / The argument of your praise, balm of your age, / The best, the dearest" (1+1'+1'+1+1') could inexplicably have become "monstrous" and "unnatural." Then, choosing to possess the dispossessed, he resists the rejections handed down by Lear and Burgundy. He does this by brilliantly weaving synonymous oxymora and paradoxes into six declarations of unqualified favorable judgment (emphasis added):

> Fairest Cordelia, that art most rich being poor,
> Most choice forsaken, and most loved despised,
> *Thee and thy virtues here I seize upon.*   1
> Be it lawful *I take up what's cast away.*   +1'
> Gods, gods! 'Tis strange that from their cold'st neglect
> *My love should kindle* to inflamed respect.   +1'
> *Thy dow'rless daughter,* King, thrown to my chance,   +1'
> *Is queen of us,* of ours, and our fair France.
> *Not all the dukes* of wat'rish Burgundy   +1'
> *Can buy this unprized precious maid of me.*
> Bid them farewell, Cordelia, though unkind
> *Thou losest here, a better where to find.*   +1'

(250–61)

The six endorsements are not mechanically parallel, their polarities being built of adjectives ("rich"/"poor") or verbs ("take up"/"cast away") or nouns ("neglect"/"respect"). And halfway through the speech the positive-to-negative order of the oxymora is reversed. Shakespeare's longer constructions rarely display complete syntactical or logical uniformity because such duplication can sound stilted, and besides would be inappropriate for a cumulation that refers to disjointed relations. Unified in purpose without being monotone, France's testimony is marked by deliberate antithesis, unlike the malevolent tirades of Lear. France does not speak with unaware self-description, as Lear does; his sarcasm does not recoil upon himself, and his acceptance of a bride seems downright heartwarming.

Most appraisals in the early scenes are not so neatly polarized. Some are not cumulative either: Burgundy refuses a princess without dowry in brusque fashion, as tersely as Cordelia characterizes her sisters' duplicity ("I know you what you are"). But Regan and Goneril copy the redundant, self-characterizing maledictions of their father, vilifying him in private with an antiphonal critique harping on his "imperfections" and "the infirmity of his age" (I.i.287–304). Similarly, when Gloucester requests that Edgar be found and condemned, his terms of abuse—nouns like "villain" (five uses in I.ii.74–77) and synonymous adjectives like "abhorred," "abominable," "unnatural, detested, brutish"—echo Lear's repetitious insults to Kent and Cordelia.

While these characters pass judgment upon themselves without realizing it, Edmund judges himself quite consciously. In a notable instance of iterative ego-assertion (I.ii.1–22), he inverts customary ethical standards, as Lear and Gloucester do, by deriding "legitimate" quality (five uses of the term) and by elevating "baseness" (six uses, in variant forms) or "bastardy" (four uses). His self-elevation produces the same result as the denunciations delivered by Gloucester, Goneril, Regan, and Lear. All their lengthy, vigorous evaluations are spurious, their inaccuracy mocking their insistence.

Such perversion of language among the aristocratic elite offers "proof and precedent" (as Edgar says) of widespread disbelief in the proprieties regulating social and family ties (as Nietzsche says). To amplify this idea, Gloucester specifies the facts that have upset his sense of decorum. The abruptness of his rhetorical questions conveys the rapidity of the disheartening events he describes (the supporting details) and the turmoil he senses (the implied predication):

Kent banished thus? and France in choler parted?	A://1+2
And the King gone to-night? Prescribed his pow'r?	+3+4
Confined to exhibition? All this done	+4'+5
Upon the gad?	

(I.ii.23–26)

He goes on, in linked nouns and parallel phrases or clauses (I.ii.101–14), to list thirteen maladies peculiar to the court or general to the time. Confused by these terrifying "disorders," he attributes them to supernatural origin.

Edmund, in a more exhaustive estimation of the "world" (115–32, 139–45), finds eleven words for human folly, nine names for "whoremaster man," and eleven "divisions" that disrupt private and public life. He ascribes such "disasters" to "the surfeits of our own behaviour," not to "heavenly compulsion" (which he mentions in twelve ways). Father and son differ on causation, but their extensive observations in just forty-three lines of compact additive prose agree on the corruption of rationality and integrity. Their generalizations about worldwide depravity, following the disturbing personal judgments that begin the play, initiate a changeover from cynical cumulative evaluations of individuals to cynical cumulative evaluations of mankind, the second undressing a speaker as shamefully as the first.[10]

3

As characters reach for precedence and power, or struggle to cope with severe reprisals, their widening pessimism is framed in complicated additions dissecting and destabilizing justice, whether defined in language that is self-oriented (the heroic "I") or community oriented (the choric "we"). By act 3, an all-encompassing censure dominates the rhetoric. Judgments continue to be published as multiple insults, accusations, and curses; and feelings continue to be vented in repetitive cries of disgust, fear, disillusionment, and vindictiveness. But now perceptions are articulated in long tallies describing the fraudulent, mean, unnatural, and immoderate character of human life. Speech becomes less symmetrical, not as artificially balanced in the classical custom, and either more exclamatory or more discursive. At one extreme, outcries reverberate in the repetition of single words ("Howl, howl, howl!"). At the other extreme, an inclination toward abstract analysis generates increased grammatical and logical complexity. Long coordinate clauses or sentences are more frequent after act 2: most of the fifteen concise parallel structures in the play occur early—many in the opening scene—while most of the twenty amplifications occur in acts 3, 4, and 5 (commas and the ubiquitous *and* continue to be the favorite bonding tools).

Aristocratic figures condemn themselves as thoroughly with their broader rhetoric of condemnation as they did with their personal reproaches. They foreclose their own importance by intemperately annulling the importance of the whole species. They assert ambition but at the same time discredit it; they abort their journey toward justification by deriding justice; they engage in self-satire. The characters of *King Lear*, like Euripides' Hecuba, stay bound to a heroic-choric system of values no matter how urgently they deny it, lament its passing, or strive to function outside it. For them, to attack a trusting ally is to wound oneself, and to denounce *everyone* is to kill oneself. Negation cannot, they find, fill a void; it imposes one. Everybody loses, both believers and skeptics, when belief in the inherited social order breaks down, when all claims to dignity and superior competence are canceled. A few, led by Cordelia, remain uncontaminated by baseness and resist it; others (Lear and Gloucester, his double) grapple with their disbelief; still others (like Edmund, Goneril, and Regan), unaware of the irony activated by universal debasement, augment it.

Among the pure-of-heart resisters, one character plays cumulative word games with a skeptical awareness. The Fool understands "how this world goes." He ridicules Lear, Goneril, and Regan, then composes a "prophecy" adding up ten generic instances of knavery or foolishness (III.ii.79–95). Further, he assumes an appropriate role; he not only *describes* man's "lowness" but also *typifies* it with his absurd appearance and gestures. Edgar typifies it too, more grimly, disguising himself as a Bedlam beggar, emblem of derangement:

my face I'll grime with filth	1
Blanket my loins, elf all my hairs in knots,	+2+3
And with presented nakedness outface	+4
The winds and persecutions of the sky.	

(II.iii.9–12)

His ragged clothing and wild actions put him "near to beast," and his lengthy additions of lowly or vicious animals (III.iv, vi) give verbal weight to his impersonation of "uncovered" man, the tragedy's central metaphor.

To survive his mad surroundings, Edgar suits his appearance to the disjointed time ("the country gives me proof and precedent") by playing a madman, a role akin to that performed by the Fool. But poor choleric Kent lacks the satirical wit or detachment to clothe himself in the insane, bestial, or absurd dream images dominating his environment, so he struggles against them and telegraphs his helplessness with his futile enumerations of villainous traits. Doggedly hanging on to his obsolete commitment to honor (seven infinitives in I.iv.12–15), he rails at the steward Oswald, who stands for a whole class of "superserviceable" panders. With invective recalling the gargantuan insults exchanged between Prince Hal and Falstaff in *1 Henry IV*, Kent in a seventy-eight-word prose sentence

(II.ii.13–22) lets fly no less than a dozen derogatory titles ("knave," "bawd," "coward," etc.) modified by fifteen derogatory adjectives and followed by another twenty-five epithets. His superabundant insults—his consciousness of depravity—indicate a weakening of self-control; he has definitely lost his sense of humor.

"Rogues," "rascals," and "slaves" answer honest Kent when three of them—Cornwall, Regan, and Edmund—put him into stocks, normally reserved for "basest and contemned'st wretches" (138). He, along with Edgar and the Fool, suffers in body as well as mind the humiliation decent individuals (in fact, *all* individuals) are brought to. Kent's rabid denunciations, Edgar's cynical performance as Tom o'Bedlam, and the Fool's sarcastic tally of familiar inequities work together with Gloucester's worried account of epidemic disorder and Edmund's contemptuous remarks on "whoremaster man" to portray man as beast, an almost ubiquitous presence.

Lear recapitulates with greater fervor these repetitive comments on the epidemic of degradation, and as a result he suffers greater shame.[11] Along with Gloucester and Edgar, he endures the severe bodily and mental distress of a fall from high place. His disappointment with one person, like Kent's disgust with Oswald, arouses towering, disproportionate indignation that opens out to the whole species. Disoriented in a deranged universe, he feels Kent's helplessness and impulsiveness, Gloucester's apprehension, Edgar's chagrin, the Fool's bemusement, and Edmund's disdain. His willfulness, like that of Edmund, Regan, and Goneril, knows no bounds, yet like Kent and Cordelia he cares deeply about protocol. During the first four acts, as attention turns from sins of individuals to sins of mankind, his iterative rhetoric intensifies the pressure of diverse voices heard judging others and demanding prerogative until at last the piling up of cynicism, frustration, guilt, and self-righteousness unbalances his sanity and speech. When he evaluates mankind negatively, he too passes judgment on himself and sinks under the weight of his mountainous spite, under an enormous crushing heap of verbal "nothing."

His descent into renunciation, begun with the assault upon Cordelia, resumes with the assault upon Goneril (I.iv.266–80). A prefatory inquiry, "Are you our daughter?" (209), resembles his repudiation of Cordelia ("we / Have no such daughter"; "thou my sometime daughter") in the first scene (I.i.120, 263). In both episodes Lear, who commands or proclaims more than he questions, describes, narrates, speculates, or exclaims, commands nature to punish Goneril with the same offense she has committed—denial of the parent-child bond. His imperatives (I.iv.266–80) amplify two forms of punishment: the goddess of nature must "convey sterility" to Goneril (three restatements) or else "create her child of spleen" (three restatements). Detailing such a choice so meticulously lends an air of deliberation to a gruesome, hysterical judgment.

By transferring Goneril's penalty to a future time Lear extends his outrage a bit beyond the immediate circumstances. However, not until Regan delivers a third blow to his pride does the scope of his evaluations start to widen. The transition unfolds gradually as Lear records his misery and orders the gods of nature to redress it. First he elaborates his curse against Goneril with six further "vengeances of heaven" (I.iv.290–92, II.iv.157–63), itemizing the discourtesies shown him (three in II.iv.154–56, another seven in 166–73) and the courtesies due him (five in 173–75). When his third appeal for respect fails ("Vengeance, plague, death, confusion!"), he hurls an iterative oath at his elder daughters (II.iv.259–81) that unveils a larger view of his dilemma. Although he still broods over his own problems, the commentary on "need" (259–65) heralds an increasing degree of abstraction. His brief complaints citing "basest beggars" and "man's life" anticipate the lengthy conclusions he will derive from his case and apply to the human condition.

Eventually, just as Edmund, Gloucester, Kent, Edgar, and the Fool discover injustice to be a global fact, so does Lear translate the rancor engendered by his "unkind daughters" into an accusation against humanity. At the beginning of act 3, an attendant reports him "contending with the fretful elements / . . . That things might change or cease" (III.i.4, 7). Lear orders nature (III.ii.1–9, 14) to take revenge on the "world" in the same way he ordered it to punish Goneril—by reciprocating in kind for "unnatural" acts. "Rain, wind, thunder, fire," the celestial elements, are to destroy the earth, the prime element in human nature. Congregations of nearly synonymous verbs—"blow," "crack your cheeks," "rage, blow"; "spout," "drench," "drown"; "singe," "spit fire"; "strike flat," "crack," "spill"—give his speech its verve, just as lively verbs animate his additions throughout the tragedy.

In acts 3 and 4, Lear's judicial imperatives become increasingly general: "Tremble, thou wretch, / . . . Unwhipped of justice"; "Take physic, pomp"; "Is man no more than this?"; "Let copulation thrive." Four amplifications predicate, illustrate, and condemn "man's faults"—deception (III.ii.49–59), frailty (III.iv.96–102), lust and infidelity (IV.vi.108–29), and the abuse of "authority" (IV.vi.148–69). Yet he still closes each passage with a postscript on its relevance to his personal grievance: Lear does not change into a disinterested philosopher. Far from it—as the inclination to draft broader issues grows, his capacity to sustain a constructive outlook shrinks. When disenchantment, rage, and intolerance of "folly" compromise his position as the kingdom's chief "justicer," his negative attitude regarding individuals and mankind decays into confusion regarding his own identity.

4

A speaker can mortify himself (to repeat a key term in *Samson Agonistes*) by condemning others. Or he can mortify himself by trying without success to *rebut* his condemnations! The first speech habit conveys contradiction through the unintentional self-deprecation implied in his denunciations; the second speech habit conveys contradiction explicitly. As his dismay turns against his own well-being, Lear attempts to counter his drift toward incoherent indignation and self-pity with appeals to "patience." But the reasonable remedies he summons to regain equilibrium and restore self-respect must contend with the vindictiveness, sorrow, and cynicism that keep pouring out. Suppressing heroic defiance cannot work for a man of "authority": a challenge to that authority will trigger murder, suicide, or insanity, not choric accommodation or insight. Instead of accommodating or reforming, he only replaces his single-minded, self-deflating invective with an unresolved polarity; he discredits himself not simply by condemning his family and society but also by acting out the same incompatible motives that drove the Athenian hero to distraction. Conceived as a masculine model requiring both unqualified self-reference and unqualified integration with others, he builds a long series of conflicting cumulations out of both "needs," intermittently perceiving the inconsistency that finally explodes his sanity.

Lear anticipates this self-dismantling early in the story, right after Goneril criticizes his "insolent retinue." He realizes that his "frame of nature" has been wrenched "from the fixed place" (I.iv.259–60), his "manhood" shaken (288). "We are not ourselves," he complains (II.iv.102). Goneril's attack upon his self-*esteem* instantly disrupts his self-*awareness:* a character who requires others to confirm his worth finds it impossible to see or judge himself accurately once denied that confirmation. He analyzes his doubt in a beautifully contrived short amplification:

Does any here know me? This is not Lear.	A:
Does Lear walk thus? speak thus? Where are his eyes?	1[a+b+c
Either his notion weakens, his discernings	+d+e]
Are lethargied—Ha! Waking? 'Tis not so.	+1'
Who is it that can tell me who I am?	:A'

(I.iv.216–21)

In the two keynote queries Lear manifests uncertainty about his coherence; between them, his elaboration queries manifest uncertainty about specific motor, sensory, and intellectual skills. All his questions address his inability to recognize a personality deprived of dignity. The answers, his own and the Fool's ("Lear's shadow"), suggest dysfunction, self-negation. "You see how full of changes his age is," Goneril says, sounding a Nietzschean theme, "yet he hath ever but slenderly known himself." "These dispositions . . . of late transport you / From what you rightly are" (I.i.287, 292–93; I.iv.212–13).[12]

But King Lear does not stay transported; he revolves between recognition of limit and mindless assertion of prerogative. His additions express with unceasing redundancy a resigned but insightful passivity side by side with rage and chronic self-righteousness. He surrenders his "power, / Preeminence, and all the large effects / That troop with majesty" (1+1'+1') but at the same time wants to "retain / The name, and all th' addition to a king": / 1'+1' (I.i.130–32, 135–36). He grants his error in denouncing Cordelia: "O Lear, Lear, Lear! Beat at this gate that let thy folly in / And thy dear judgment out" (I.iv.261–63). Yet he repetitiously blames his "pelican daughters" or "man's nature" for his pain. He pictures himself as a "slave, / A poor, infirm, weak, and despised old man," then calls forth "noble anger," swears revenge, and accuses nature itself (III.ii.21–24). Though unconcerned with physical hardship, as opposed to mental anguish (three statements, III.iv.6–14), he decides that exposure to such hardship would sharpen his knowledge of injustice (two statements, III.iv.28–36). He describes his kinship with "unaccommodated man," that "poor, bare, forked animal," and demonstrates it by undressing during the storm on the heath: "Thou ow'st the worm no silk, the beast no hide, the sheep no wool, the cat no perfume" (III.iv.97–101). But such exposure fills him with disgust; while "not ague-proof," he labors to be "every inch a king" (IV.vi.104, 106).

At times he believes his chief asset to be "patience," his chief need to "say nothing." Acting in that diminished mode, however, would preclude a king's "revenges," so in widely dispersed cumulations and antitheses, he gyrates between the two "states," crying out for sufficient self-control (1) to deal with his immense indignation and its accompanying threat of insanity (2):

O, let me not be mad, not mad, sweet heaven!   1[a+a]
Keep me in temper; I would not be mad!   +1'+1

(I.v.40–41)

> O, how this mother swells up toward my heart! /2
> Hysterica passio, down, thou climbing sorrow; /1'
> Thy element's below. +1'
>
> (II.iv.54–56)
>
> > I'll forbear; +1'
> > And am fallen out with my headier will +1'
> > ....
> > Death on my state! /2'
> > ....
> > O me, my heart, my rising heart! But down! +2'/1'
>
> (II.iv.104–5, 107, 116)
>
> > I prithee, daughter, do not make me mad. +1
> > ....
> > I can be patient .... +1'
>
> (II.iv.213, 225)
>
> > You heavens, give me that patience, patience I need. +1'[a+a]
> > ....
> > O fool, I shall go mad! /2'
>
> (II.iv.266, 281)
>
> > O, ho! 'tis foul. +2'
> > ....
> > No, I will be the pattern of all patience; /1'
> > I will say nothing. +1'
>
> (III.ii.24, 37–38)

Lear's outrage constantly threatens to overwhelm his desire for patience: a repeated, ineffectual injunction against weeping—stereotypical sign of feminine or childish weakness—works against the repeated, ineffectual injunction against raving like a madman. In his peremptory iterative style, the king fluctuates between tearful grief issuing from shame, helplessness, or profound deprivation (1) and angry impatience with tears (2):

> *[to Goneril]* Life and death, I am ashamed   1
> That thou has power to shake my manhood thus!

> That these hot tears, which break from me perforce,
> Should make thee worth them.
> . . . .
>   Old fond eyes, /2
> Beweep this cause again I'll pluck ye out
> And cast you, with the waters that you loose,
> To temper clay.
>
> (I.iv. 287–90, 292–95)

> *[to the gods]* . . . fool me not so much   +2'
> To bear it tamely; touch me with noble anger,   +2'
> And let not women's weapons, water drops,   +2'
> Stain my man's cheeks.
> . . . .
> You think I'll weep.   /1'
> No, I'll not weep.   /2'
> *Storm and tempest.*
> I have full cause of weeping, but this heart   /1'/2'
> Shall break into a hundred thousand flaws
> Or ere I'll weep. O fool, I shall go mad!   +2'
>
> (II.iv.270–73, 277–81)

By stimulating "noble anger," which he hopes will combat the urge to cry like a child, he undermines his intention to *refrain* from anger, which will make him howl like a lunatic. These recurring contradictions evidence the degeneration of a stance ideally incorporating sagacity with imperturbable stamina—a lapse from "everything" into "nothing." For three acts he alternates between references to himself as a tearful "natural fool of fortune" (1) and a grim avenger (2):

>   Filial ingratitude,   1
> Is it not as this mouth should tear this hand
> For lifting food to't? But I will punish home.   /2
> No, I will weep no more. In such a night   +2'/1'
> To shut me out! Pour on; I will endure.   /2'+2'
> In such a night as this! O Regan, Goneril,   /1'
> Your old kind father, whose frank heart gave all—   +1'
> O, that way madness lies; let me shun that.   +1'+1'
> No more of that.   +1'
>
> (III.iv.14–22)

He classifies forbearance as a virtue when opposed to insane fury but as an enervating evil when it permits self-pity and tears. His vacillation between virtue and vice—his failure to distinguish between them—would have offended Plato as much as it did Hegel.[13]

In fact, after his "dear judgment" collapses under the stress of this internal debate, Lear adds the role of evildoer to his incompatible personalities as mad avenger and pitiful victim. His enactment of a magistrate who sanctions corruption (IV.vi.90–199) perpetuates and yet parodies his consecration to "the great image of authority." He pardons adultery and encourages copulation, at the same time indicating his revulsion (127–29) in linked repetitive descriptions ("There's hell, there's darkness," etc.) and exclamations ("Fie, fie, fie! pah, pah!"). To back up his contention (revised four times) that justice is anarchic ("a dog's obeyed in office"), he lists five pairs of creatures (judge and thief, beggar and dog, beadle and whore, and so on) who invert proper precedence (148–69). Yet he zealously carries out the "power" of office by authorizing such a turnabout. He counsels humility because a judge like a child can be prone to tears, then cries out for revenge ("kill, kill, kill, kill, kill, kill!").[14]

Lear, in short, broadcasts a huge quantity of additive rhetoric boosting his willfulness and self-righteousness alongside an equally large quantity of additive rhetoric conceding his fragility or complicity in base practices. Obdurate innocence coexists with painful realization, the conflicting states of a stereotype that seeks the benefits of both priority and accommodation, a dispute handed down by the Athenians. As in Athenian tragedy, a model of manhood splits apart, each part changing into a caricature, one a judge-prosecutor turned outraged criminal, the other a dependent partner in a crucial social relationship who has become a dupe or scapegoat. Unable to knit together heroic aggressiveness with choric pragmatism, moderation, and decorum, Lear clings to the composite model while corrupting and relinquishing it. Occasionally riotous anger reduces iterative speech to iterative *fragments,* as in his last, inarticulate threat to Goneril and Regan:

I will have such revenges on you both	1
That all the world shall—I will do such things—	+1'
What they are, yet I know not; but they shall be	+1'
The terrors of the earth.	

(II.iv.274–77)

One question lingers: "Who is it that can tell me who I am?"

5

In *King Lear* few identities remain constant: Regan, Goneril, and Edmund dissemble, Edgar and Kent put on disguises, Lear and Gloucester undergo violent "changes." The entire human species seems to have become "degenerate." The problem of accurate identification (Aristotle's "recognition") thus beclouds the problem of proper judgment and deference. Before precedence can be established to organize a just society, individuals must be appraised correctly, but individuals cannot be appraised correctly unless they can be perceived clearly.

Questions about knowing, therefore, succeed questions about ranking, as in all major Shakespearean and Athenian tragedies. Regan and Goneril have no stake in bringing such issues to light, and their speech is consequently of little rhetorical interest in the last two acts. In those acts, other characters cumulate truths that reapportion status according to merit and work to counteract the movement toward devaluation. Their additions build up rather than tear down mutual trust. Their positive, unambivalent statements differ markedly from the negative outcries or self-contradictions of Lear; they help dispel the Dionysian nightmare; they would have gladdened Plato's heart and made Hegel happy. The king, however, stays bound upon his wheel of fire, commuting to the end between "best" and "worst," knowledge and darkness, communion and exclusion.

Albany makes Miltonic proclamations on the workings of justice. Perceiving Goneril's "deformity," he reinstates Lear, then Kent and Edgar, in an aristocrat's conventional distribution of punishment and reward:

All friends shall taste	1
The wages of their virtue, and all foes	+2
The cup of their deservings.	

(V.iii.303-5)

In contrast to Albany, Kent knew from the outset (when he advised Lear to "see better") that vice and decency may be hard to distinguish. Free to "speak" again without constraint, he summarizes in a short addition Lear's "unkindness" and "sovereign shame" (IV.iii.42–47).

If Kent's loyalty obligated him to tell unpleasant truths concerning the king early in the play and late, Cordelia chose the path of silence. At last, however, she can publicly declare her "love, dear love." Her reiterated pleas for aid from soldiers (1) and medicines (2) are as urgent as her father's imperatives but more compassionate than either his commands or her own earlier formula ("Obey you, love you, and most honor you"):

> A century *send forth!*   1[a
> *Search* every acre in the high-grown field   +b
> And *bring* him to our eye.   +c]
> . . . . .
> All blessed secrets   +2
> All you unpublished virtues of the earth,
> *Spring* with my tears; *be aidant and remediate*   [d+e+e']
> In the good man's distress. *Seek, seek* for him.   +1'[b'+b']

(IV.iv.6–8, 15–18)

While Albany, Kent, and Cordelia wish to assist others, like the arbitrators in Athenian tragedy, Edmund keeps up his preoccupation with himself. But he does change his *style* of self-assertion. Prior to Edgar's challenge he concealed his motives; following it, he elects to "maintain [his] truth and honor" openly, to "disdain and spurn" devious maneuvers. He even disdains the usual rules guiding duelists, for "by th'law of war" Edgar as challenger should prove his noble "quality or degree" (ironically, it is the honest brother who again conceals his identity). As forthright in defeat as in combat, Edmund verifies the victor's verdict with a concise addition: "The wheel is come full circle; I am here" (V.iii.175). And his compensation sounds as frank and laconic as his confession:

> Yet Edmund was beloved.   A:
> The one the other poisoned for my sake,   1
> And after slew herself.   +2

(V.iii.240–42)

His closing testament copies the simplicity and honesty of pronouncements made by Cordelia, Kent, and Albany.

These four characters express self-respect or respect for another individual; Gloucester and Edgar articulate respectful truths about mankind. Gloucester refers to his own misery in the laconic addition, "I am tied to th' stake, and I must stand the course" (III.vii.54), but his penchant for relating private happenings to universal principles directs his belated commentaries on suffering and seeing. Formerly his logic was deductive, matching records of facts ("machinations, hollowness, treachery") to an initial truism ("These late eclipses . . . portend no good"). After his privations, he draws his own inferences. As a result, the information in his amplifications shrinks to one or two touching examples that introduce, instead of follow, the generalization:

> I stumbled when I saw. Full oft 'tis seen   1
> Our means secure us, and our mere defects   :A[a+b]
> Prove our commodities.
>
> (IV.i.19–21)

If justice is defined as correct deference, it is essential to distinguish genuine quality from counterfeit; in *King Lear,* as in Athenian tragedy, observations on sight and insight call attention to the frequent divergence between visual and intellectual acuity.

Heartbroken by his discovery that he discredited the superior son, Gloucester attempts suicide, but his last inductions, though sometimes issued in Lear's magisterial manner, get beyond Lear's inconsistency. They testify to providential order as unambiguously as Milton's solemn pieties do:

> That I am wretched   1
> Makes thee the happier. Heavens, deal so still!
> Let the superfluous and lust-dieted man,   :A[a+a']
> That slaves your ordinance, that will not see   [b+b']
> Because he does not feel, feel your pow'r quickly;
> So distribution should undo excess,   +A'[c
> And each man have enough.   +c']
>
> (IV.i.65–71)

A chastened Gloucester, asking for divine intervention to guarantee equity, attests to the value of integrating principle ("ordinance"), sensitivity (to "feel"), and awareness (to "see")—a balance that escaped Lear too.

Learning from misfortune, Edgar outdoes his father in distilling sweeping abstractions from disheartening experiences and publishing them in pithy cumulative constructions. He seconds Gloucester's argument, which he illustrates with Gloucester's history, that heaven punishes those who abuse privilege. "The gods are just, and of our pleasant vices / Make instruments to plague us," he tells Edmund; "The dark and vicious place where thee he got / Cost him his eyes": A+A':1 (V.iii.171–74).

But Edgar, like his brother, relies more on human resourcefulness for survival than on divine regulation. Having lived through the "strange mutations" that afflict people regardless of station, he arrives at secular wisdom on how to "endure" (the unheroic half of Lear's quest). Like Gloucester and Edmund, he supports his conclusions with only one or two telling references to facts while announcing a general proposal twice in III.vi.100–105 ("We scarcely think our miseries our foes"), three times in IV.i.1–6 ("Yet better thus, and known to be contemned"), three times in IV.i.25–28 ("Who is't can say 'I am at the worst'?"), and twice in V.ii.9–11 ("Men must endure / Their going hence"). His longing to "see," to "think," and to "know" offsets Gloucester's momentary impulse to commit suicide and Lear's to kill or go berserk. For Edgar, and eventually for his father, understanding the positive conditions that govern all humans becomes more important than passing negative judgment on individuals.

After Lear emerges from his round of denunciation, inconsistency, and humiliation, his insights are as clear-cut and constructive as conclusions drawn by Albany, Kent, Cordelia, Edmund, Edgar, and Gloucester. But mindless egomania once more refutes mature self-effacement, and his inconstancy in matters of perception, feeling, and belief persists to his death. He gains equilibrium, paradoxically, so long as he accepts his mental (a) and physical (b) fallibility:

I am a very foolish fond old man	1[a+a'+b]
. . . .	
I fear I am not in my perfect mind.	+1'[a']
. . . .	
I am old and foolish.	+1'[b+a]
(IV.vii.60, 63, 84)	

Rather than despise weeping as unmanly, he humbly admits that his "tears / Do scald like molten lead." Rather than fear disorientation, as earlier ("I shall go mad"; "This is not Lear"; "Are you our daughter?"), he humbly admits his perplexity regarding identities. He does not know his own "condition" nor does he remember Cordelia or Kent, his present location or previous lodging (IV.vii.47–48, 52–57, 64–68). Even his commands seem contrite; rather than demand vengeance from the gods, he petitions Cordelia's forgiveness:

Pray, do not mock me.	1
. . . .	
Do not laugh at me.	+1'
. . . .	
I pray weep not.	+2
. . . .	
Do not abuse me.	+3
. . . .	
You must bear with me.	:A
Pray you now, forget and forgive.	+A'[a+b]
(IV.vii.59, 68, 71, 77, 83–84)	

The penitent Lear continues to organize his speech by accumulating references to robust actions. In a winding amplification, biblical in cadence, that joins twenty-three lively verbs with a dozen *ands* in only twelve lines, he envisions a creative reversal of precedence. In prison, he and Cordelia will live as peers; he will defer to her charity, and together they will survive fortune's changes:

Cordelia: Shall we not see these daughters and these sisters?	
Lear: No, no, no, no! Come, let's away to prison.	A:
We two alone will sing like birds i' th' cage.	1
When thou dost ask me blessing, I'll kneel down.	+2[a
And ask of thee forgiveness. So we'll live,	+b]+3
And pray, and sing, and tell old tales, and laugh	+2'+1+4+5
At gilded butterflies, and hear poor rogues	+6
Talk of court news; and we'll talk with them too—	+7
Who loses and who wins; who's in, who's out—	[c+d+d'+c']
And take upon's the mystery of things	+8
As if we were God's spies; and we'll wear out,	+9
In a walled prison, packs and sects of great ones	[e+f]
That ebb and flow by th' moon.	[g+h]

(V.iii.7–19)

Lear as a prisoner will honor values—wise judgment, patience, altruism—he could not honor while impersonating a magistrate. He imagines activities that would have satisfied Edgar's stoic-choric goal of detachment from aristocratic prerogative, ambition, and deceit, then enriches such detachment with a prescription for spiritual growth and heartfelt cooperation between equals. Apparently he has terminated his Nietzschean journey of discontinuity and repetition, achieving at last a nontragic condition of certitude, security, and higher consciousness—Hegel's heaven, Plato's paradise.

Beatitude, however, did not come any easier to Shakespeare's characters than it did to those of Aeschylus, Sophocles, and Euripides. As usual, Lear's words in this passage belie his dream of harmony; they reflect a continuation of stereotypical conflict. The more the king changes for the better, the more he remains inconsistent, a choric sense of subordination still at odds with a heroic emotional thrust directed toward supremacy. His resigned command "let's away to prison" follows a typically vindictive (and typically iterative) rejection ("No, no, no, no!") of Goneril and Regan. The temperate pastimes he forecasts—praying, singing, gossiping, contemplating—climax in an intemperate triumph over "great ones," endurance now turned into a weapon for the reclamation of position. His

152 / The Excess of Heroism in Tragic Drama

humility as a prisoner takes second place to his vanity as a divinely graced "sacrifice," accommodation reverts to a stubborn refusal to yield to enemies ("We'll see 'em starved first"), and crying again becomes a sign of weakness and defeat ("Wipe thine eyes"). Despite his admission of guilt and his prescription for healing communion, Lear cannot escape the antique fixation on self-defense and vindication; despite his recent intimacy with "nothing," he is locked into an eternal courtship of "all."

The murder of Cordelia provokes the king to act out a last set of law-court roles—witness to a killing, executioner, and condemned man. It moves him to a concluding display of his incompatible liabilities (V.iii.258–80): emotional extravagance ("Howl, howl, howl!"), rash judgment ("You are men of stones"), an inclination to condemn humanity for the sins of individuals ("heaven's vault should crack," "A plague upon you murderers, traitors all"), inconsistency ("She's dead as earth. Lend me a looking glass"), tenacity in substituting desire for reality ("This feather stirs; she lives!"), vanity and vengefulness ("I killed the slave"), self-pity ("I am old now"), an unappeasable sense of deprivation ("Cordelia, Cordelia, stay a little"), and faulty perception ("Who are you?").

In his closing speech, Lear's problem with discernment and evaluation shrinks to a pathetic inability to discriminate between death (1) and life (2):

She's gone for ever.	1
I know when one is dead, and when one lives.	+1'/2
She's dead as earth. Lend me a looking glass.	/1'
If that her breath will mist or stain the stone,	
Why then she lives.	/2
. . . .	
This feather stirs; she lives!	+2
. . . .	
now she's gone for ever.	/1
. . . .	
And my poor fool is hanged: no, no, no life?	+1'+1'[a+a+a]
Why should a dog, a horse, a rat, have life,	/2'
And thou no breath at all? Thou'lt come no more,	/1'+1'
Never, never, never, never, never.	[b+b+b+b+b]
. . . .	
Do you see this? Look on her! Look her lips,	/2'[c+c
Look there, look there—	+c+c]

(V.iii.260–64, 266, 271, 306–9, 311–12)

Lear makes his divided vision known through repetitive misperceptions, just as previously he made his impotence known through repetitive bids for precedence, his poor judgment through repetitive condemnations, and his illogic through repetitive pleas for sanity. His iterations of the ultimate dualism, though much simpler than his earlier rhetorical barrages, are equally unresolved. Terms testifying to life vie strenuously with but are sadly outnumbered by negative terms ("dead," "gone," "no," "never"). To the end, Lear bears witness to the uncertainty of our certainties.

King Lear may be inconsistent, yet his self-contradictions, issued so vividly and repetitiously through those piercing verbs, pungent or pitiable nouns, and smoking adjectives, dominate the characters around him. The other characters are not complete, neither the good ones nor the bad. Both camps are limited, insufficient, "one-sided." Evil "must perforce prey on itself, / Like the monsters of the deep" (IV.ii.49–50), vanquished by its own moral void, not by divine agents or the pure of heart. As in a Greek tragedy, justice requires no all-powerful redeemer because for individuals conditioned by a code of aristocratic behavior, retribution is automatic: unbalanced self-indulgence elicits a chain of reactions, psychological and social, that generates retributive shame or guilt. Rules governing enlightened egoism call for discipline and accountability; they give passion a substantive objective (Hegel's language) or semblance of "Apollonian" unity (Nietzsche's language), without which passion whirls in meaningless sound and fury (as Macbeth put it) or in barren, directionless desires (as Plato put it). Shakespeare's evildoers illustrate the Platonic lesson that coherent extension in the world requires moral solidity.

For Regan and Goneril, self-interest does not come into contact (as Plato and Hegel proposed it should) with wider insights and sympathies, yet they cannot escape the power of those insights and sympathies; they are victims of their escape into nothingness as well as predators. Because their typical means of augmenting themselves is to deny ethical authority, moreover, Regan and Goneril lack *verbal* authority. They do not participate much even in the piling up of negatives: they lack the degree of engagement with conventional law that gives point to arguments on or exclamations about the inadequacy of that law. Pernicious as Edmund may be, in contrast, his sensitivity to traditional rules of precedence makes him momentarily articulate, first about their perversion ("Now, gods, stand up for bastards") and later about their restoration. Criminals, he realizes, commonly come "full circle" to the dead end of an exhausted nihilism.

The virtuous nobles of *King Lear* are not much better off than the evil nobles. Their one-sided nature limits *them* too; they are unable to nullify the nullifiers with their sincerity. Edgar, Kent, Cordelia, Albany, and the King of France, though wise, comforting, and serviceable at times, just as often prove to be useless. Their kindness and naive truths do not forestall the errors of Lear and Gloucester or defeat the usurpers' army. They become acquainted with grief, they learn how "this world goes," and they work to counterbalance cynicism or disenchantment with constructive actions and words. But their purity withholds from them a final knowledge or potency that can resist the onslaught of steadfast, unmitigated selfishness, that can heal the disparities they observe, that can triumph as well as "endure." When they operate as arbiters their comments about honesty, loyalty, and fairness, like comments made by peacemakers in Shakespeare's other tragedies, do not generally provide them with rhetorical opportunities to build up energy intense enough to neutralize their opponents until after the damage has been done.

So gentility is inefficient, and self-dedication is self-restrictive. Only the man in the middle, as Aristotle described him, or more accurately the individual who swings compulsively between extremes, makes those extremes believable. Participating in both and unable to integrate them, he is neither a champion of social equity nor a Satan (or Nietzsche's joyfully satanic savior). After Lear disinherits honesty, his aggressive additions project the defenselessness of trust and the impulsiveness of greed, the paralysis of pessimism and the tough wisdom of humility. These polar values may take up separate residence in secondary figures, but they sustain a constant flux in Shakespeare's major protagonists, each of whom is bracketed by a two-character constellation that symbolizes his two-sided existence—Macbeth between Duncan and Lady Macbeth, Othello between Desdemona and Iago, Hamlet between his father and his uncle, and Lear between his youngest and elder daughters. Lear participates in the egomania of Goneril and Regan just as Macbeth participates in his wife's, Othello in Iago's, and Hamlet in his uncle's.

In addition, smaller constellations usually duplicate these stellar triumvirates: Malcolm is flanked by Macduff and a fictitious villain he invents to test Macduff's loyalty; innocent Ophelia and manipulative Polonius surround Laertes (Hamlet's "brother"); and Lear's alter ego, Gloucester, with his contrasting sons, seconds Lear with his daughters (*Othello* lacks a second trio). "No contraries hold more antipathy," Kent says (II.ii.82), but at the same time they are (to adapt Hegel and take issue with Plato again) related and inseparable. Perhaps it takes so explosive a split to dramatize the force holding them together. The individual who hurtles between honesty and anarchy gives their antagonism and dependence a recognizable shape, and Shakespeare conveys that shape through the technical resources Plato found defective.

Summary and Speculation

The time to tie things together has come, for as Edgar remarks, "To amplify too much would . . . top extremity." We end with a theory about tragedy that draws upon divergent ideas contributed by Plato, Hegel, and Nietzsche, with an assist from Aristotle. Melodrama in the West has customarily presented conflict between a Hegelian stock character devoted to altruistic duty (accommodation, responsibility) and a Dionysian or Satanic figure devoted to self-enlargement ("I grow, I prosper," Edmund gloats). In tragedy, composite theatrical creatures, depicted until recent times as highborn elitists, take on both roles in a battle for honor, respect, justice. These creatures dress self-interest in idealized garments, intending to attain social acclamation by fulfilling a stereotypical standard of manly excellence.

But their disparate motives cohabit in an uneasy alliance that is shattered by an irrational response to disrespect. Threats to pride, delivered by supernatural power, peer judgment, choric criticism, and feminine betrayal, release an overpowering fear of shame, immense sorrow at the deprivation of status, and insane lust to retaliate. Transformed by some real or imagined challenge to their authority, these characters go from an exemplary to a dysfunctional posture, from confidence in a glorious identity confirmed by unconditional family and community approval to compulsive, usually violent, protests against insult, reevaluation, or restriction. Their fanatical efforts to enforce their twin causes (self-respect and family or public respect) exaggerate their aggressiveness, disassociate self-service from social approval, and desecrate their code of honor.

In Athenian tragedy, their radical acts (or radical inaction) compromise their reputation; in Shakespearean tragedy, they damage, after brooding on their fallibility, both reputation and self-esteem. In both theaters, the division between mutually dependent premises menaces their moral integrity as well as their physical existence: polarization of identity amounts to disintegration of identity, competition between values elicits negation of values. Self-sufficiency, for example, becomes opposed not only by the principle of accountability but also by weakness, insecurity, and fear; constancy becomes opposed not only by flexibility but also by inconstancy, flux, metamorphosis. Unbalanced by insult, the composite protagonists of tragedy break apart their tenuous union of divergent principles, move toward murder, suicide, or insanity, and (ironically) enact rather than disinherit traits, such as frailty and inconsistency, they had scorned. Having promoted a glorious two-sided ideal, they mourn its passing but contribute to its mutilation.

Yet they keep circulating between the poles of egoism and responsibility; if they endanger their code, they also reaffirm it, hanging onto a lacerated but tough remnant of good faith. While their transformation publicizes, in a predictable succession of events, an uncontrollable volatility, their dual allegiance (however mutilated) energizes them to the end. An inertial force keeping these exceptional individuals intact seems to resist any disruptive force. So they commute between invalidation, whether inwardly or socially imposed, and reassertion. And their fluctuations are given dramatic presence by a double-edged rhetoric, a two-faced imagery, and a back-and-forth narrative.

This juggling act, one might imagine, would address a spectator's intelligence as well as feelings, but Plato did not think so. He particularly disliked crafty poets (those rivals of philosophers) who connived to impress and persuade, frighten and sadden, question and equivocate—poets who said contrary things instead of *one* thing. He preferred unity and "high-mindedness," guidance by those with access to immortal, unchanging realities. His anxiety about the rift between those unchanging essences and inconstant passions or untrustworthy senses cut his discussion of poetry in the *Republic* right down the middle.

At first, just like a tragic hero, he was antinegative: he despised the decadent activity of spectators witnessing (and possibly imitating) massive mistakes—which Aristotle later declared to be at the heart of tragedy—so he advised storytellers to stop reviewing (imitating) the fickle facts of failure or imperfection and start paying more attention to successful virtue. Then, after criticizing their inclination to *disregard* "standards of rightness" (in favor of improper subjects), he turned to their inclination to *misrepresent* those standards (through their faulty medium and artistic manner). Tragic tales either deliberately or (worse) unwittingly told lies. Feeling increasingly distrustful after he shifted his interpretation of imitation to the second danger, increasingly doubtful whether even respectable poets were capable of conforming to his advice, he threw them all out of his republic. Plato did not care for the paradox that drama, like his own dialogues, might get at truth by reporting false starts and dismal conclusions, by encompassing (imitating) both predication and denial, addition and diminishment, the two sides to every story.

Aristotle, Hegel, and Nietzsche tried to solve that paradox. Aristotle agreed that poets knew nothing except how to imitate and what they often imitated was heroic error and disaster; but in those two facts lay poetry's power and truthfulness, not its defects. Following Aristotle's ingenious though incomplete adaptation of Plato's views, Nietzsche too found a value in the capacity of tragedy to picture pitiful and fearful events. Nietzsche saw "turbulence" as the denominator common to the morally laudable and despicable, replacing divine forms at the core of the universe. All good and bad things withered, disappeared, and then recurred spontaneously, dissonantly, pointlessly, cyclically—all thoughts, objects, lives. Laws or examples of orderly existence came and went randomly, always changing into annulments, continuity being provided solely by their recurrence and our readiness to enjoy the tumult. Poets could capture a sense of the whirlpool through dream images; they could mirror the amoral swirl of ego-vitality in clearly drawn, evanescent pictures of (in Strindberg's words) "disconnected but apparently logical" polarities. Nietzsche concurred with Plato's conclusion on the duplicity and hollowness of poetic language, but he put it to good artistic use.

Hegel, on the other hand, rehabilitated Plato's insistence that the merit of poetry hangs on its service as a message-bearer of definitive truth. If Nietzsche proposed that unmediated energy was the sole source of creation and destruction, Hegel proposed that unmediated spirit united them. Wishing to preserve the sanctity of social laws, he tried to have them both ways—imperfectly realized when we watch them clash, fully realized when we understand their conflict to be evidence of an implied spiritual totality.

When Hegel assumed, with Plato, that the totality (ethical substance) was godlike, constant, and coherent, he supported his assumption by citing Greek characters who reach out for those attributes in their standards of conduct. Unfortunately, as Plato had glumly observed, their reaching out often turns mercurial, nonrational, and hurtful at the same time that it seeks transcendent blessings. According to Hegel's famous interpretation of *Antigone*, a contest between duty to the state and duty to family provides the contestants with a golden opportunity to articulate ethical sentiments. In most tragedies, however, as in this play, any high-minded debate on the subject of noble social objectives carried on by an aggressive male and a rebellious female, or between two competitive males or females, quickly deteriorates into a ruinous effort to compel respect—to reinforce two inflated egos. Nietzsche taught us that the irony then opens out to wider and wilder oppositions involving belief and cynicism, order and flux, endurance and annihilation.

Following Nietzsche, we must revise Hegel's and Plato's prescriptions for tragic paragons by questioning the reliability of those paragons as symbols of laudable conduct. Hegel argued sensibly for a rhythm of assertion and counterassertion, but he limited this rhythm to declarations he considered morally sound. He could not fathom that positive and negative acted like electrical currents engaged in perpetual alternation, as tightly connected as the terms in King Lear's additions. He rationalized not only contingency, since collision and retribution were inevitable, but also evil (negation), since in his view spiritual being completed itself by absorbing and justifying (never devastating) its conflicting principles. He therefore missed the schism within the individual that temporarily empties principle of content. He missed the ethical turbulence contained within the psychological uproar, the sorrowful and fearful progress toward suicide of a venerated model transformed into a monster or maniac by an impossible masculine dream of perfection ("it is the thoughts of *men* that are deceitful," the chorus of *Medea* says).

Hegel gave us invaluable aid: his heroic exertions to find a wholeness—a purposefulness—underlying tragic contention renewed an important cultural task, and his account of collision between values outlined a central dramatic fact. But he did not see the internalization of that fact, the troublesome *two-sidedness* of a bipolar paranoiac hero who was mighty and also mighty vulnerable. He did not see how the collision brought about invalidation in classical tragedy or revalidation in Shakespeare. And he would have condemned modern writers who focus on the failure of choric rather than heroic values—on timidity rather than arrogance. Yet tragic drama favors literary mechanisms that reflect the entirety of existence, not mechanisms that exalt the best and ban the worst; the protagonist conducts a dialogue, in binary fashion, between Mr. Big One and Mr. Zero.

Hegel, Nietzsche, and Plato each addressed the dark side of tragedy—injustice, frailty, and error; shame, self-defeat, and betrayal; disillusion, demoralization, and panic; inconsistency, bestiality, and madness. They observed the dramatization of treason, flux, and duplicity in manly models, every "excess of heroism, absurdity, or abomination," and their responses differed. Plato rejected that dark side, Hegel sanitized it, and Nietzsche reveled in it (Aristotle translated it into plot formulas). Their incisive, biased revelations distorted the equality of light and darkness, the tortuous relationship that threatens disorder but guarantees renewal.

Like the philosophers, Shakespeare and later authors joined the Athenian dramatists in their attention to moral dualisms (duel-isms), which seem to fascinate the Western male mentality.[1] Unlike the philosophers, however, they usually volunteered no final solution, no resolution of polarity. They found that competition could lead to moving climaxes (the goal of drama for Aristotle). But they made it clear that the cleavage into contraries caused carnage, and they told their stories the way they did in order to ask certain questions. Was it realistic to conceive conduct in terms of polarities, or plausible to isolate the components and call one good or bad? Does manly competition affirm value or destroy it? Is the universe that gives rise to hostile contenders an All or a Nothing? Or both? And, recent writers have asked, can a unifier be visualized that is less hypothetical than Plato's divine forms or Hegel's world spirit (the definitive father), less deranged than Nietzsche's natural force, less arbitrary and more healing ("aidant and remediate," Cordelia says) than the arbiters improvised by previous playwrights? The playwrights delivered an unresolved critique of ancient masculine priorities, not a celebration.

But conflict was not their last word. In their strongest works, tragedians simulated (imitated) not only the opposition but also the convertibility or close association or equivalence of contraries. The repetitions and antitheses, the metamorphoses and oscillations in a play like *King Lear* managed to suggest a tense interplay, even a bond, between illusion and essence in Plato's terms; or lust and law in Hegel's; or personality and power in Nietzsche's. We *do* gain a sense of wholeness, although it is a distressed realization, learned from the hero's inability either to divorce negative from positive or to reconcile them.

So much uncertainty and compassion paraded across the stage, so much impatience and anxiety—and all for what purpose? Perhaps authors manipulate those sensitive linguistic, metaphorical, and narrative devices in order to reproduce (imitate) a primeval double objective that has occupied the human animal in its long evolution, pushing that animal now toward fanatical rigidity, intensity, and exclusion, now toward choric adaptability, temperance, and cooperation—at times motivating some magnificent competitive breakthrough to a new level of functioning, at other times creating an impasse that predicts the extinction of a species. Perhaps experiencing these swings during a performance induces in audiences the emotional discharge Aristotle described, preparing them to work out their own solutions, evolve their own perspective, get at meanings vital for their own well-being. Of course, Plato might have been right about the superiority of philosophical instruction and moral conditioning over poetic transportation in helping us locate happiness or evade unhappiness. And yet there may be a need (reason not the need) to live through the harsh, confusing antagonisms keenly but also distantly, to rehearse them, to know them in dreams before we wake.

Notes

Preface

1. Translations by David Grene (*Philoctetes*) and Robert Fitzgerald (*Oedipus at Colonus*) in *The Complete Greek Tragedies* (*CGT*), ed. David Grene and Richmond Lattimore, 4 vols. (Chicago: University of Chicago Press, 1959), vol. 2.
2. The *Iliad*, trans. E. V. Rieu (Baltimore: Penguin, 1950), 292.

1. Hegel's Theory

1. *Shakespearean Tragedy*, 2nd ed. (London: Macmillan, 1905), ch. 1; and "Hegel's Theory of Tragedy" in *Oxford Lectures on Poetry* (London: Macmillan, 1909). In both books Bradley adapts Hegel's theory because it "applies only imperfectly to the works of Shakespeare."
2. Kenneth Burke, *A Grammar of Motives* (New York: Prentice-Hall, 1945), 39, 267. Burke's triad, "*poiema, pathema, mathema*," was translated into the English version by Francis Fergusson in *The Idea of a Theater* (New York: Doubleday, 1949), 31.
3. *The Paradox of Tragedy* (Bloomington: Indiana University Press, 1960), 23. In an extensive survey of the interpretation of tragedy in the "past three or four decades," George Kimmelman, "The Concept of Tragedy in Modern Criticism," *Journal of Aesthetics and Art Criticism* 4 (1946): 141–60, referred to Hegel only in passing.
4. They included Carl J. Friedrich, ed., *The Philosophy of Hegel* (New York: Modern Library, 1953), lvii; Jack Kaminsky, *Hegel on Art* (Albany: State University of New York Press, 1962), 167–77; René Wellek, *Concepts of Criticism* (New Haven: Yale University Press, 1963), 363–64; Albert Hofstadter and Richard Kuhns, eds., *Philosophies of Art and Beauty* (New York: Modern Library, 1964), 380; and Lionel Abel, "Is There a Tragic Sense of Life?" *Theatre* (Lincoln Center) 2 (1965): 37. In their introduction to *Hegel on Tragedy* (Garden City, N.Y.: Doubleday, 1962), xii, Anne and Henry Paolucci comment that in contrast to his generally unfavorable current reception in Great Britain and the United States, Hegel is still well received by literary scholars in Germany, France, Italy, and Spain. This is not the place to survey twentieth-century Continental thinkers, from Kierkegaard to Derrida, who have shown Hegel's influence.

5. On this sort of contradiction see my essay, "The Unrecognized Influence of Hegel's Theory of Tragedy," *Journal of Aesthetics and Art Criticism* 28 (1969): 91–97. I acknowledge my own debt to my cherished undergraduate mentor at the University of Oklahoma, Professor Gustav E. Mueller—a poetic Hegelian who subtitled one of his books "The Certainty of Our Uncertainties."

6. References are to the translation by T. M. Knox, *Aesthetics: Lectures on Fine Art*, 2 vols. (Oxford: Clarendon Press, 1975).

7. "Pragmatism and the Tragic Sense of Life," *Commentary* 30 (Aug. 1960): 146. More recently, Michelle Gellrich, in her superb *Tragedy and Theory* (Princeton: Princeton University Press, 1988), comments that for Hegel "the moral confusion that conflict brings in its wake is merely a stage in a larger process that discloses to the mind of reason the immanent power of *Geist* in human struggles. . . . [But] Greek tragedy . . . does not validate systematic expectations of order so much as complicate or subvert them" (47, 94).

Others writing in English in the past hundred years who have protested that Hegel rationalizes the presence of evil or disorder in tragedy include Bradley, "Hegel on Tragedy" 379; Prosser Hall Frye, *Romance and Tragedy* (Lincoln: University of Nebraska Press, 1922), 50–53; John S. Smart, "Tragedy," *Essays and Studies* 8 (1922): 9–36; F. L. Lucas, *Tragedy in Relation to Aristotle's Poetics* (London: Hogarth, 1928), 40–43; Morris R. Cohen, "Hegel's Rationalism," *Philosophical Review* 41 (1932): 283–301; Herbert J. Muller, *Modern Fiction* (New York: Funk & Wagnells, 1937), 21, 34; Katharine Everett Gilbert and Helmut Kuhn, *A History of Esthetics*, rev. ed. (Bloomington: Indiana University Press, 1953), 453; René Wellek, *A History of Modern Criticism: 1750–1950*, vol. 2, *The Romantic Age* (New Haven: Yale University Press, 1955), 333; and A. M. Quinton, "Tragedy," *Aesthetics and the Philosophy of Criticism*, ed. Marvin Levich (New York: Random House, 1963), 185–203.

These writers often simplify Hegel's "rationalism." For an excellent analysis correcting popular misconceptions of Hegel as a "manic rationalist" or a "transcendent metaphysician," see J. N. Findlay, *Hegel: A Re-examination* (New York: Macmillan, 1958). In a similar vein, Gustav E. Mueller, "The Hegel Legend of 'Thesis-Antithesis-Synthesis,'" *Journal of the History of Ideas* 19 (1958): 411–14, warns against simplistic interpretation; see also Mueller's *Hegel* (New York: Pageant, 1968), and "The Dialectical Development of Hegel's Aesthetics," *Origins and Dimensions of Philosophy* (New York: Pageant, 1965), 445–557.

8. "Hegel's Theory of Tragedy," in Paolucci, *Hegel on Tragedy* 377. Writers who have defended the "noble individual" against Hegel's disregard include Lewis Campbell, *Tragic Drama in Aeschylus, Sophocles, and Shakespeare* (London: Smith & Elder, 1904), 10; Lucius Walter Elder, "A Criticism of Some Attempts to Rationalize Tragedy," diss., University of Pennsylvania, 1915, 54; W. Macneile Dixon, *Tragedy* (London: Arnold, 1924), 180; Israel Knox, *The Aesthetic Theories of Kant, Hegel, and Schopenhauer* (New York: Columbia University Press, 1936), 111; Newton P. Stallknecht and Robert Brumbaugh, *The Spirit of Western Philosophy* (New York: Longmans, Green, 1950), 398–99, 409; John Crowe Ransom, "The Concrete Universal,"

pt. 1, *Kenyon Review* 16 (1954): 556; and William K. Wimsatt Jr. and Cleanth Brooks, *Literary Criticism* (New York: Knopf, 1957), 561.

9. Hegel did not originate this distinction between classical and "modern" art. In Germany earlier formulations were proposed by Schiller, Friedrich Schlegel, and Schelling. Benedetto Croce, in his *Aesthetic*, trans. Douglas Ainslie, 2nd ed. (London: Macmillan, 1922), 301–3, and *What Is Living and What Is Dead of the Philosophy of Hegel*, trans. Douglas Ainslie (London: Macmillan, 1915), 120–33, claims that for Hegel the arts had become moribund in the modern era. Croce's interpretation has been disputed by, among others, Bernard Bosanquet, *Science and Philosophy* (New York: Macmillan, 1927), 428–37. Anne Paolucci, "Bradley and Hegel on Shakespeare," *Comparative Literature* 16 (1964): 211–25, argues (unconvincingly, I believe) that Hegel did not find Greek tragedy superior to Shakespeare.

10. William Arrowsmith's term, along with "disorder," "crisis," and "chaos," in "The Criticism of Greek Tragedy," *Tulane Drama Review* 3.3 (1959): 31–57; and "A Greek Theater of Ideas," *Ideas in the Drama*, ed. John Gassner (New York: Columbia University Press, 1964), 1–41.

11. For further remarks on Aristotle's *Poetics*, see chapter 8.

2. The Male Model

1. Scholarly judgment relating fifth-century politics to tragedy, though divided, tends to support this conclusion. For example, Norman O. Brown, "Pindar, Sophocles, and the Thirty Years' Peace," *Transactions of the American Philological Association* 82 (1951): 1–28, sees the suicide of Sophocles' Ajax symbolizing "the historic defeat of the aristocratic ideal in the middle of the fifth century B.C., ratified by the Thirty Years' Peace in 446/445 B.C." (18). Similarly, George Thomson, *Aeschylus and Athens*, 3rd ed. (London: Lawrence & Wishart, 1966), claims that Aeschylean tragedy celebrates the establishment of democracy in Athens. Yet as Charles Segal comments, *Tragedy and Civilization* (Cambridge: Harvard University Press, 1981), 12, "the fifth-century polis is still not so secure that it can dispense with or fail to admire the heroic energy, the sheer physical strength, or the mental acumen that might be needed to defend it." See also M. T. W. Arnheim, *Aristocracy in Greek Society* (London: Thames & Hudson, 1977); Christian Meier, *The Political Art of Greek Tragedy*, trans. Andrew Webber (Baltimore: Johns Hopkins University Press, 1988); John J. Winkler and Froma I. Zeitlin, eds., *Nothing to Do with Dionysos?* (Princeton: Princeton University Press, 1990); Peter W. Rose, *Sons of the Gods, Children of Earth* (Ithaca: Cornell University Press, 1992); Alan H. Sommerstein et al., eds., *Tragedy, Comedy and the Polis* (Bari: Levante Editori, 1993); Barbara Goff, ed., *History, Tragedy, Theory* (Austin: University of Texas Press, 1995); Christopher Pelling, ed., *Greek Tragedy and the Historian* (Oxford: Clarendon Press, 1997); and Jasper Griffin, "The Social Function of Attic Tragedy," *Classical Quarterly* 48 (1998): 39–61.

For negative observations on Greek narcissism and competitiveness in both literature and society, see Alvin W. Gouldner, *Enter Plato* (New York: Basic, 1965),

13–102; and Philip E. Slater, *The Glory of Hera* (Boston: Beacon, 1971), esp. 36–43 and 420–57. For studies relating Greek society to tragedy and mythology, see the incisive essays by Jean-Pierre Vernant and Pierre Vidal-Naquet, *Myth and Tragedy in Ancient Greece*, trans. Janet Lloyd (New York: Zone, 1988); also David J. Bradshaw, "The Ajax Myth and the Polis," *Myth and the Polis*, ed. Dora C. Pozzi and John M. Wickersham (Ithaca: Cornell University Press, 1991), 99–125; and Richard Seaford, *Reciprocity and Ritual* (Oxford: Clarendon Press, 1994).

2. On the "heroic ideal," see (among many others) Werner Jaeger, *Paideia: The Ideals of Greek Culture*, trans. Gilbert Highet, 2 vols. (New York: Oxford University Press, 1939, 1943), 1: 1–54; M. I. Finley, *The World of Odysseus* (New York: Viking, 1954), 121–41; C. M. Bowra, *The Greek Experience* (Cleveland: World, 1957), 20–41; Cedric H. Whitman, *Homer and the Heroic Tradition* (Cambridge: Harvard University Press, 1958); A. W. H. Adkins, *Merit and Responsibility* (New York: Oxford University Press, 1960), and *Moral Values and Political Behaviour in Ancient Greece* (New York: Norton, 1972); and Mary Whitlock Blundell, *Helping Friends and Harming Enemies* (Cambridge: Cambridge University Press, 1989). Excellent accounts of evolving aristocratic ideals from Homer to the fifth century BC are offered by Walter Donlan, *The Aristocratic Ideal in Ancient Greece* (Lawrence, Kans.: Coronado Press, 1980), and Joseph M. Bryant, *Moral Codes and Social Structure in Ancient Greece* (Albany: State University of New York Press, 1996). For a summary of "heroic" attributes, see Michael Grant, *Myths of the Greeks and Romans* (New York: New American Library, 1962), 44–50.

3. On shame, social responsibility, and divine order, see Douglas L. Cairns, *Aidōs: Honour and Shame in Ancient Greek Literature* (Oxford: Clarendon Press, 1993); Bernard Williams, *Shame and Necessity* (Berkeley: University of California Press, 1993); and William F. Zak, *The Polis and the Divine Order* (Lewisburg, Pa.: Bucknell University Press, 1995). Cairns rightly emphasizes the internalization of shame and guilt.

4. D. A. Hester, "Sophocles the Unphilosophical," *Mnemosyne* 24 (1971): 11–59, uses this term to describe the plays of Sophocles: "we can abandon the futile search for deep theological insights; . . . the apparent moral issues are incidental to the drama" (47). But I would apply "unphilosophical" only to the *protagonists*, not to the playwrights or the plays.

5. Scholars who laud Prometheus as an exemplar of noble perfection include E. A. Havelock, *Prometheus* (Seattle: University of Washington Press, 1951, 1968), 2–109; L. A. Post, *From Homer to Menander* (Berkeley: University of California Press, 1951), esp. 74; John H. Finley Jr., *Pindar and Aeschylus* (Cambridge: Harvard University Press, 1955), 179–290; Thomas G. Rosenmeyer, *The Masks of Tragedy* (Austin: University of Texas Press, 1963), 49–102; and Lois Spatz, *Aeschylus* (Boston: Twayne, 1982), 158–63. Many others could be cited. In the minority, George Thomson, *Aeschylus and Athens* 304, calls the "unrestraint of Prometheus . . . a disease."

The adulation of Prometheus by critics, poets, artists, and composers in Britain and America probably started with Shelley's comments in the preface to *Prometheus Unbound* (1820): "in addition to courage, and majesty, and firm and patient opposition to omnipotent force, he is susceptible of being described as exempt from the taints of ambition, envy, revenge, and a desire for personal aggrandisement.... Prometheus is, as it were, the type of the highest perfection of moral and intellectual nature, impelled by the purest and the truest motives to the best and noblest ends."

6. Thomson, *Aeschylus and Athens* 309–16, reconstructs the events of the second and third plays from surviving fragments.

7. Bernard M. W. Knox, *The Heroic Temper* (Berkeley: University of California Press, 1964), 44–50, points out similar correspondences. Ambiguities in *Philoctetes* and *Ajax* (and Sophocles' other works) have been noticed more often since Edmund Wilson, "Philoctetes: The Wound and the Bow," *The Wound and the Bow* (New York: Oxford University Press, 1947), 272–95, discussed "the conception of superior strength as inseparable from disability" (287); "these insane or obsessed people of Sophocles all display a perverse kind of nobility" (292). Similarly, Michelle Gellrich, *Tragedy and Theory* (Princeton: Princeton University Press, 1988), 75–76, writes that "Oedipus is simultaneously a noble ruler and a criminal contaminated with *miasma* [pollution].... He is at once both the positive term of an opposition and the negative."

On this point see also G. M. Kirkwood, *A Study of Sophoclean Drama* (Ithaca: Cornell University Press, 1958); Jan Kott, *The Eating of the Gods*, trans. B. Taborski and E. J. Czerwinski (New York: Vintage, 1974); and Joe Park Poe, *Heroism and Divine Justice in Sophocles' Philoctetes* (Leiden: Brill, 1974). The idea of ambiguity is extended to Greek tragedy generally by Segal, *Tragedy and Civilization*, and "Greek Tragedy and Society: A Structuralist Perspective," *Greek Tragedy and Political Theory*, ed. J. Peter Euben (Berkeley: University of California Press, 1986), 43–75; and by Vernant and Vidal-Naquet, *Myth and Tragedy in Ancient Greece* ch. 2–3.

In contrast, authors inclined to emphasize "excellence" and "nobility" in Sophocles' protagonists include John A. Moore, *Sophocles and "Aretê"* (Cambridge: Harvard University Press, 1938); Cedric H. Whitman, *Sophocles* (Cambridge: Harvard University Press, 1951); Ivan M. Linforth, "Three Scenes in Sophocles' *Ajax*," *University of California Publications in Classical Philology* 15 (1954): 1–28; and Martha Nussbaum, "Consequences and Character in Sophocles' *Philoctetes*," *Philosophy and Literature* 1 (1976): 25–53.

8. R. P. Winnington-Ingram, *Sophocles* (Cambridge: Cambridge University Press, 1980), 63, makes a similar point.

9. Brown, "Pindar, Sophocles, and the Thirty Years' Peace," 18, may be overstating his case when he finds *Ajax* portraying the conclusive "defeat of the aristocratic ideal" in 446 B.C., with Odysseus as "the symbol of the new 'bourgeois' order which had won the victory." "Bourgeois" (choric) values were operative long before 446, and "aristocratic" values have proved their resilience long after.

10. On Euripides as critic of Athenian values, see E. R. Dodds, "Euripides the Irrationalist," *Classical Review* 43 (1929): 97–104; and Arrowsmith, "A Greek Theater of Ideas."

11. For professional diagnoses of Pentheus' mental condition, see William Sale,

"The Psychoanalysis of Pentheus in the *Bacchae* of Euripides," *Yale Classical Studies* 22 (1972): 63–82; and Charles Segal, "Pentheus and Hippolytus on the Couch and on the Grid: Psychoanalytic and Structuralist Readings of Greek Tragedy," *Classical World* 72 (1978): 129–48.

12. On gender role reversals, see Charles Segal, "The Menace of Dionysus: Sex Roles and Reversals in Euripides' *Bacchae*," *Arethusa* 11 (1978): 185–202.

13. On the hunting image, see R. P. Winnington-Ingram, *Euripides and Dionysus* (Cambridge: Cambridge University Press, 1948), 93–134.

3. Women

1. Scholarly opinion is divided on how accurately the tragedies reflect the social and legal position of fifth-century Athenian women. Those who believe that Athenian women enjoyed generally favorable status include Hans Licht, *Sexual Life in Ancient Greece* (London: Abbey Library, 1932); A. W. Gomme, "The Position of Women in Athens in the Fifth and Fourth Centuries B.C.," *Essays in Greek History and Literature* (Oxford: Blackwell, 1937), 89–115; H. D. F. Kitto, *The Greeks* (Baltimore: Penguin, 1951), 219–36; Charles Seltman, "The Status of Women in Athens," *Greece and Rome* 2 (1955): 119–24, and *Women in Antiquity* (New York: St. Martin's, 1956); W. K. Lacey, *The Family in Classical Greece* (Ithaca: Cornell University Press, 1968); Donald C. Richter, "The Position of Women in Classical Athens," *Classical Journal* 67 (1971): 1–8; David M. Schapp, *Economic Rights of Women in Ancient Greece* (Edinburgh: Edinburgh University Press, 1979); Mary R. Lefkowitz, "Women in Greek Myth," *American Scholar* (Spring 1985): 207–19, and *Women in Greek Myth* (Baltimore: Johns Hopkins University Press, 1986); and Raphael Sealey, *Women and Law in Classical Greece* (Chapel Hill: University of North Carolina Press, 1990).

Authors who contend that Athenian women were severely restricted and maligned include H. Blümner, *The Home Life of the Ancient Greeks*, trans. Alice Zimmern (New York: Funk & Wagnalls, n.d.); J. P. Mahaffy, *Social Life in Greece from Homer to Menander*, 3d ed. (London: Macmillan, 1877); Alfred Zimmern, *The Greek Commonwealth*, 5th ed. (New York: Modern Library, 1956 [1st ed. 1912]), 341–50; F. A. Wright, *Feminism in Greek Literature* (London: Routledge, 1923), 57–134; R. P. Winnington-Ingram, "Clytemnestra and the Vote of Athena," *Journal of Hellenic Studies* 68 (1948): 130–47; Kenneth Burke, "Form and Persecution in the *Oresteia*," *Sewanee Review* 60 (1952): 377–96; Robert Flacèliere, *Daily Life in Greece at the Time of Pericles*, trans. Peter Green (New York: Macmillan, 1965); Katherine M. Rogers, *The Troublesome Helpmate* (Seattle: University of Washington Press, 1966); Marylin B. Arthur, "Early Greece: The Origins of the Western Attitude toward Women," *Arethusa* 6 (1973): 7–58; Roger Just, "Conceptions of Women in Classical Athens," *Journal of the Anthropological Society of Oxford* 6 (1975): 153–70; Sarah B. Pomeroy, *Goddesses, Whores, Wives, and Slaves* (New York: Schocken, 1975); Philip Vellacott, *Ironic Drama* (Cambridge: Cambridge University Press, 1975), 82–126, 206–25; Helene P. Foley, "The Conception of Women in Athenian Drama," *Reflections of Women in Antiquity*, ed. Helene P. Foley (New York: Gordon & Breach, 1981), 127–

68; Page duBois, *Sowing the Body* (Chicago: University of Chicago Press, 1988); and Roger Just, *Women in Athenian Law and Life* (London: Routledge, 1989).

By the fourth century, A. R. W. Harrison writes, in *The Law of Athens* (Oxford: Clarendon Press, 1968), "there can be no doubt that a woman remained under some sort of tutelage during the whole of her life. She could not enter into any but the most trifling contract, she could not engage her own hand in marriage, and she could not plead her own case in court" (108). In an intriguing speculation, Philip E. Salter, *The Glory of Hera* (Boston: Beacon, 1971), 7, 453, explains the "rejection and derogation of women" as a psychological "disease"; see also Slater, "The Greek Family in History and Myth," *Arethusa* 7 (1974): 9–44. K. J. Dover states, in "Classical Greek Attitudes to Sexual Behaviour," *Arethusa* 6 (1973): 65, "it seems to have been believed that women enjoyed sexual intercourse more intensely than men . . . and that if not segregated and guarded women would be insatiably promiscuous."

On pejorative judgments of women in tragedy, see Philip Vellacott, "Woman and Man in Ancient Greece: The Evidence from Tragic Drama," *Carleton Miscellany* 18.2 (1980): 7–30; Ruth Padel, "Women: Model for Possession by Greek Daemons," *Images of Women in Antiquity*, ed. Averil Cameron and Amélie Kuhrt (Detroit: Wayne State University Press, 1983), 3–19; Froma I. Zeitlin, "Playing the Other: Theater, Theatricality, and the Feminine in Greek Drama," *Representations* 11.3 (1985): 63–94; Synnøve Des Bouvrie, *Women in Greek Tragedy* (Oslo: Norwegian University Press, 1990); Linda Kintz, *The Subject's Tragedy* (Ann Arbor: University of Michigan Press, 1992); Nancy Sorkin Rabinowitz, "Tragedy and the Politics of Containment," *Representation in Greece and Rome*, ed. Amy Richlin (New York: Oxford University Press, 1992), and *Anxiety Veiled: Euripides and the Traffic in Women* (Ithaca: Cornell University Press, 1993); and Bernd Seidensticker, "Women on the Tragic Stage," in Barbara Goff, ed., *History, Tragedy, Theory* (Austin: University of Texas Press, 1995), 151–73. According to George Thomson, *Aeschylus and Athens*, 3rd ed. (London: Lawrence & Wishart, 1966), 269, Aeschylus in the *Oresteia* "regarded the subordination of women, quite correctly, as an indispensable condition of democracy. . . . The subjection of women was a necessary consequence of the development of private property."

Charles Segal, "The Menace of Dionysus," *Arethusa* 11 (1978): 185–202, points out that the picture of women presented by Greek tragedians is "ambivalent"; using other sources, John Gould, "Law, Custom and Myth: Aspects of the Social Position of Women in Classical Athens," *Journal of Hellenic Studies* 100 (1980): 38–59, sees the same "ambivalence." On male-female antagonism as "mythic argument," see Froma I. Zeitlin, "The Dynamics of Misogyny: Myth and Mythmaking in the *Oresteia*," *Arethusa* 11 (1978): 149–84; and P. Walcot, "Greek Attitudes towards Women: The Mythological Evidence," *Greece and Rome* 31 (1984): 37–47. Juliet DuBoulay, *Portrait of a Greek Mountain Village* (Oxford: Clarendon Press, 1974), 101–39, reports that in a Greek village she studied, "a series of opposites delineates the differentiation [between] male and female nature" (104). Her list of female attributes corresponds closely to the fifth-century stereotype, which suggests continuity between past and present attitudes.

Women in the Ancient World, ed. John Paradotto and J. P. Sullivan (Albany: State University of New York Press, 1984), reprints thirteen essays that appeared in *Arethusa* and also provides a useful "Selected Bibliography on Women in Classical Antiquity" by Sarah B. Pomeroy (315–72). Foley, *Reflections of Women in Antiquity;* Cameron and Kuhrt, *Images of Women;* Mary DeForest, ed., *Women's Power, Man's Game* (Wauconda, Ill.: Bolchazy-Carducci, 1993); and Elaine Fantham et al., *Women in the Classical World* (New York: Oxford University Press, 1994), bring together additional essays on women in classical literature and society.

2. According to Zeitlin, "Playing the Other," 81, Greek tragedy "arrives at closures that generally reassert male, often paternal, structures of authority, but before that the work of the drama is to open up [either disrupt or redeem] the masculine view of the universe."

3. Translation by Philip Vellacott, *The Oresteian Trilogy* (Baltimore: Penguin, 1956). Winnington-Ingram, "Clytemnestra and the Vote of Athena," comments extensively on Clytemnestra's masculine force, as does Aya Betensky, "Aeschylus' *Oresteia:* The Power of Clytemnestra," *Ramus* 7 (1978): 11–25. See also Vellacott's introduction, esp. 21–26; and Richmond Lattimore, *The Complete Greek Tragedies*, ed. David Grene and Richmond Lattimore, 4 vols. (Chicago: University of Chicago Press, 1959), 1: 12–14.

4. But Michelle Gellrich, *Tragedy and Theory* (Princeton University Press, 1988), 154, finds that the "Furies' new role in Athens . . . [retains] the principle of retribution."

5. Electra's emotionality, negativity, and addiction to "fruitless words" are emphasized by Thomas M. Woodard, "*Electra* by Sophocles: The Dialectical Design," pt. 1, *Harvard Studies in Classical Philology* 68 (1964): 163–205; and by Charles Paul Segal, "The *Electra* of Sophocles," *Transactions of the American Philological Association* 97 (1966): 473–546.

6. See George B. Walsh, "Public and Private in Three Plays of Euripides," *Classical Philology* 73 (1978): 294–309; and B. M. W. Knox, "The *Medea* of Euripides," *Yale Classical Studies* 25 (1977): 193–226, esp. 210–11. Vellacott, *Ironic Drama*, 125, states that in Euripides' plays "women of notable character were likely to find in the life allotted to them an intolerable contradiction [between domestic and public roles] which led to tragedy." Medea's "manly" qualities have been discussed by Michael Shaw, "The Female Intruder: Women in Fifth-Century Athens," *Classical Philology* 70 (1975): 255–66; Elizabeth Bryson Bongie, "Heroic Elements in the *Medea* of Euripides," *Transactions of the American Philological Association* 107 (1977): 27–56; Shirley A. Barlow, "Stereotype and Reversal in Euripides' *Medea*," *Greece and Rome* 36 (1989): 158–71; and Helene Foley, "Medea's Divided Self," *Classical Antiquity* 8 (1989): 61–85. Medea "comes closest to the demand for an equivalence of that feminine self to the male," Zeitlin remarks in "Playing the Other," 68, "yet her spectacular departure from the city on the dragon chariot of her immortal ancestor, the Sun, suggests that there can be no place for her in the social structure." On

the theme of "foreignness," see Helen H. Bacon, *Barbarians in Greek Tragedy* (New Haven: Yale University Press, 1961).

4. The Sequence of Athenian Tragedy

1. Arnold J. Toynbee, *A Study of History* (New York: Oxford University Press, 1945). Dorothea Krook, *Elements of Tragedy* (New Haven: Yale University Press, 1969), 8–11, finds that an "act of shame" ("betrayal or rejection") precipitates tragic suffering, knowledge, and affirmation; Bernard M. W. Knox, *The Heroic Temper* (Berkeley: University of California Press, 1964), 10ff., discusses the pressure to "yield" exerted upon "heroic resolve."

2. In a well-known passage (*Aesthetics* 2: 1213), Hegel disregarded the huge concern for personal vindication shown by both Antigone and Creon, arguing that the contenders fought primarily for family or social principles. Martha C. Nussbaum, *The Fragility of Goodness* (Cambridge: Cambridge University Press, 1986), 63–79, presents a modified Hegelian interpretation, and George Steiner, *Antigones* (New York: Oxford University Press, 1984), 19–42, after an exhaustive inventory of Hegel's references to the play, concludes that the philosopher's interpretation remains valid.

Cedric H. Whitman, *Sophocles* (Cambridge: Harvard University Press, 1951), 84–85, disputes this reading of *Antigone*, as do D. W. Lucas, *The Greek Tragic Poets*, 2nd ed. (New York: Norton, 1959), 139; Hester, "Sophocles the Unphilosophical" (Hester surveys Hegelian criticism on the play); Gerald F. Else, *The Madness of Antigone* (Heidelberg: Winter, 1976), 96–97; T. C. W. Oudemans and A. P. M. H. Lardinois, *Tragic Ambiguity* (Leiden: Brill, 1987), 110–17; Gellrich, *Tragedy and Theory* 44–71; and Cynthia Willett, "Hegel, Antigone, and the Possibility of Ecstatic Dialogue," *Philosophy and Literature* 14 (1990): 268–83. "The negation of Antigone's commitment to family," Gellrich writes (53), "does not initially come from without, in Creon's denial of her moral priority, but is contained within her actions from the outset." My own point is that both Antigone and Creon, like the protagonist and antagonist in most Athenian tragedies, come to grief (and bring it to others) by allowing an inflated ego to overcome their responsibility for family and social well-being—however vocal they may be in defense of some "one-sided" cause.

3. Bernard Knox writes in *Word and Action* (Baltimore: Johns Hopkins University Press, 1979), 235, "a change of mind appears in Aeschylean and Sophoclean drama as something imposed and hence a sign of weakness." See Jacqueline Duchemin, "*L'agon*" *dans la tragédie grecque*, 2nd ed. (Paris: Belles Lettres, 1968); Philip Holt, "The Debate-Scenes in the *Ajax*," *American Journal of Philology* 102 (1981): 275–88; R. G. A. Buxton, *Persuasion in Greek Tragedy* (Cambridge: Cambridge University Press, 1982); Kathy Eden, *Poetic and Legal Fiction in the Aristotelian Tradition* (Princeton: Princeton University Press, 1986); Michael Lloyd, *The Agon in Euripides* (Oxford: Clarendon Press, 1992); and C. Collard, "Formal Debates in Euripides' Drama," *Greek Tragedy*, ed. Ian McAuslan and Peter Wolcot (Oxford: Oxford University Press, 1993).

4. "As long as there exists a prize, eminently desirable and thoroughly abstract,

that men strive constantly to wrest from one another," observes René Girard, *Violence and the Sacred*, trans. Patrick Gregory (Baltimore: Johns Hopkins University Press, 1977), "there can be no transcendent force capable of restoring peace" (152).

5. Of these two kinds of madness, externally imposed and internally generated, Ruth Padel, *Whom Gods Destroy* (Princeton: Princeton University Press, 1995), credits only the first: "the idea that greatness comes from the same source as madness is a Renaissance input, not a fifth-century idea. . . . Greek tragic madness is caused by gods" (63). On this subject, see also E. R. Dodds, *The Greeks and the Irrational* (Berkeley: University of California Press, 1951); and Philip E. Slater, appendix 2, "Greek Madness," *The Glory of Hera* (Boston: Beacon, 1971).

5. Shakespeare's Fatal Female

1. Quotations are taken from Alfred Harbage, gen. ed., *The Complete Pelican Shakespeare* (Baltimore: Penguin, 1974). How can we account for such specific continuity between the Athenian tragic dramatists and Shakespeare if Shakespeare did not know much (or any) Greek? The question has puzzled scholars for generations. Some of their answers: he knew several Greek tragedies in English translation; he was quite familiar with Seneca and other Roman playwrights who adapted Athenian plays; he was also acquainted, either through Latin or English translation, with Greek myths and nondramatic literature; and he had mastered classical rhetoric at school. Shakespeare probably read Chapman's translation of the *Iliad*, but according to Reuben Brower, *Hero and Saint: Shakespeare and the Graeco-Roman Tradition* (Oxford: Clarendon Press, 1971), 350, he knew Greek tragedy "only through the distorted versions of Seneca and his translators." Brower also mentions the influence of Virgil, Ovid, Plutarch, and others. In any case, reference to classical heroes, heroines, and gods was common in Elizabethan drama and in European literature generally; Shakespeare could assume that his playgoers, educated or not, were familiar with many themes, stories, and archetypes derived, however indirectly, from ancient Greece and Rome.

On Shakespeare's classicism, see T. S. Eliot, *Shakespeare and the Stoicism of Seneca* (London: Oxford University Press, 1927); Thomas W. Baldwin, *William Shakspere's Small Latine and Lesse Greeke*, 2 vols. (Urbana: University of Illinois Press, 1944); J. A. K. Thomson, *Shakespeare and the Classics* (New York: Barnes & Noble, 1952); Curtis Brown Watson, *Shakespeare and the Renaissance Concept of Honor* (Princeton: Princeton University Press, 1960); Virgil K. Whitaker, *Shakespeare's Use of Learning* (San Marino, Cal.: Huntington, 1964); Paul A. Cantor, *Shakespeare's Rome* (Ithaca: Cornell University Press, 1976); John Alvis, "Coriolanus and Aristotle's Magnanimous Man Reconsidered," *Interpretation* 7.3 (1978): 4–28; Vivian Thomas, *Shakespeare's Roman Worlds* (London: Routledge, 1989); Charles and Michelle Martindale, *Shakespeare and the Uses of Antiquity* (London: Routledge, 1990); Robert S. Miola, *Shakespeare and Classical Tragedy: The Influence of Seneca* (Oxford: Clarendon Press, 1992); and Jonathan Bate, *Shakespeare and Ovid* (Oxford: Clarendon Press, 1993).

2. On women and gender relations in Shakespeare, see Juliet Dusinberre, *Shake-

speare and the Nature of Women (London: Macmillan, 1975); *The Woman's Part: Feminist Criticism of Shakespeare*, ed. Carolyn Ruth Swift Lenz, Gayle Greene, and Carol Thomas Neely (Urbana: University of Illinois Press, 1980); Marilyn French, *Shakespeare's Division of Experience* (London: Abacus, 1982); Marianne Novy, *Love's Argument: Gender Relations in Shakespeare* (Chapel Hill: University of North Carolina Press, 1984); Catherine Belsey, *The Subject of Tragedy* (London: Routledge, 1985); Elaine Showalter, "Representing Ophelia: Women, Madness, and the Responsibilities of Feminist Criticism," *Shakespeare and the Question of Theory*, ed. Patricia Parker and Geoffrey Hartman (London: Methuen, 1985), 77–94; and Evelyn Gajowski, *The Art of Loving* (Newark: University of Delaware Press, 1992).

3. Other versions of Shakespeare's tragic sequence are offered by Ruth Nevo, *Tragic Form in Shakespeare* (Princeton: Princeton University Press, 1972); and J. Leeds Barroll, "Structure in Shakespearean Tragedy," *Shakespeare Studies* 7 (1974): 345–78.

4. A bit more textual information in chapter 10 will flesh out this skeletal outline of *King Lear*.

6. Nietzschean Dream Imagery in Aeschylus and Seneca

1. *The Birth of Tragedy* and *The Genealogy of Morals*, trans. Francis Golffing (New York: Doubleday Anchor, 1956). For a careful exposition and critique, see George A. Wells, "*The Birth of Tragedy*," *Trivium* 3 (1968): 59–75; also Allan Megill, "Friedrich Nietzsche as Aestheticist," *Prophets of Extremity* (Berkeley: University of California Press, 1985), 27–102. For bibliographies covering studies of Nietzsche's literary theory and its influence, see "*The Birth of Tragedy*: A Checklist of Criticism, 1872–1972," *Malahat Review* 24 (1972): 177–82, and the reference section on the theory of tragedy in this book.

2. *The Will to Power*, trans. Walter Kaufmann and R. J. Hollingdale (New York: Random House, 1967).

3. See also *Twilight of the Idols*, trans. Anthony M. Ludovici, in *The Complete Works of Friedrich Nietzsche*, ed. Oscar Levy, 18 vols. (New York: Macmillan, 1909–11; reprint, New York: Russell and Russell, 1964), 16: 237–57; *The Joyful Wisdom*, trans. Thomas Common, *Works* 10: 270–71, 332–33; and *Thus Spoke Zarathustra*, ed. and trans. Walter Kaufmann, *The Portable Nietzsche* (New York: Viking, 1954), 329–33. On "eternal recurrence," see Karl Löwith, "Nietzsche's Revival of the Doctrine of Eternal Recurrence," *Meaning in History* (Chicago: University of Chicago Press, 1949), 214–22; Joan Stambaugh, *Nietzsche's Thought of Eternal Return* (Baltimore: Johns Hopkins University Press, 1972); M. C. Sterling, "Recent Discussion of Eternal Recurrence," *Nietzsche Studien* 6 (1977): 261–91; and Lawrence J. Hatab, *Nietzsche and Eternal Recurrence* (Washington, D.C.: University Press of America, 1978).

4. Daniel Breazeale, "The Hegel-Nietzsche Problem," *Nietzsche Studien* 4 (1975): 146–64, contends that "they are *allies* in the struggle against . . . dualism. [They both try to answer] What is the relationship between affirmation and negation?" (162). See also Stephen Houlgate, "Hegel and Nietzsche on Tragedy," *Hegel, Nietzsche, and the Criticism of Metaphysics* (Cambridge: Cambridge University Press, 1986), 182–220.

5. On the influence of Heraclitus, see Stephen Barker, *Autoaesthetics* (Atlantic Highlands, N.J.: Humanities, 1992), 214–27; on other Greek influences, see James C. O'Flaherty, Timothy F. Sellner, and Robert M. Helm, eds., *Studies in Nietzsche and the Classical Tradition* (Chapel Hill: University of North Carolina Press, 1976); M. S. Silk and J. P. Stern, *Nietzsche on Tragedy* (Cambridge: Cambridge University Press, 1981); and V. Tejera, *Nietzsche and Greek Thought* (Dordrecht: Nijhoff, 1987).

6. Comments on light and darkness in the *Oresteia* have been made by Jean Dumortier, *Les Images dans la poèsie d'Eschyle* (Paris: Belles Lettres, 1935), 114–18; Robert F. Goheen, "Aspects of Dramatic Symbolism: Three Studies in the *Oresteia*," *American Journal of Philology* 76 (1955): 124–25; John H. Finley Jr., *Pindar and Aeschylus*, 248, 251; John J. Peradotto, "Some Patterns of Nature Imagery in the *Oresteia*," *American Journal of Philology* 85 (1964): 388–93; and B. Hughes Fowler, "Aeschylus' Imagery," *Classica et Mediaevalia* 28 (1970): 50–51, 64–65, 73–74. Dorothy Tarrant, "Greek Metaphors of Light," *Classical Quarterly* 54 (1960): 180–87, discusses differing usages of the term *light* in Greek authors from Homer to Plato; Ruth Padel, *Whom Gods Destroy* Princeton: Princeton University Press, 1995), 45–96, associates blackness with both madness and vision. For a succinct general discussion of classical imagery, see Robert F. Goheen, *The Imagery of Sophocles'* Antigone (Princeton: Princeton University Press, 1951), 101–19.

7. Translation by Richmond Lattimore in *The Complete Greek Tragedies*, ed. David Grene and Richmond Lattimore, 4 vols. (Chicago: University of Chicago Press, 1959), vol. 1. Brief quotations as well as longer passages are cited by line number since their location bears on the argument.

8. Philip Vellacott, *The Oresteian Trilogy* (Baltimore: Penguin, 1956), 42, translates this as "kindling night to glorious day."

9. For a painstaking reconstruction and map of the beacon route, see J. H. Quincey, "The Beacon-sites in the *Agamemnon*," *Journal of Hellenic Studies* 83 (1963): 118–32. Timothy Nolan Ganz, "The Fires of the *Oresteia*," *Journal of Hellenic Studies* 97 (1977): 28–38, feels that "fire repeatedly serves to symbolize destructive aspects of vengeance" (28).

10. On "forebodings of disaster" in the play, see Bengt Alexanderson, "Forebodings in the *Agamemnon*," *Eranos* 67 (1969): 1–23. On the predicament of the chorus in *Agamemnon*, see William C. Scott, "The Confused Chorus," *Phoenix* 23 (1969): 336–46.

11. On this subject, see G. S. Rousseau, "Dream and Vision in Aeschylus' *Oresteia*," *Arion* 2 (1963): 101–36; and George Devereux, *Dreams in Greek Tragedy* (Berkeley: University of California Press, 1976).

12. Vellacott, *Oresteian Trilogy* 69: "But Justice with her shining eyes / Lights the smoke-begrimed and mean / Dwelling."

13. Peradotto, "Nature Imagery" 390–93, comes to a similar conclusion on the incomplete resolution of light and darkness images in the trilogy.

14. Brief remarks on light and darkness in Seneca's *Oedipus* may be found in Norman T. Pratt, "Major Systems of Figurative Language in Senecan Melodrama," *Transactions and Proceedings of the American Philological Association* 94 (1963): 224;

William H. Owen, "Commonplace and Dramatic Symbol in Seneca's Tragedies," *Transactions and Proceedings of the American Philological Association* 99 (1968): 308–12; and Donald J. Mastronarde, "Seneca's *Oedipus:* The Drama in the Word," *Transactions and Proceedings of the American Philological Association* 101 (1970):294–96, 301.

15. "There is no difference for Seneca," C. J. Herington comments in "Senecan Tragedy," *Arion* 5 (1966): 433, "between physical and moral light and darkness." A similar point is made by Pratt, "Major Systems" 233, and by Mastronarde, "Seneca's *Oedipus*" 301. Quotations are from the fine translation of *Oedipus* by E. F. Watling, *Seneca: Four Tragedies and Octavia* (Baltimore: Penguin, 1966). I indicate page numbers for the longer quotations since lines are not numbered in this edition.

16. Frank Justus Miller, in his older prose translation, *Seneca's Tragedies* (Loeb Library), 2 vols. (Cambridge: Harvard University Press, 1917), vol. 1, may be more accurate here in rendering *mitior* as "milder" rather than "brighter."

7. Nietzschean Dream Imagery in Strindberg and Kafka

1. See also *The Birth of Tragedy and the Genealogy of Morals,* trans. Francis Golffing (New York: Doubleday Anchor, 1956), 24, 37–41; and *The Will to Power,* trans. Walter Kaufmann and R. J. Hollingdale (New York: Random House, 1967), 434, 449–51, 536, 539, 550. Carl P. Ellerman, "Nietzsche's Madness: Tragic Wisdom," *American Imago* 27 (1970): 338–57, speculates that Nietzsche's "collapse into insanity" demonstrates some serious dangers in this enterprise; see also Lesley Chamberlain, *Nietzsche in Turin* (New York: Picador, 1998).

2. The correspondence, with texts of the letters, is treated fully by Herman Scheffauer, "A Correspondence between Nietzsche and Strindberg," *North American Review* 198 (1913): 197–205. See also Karl Strecker, *Nietzsche und Strindberg* (Munich: Müller, 1921); V. J. McGill, *August Strindberg: The Bedeviled Viking* (New York: Brentano, 1930), 286–94; and Michael Robinson, ed., *Strindberg's Letters,* 2 vols. (Chicago: University of Chicago Press, 1992), 1: 293–99. Works of Nietzsche alluded to in the letters, and therefore almost surely read by Strindberg, are *Thus Spoke Zarathustra* (pub. 1883–85, 1892), *On the Genealogy of Morals* (pub. 1887), and *The Twilight of the Idols* (written 1888, pub. 1889). In one letter Nietzsche asked Strindberg to translate *Ecce Homo* (written 1888, pub. 1908) into French, but there is some question whether Strindberg, who refused, ever saw a manuscript copy.

3. I have found no appreciable commentary relating Strindberg's *Dream Play* to Nietzsche. Most writers referring to Nietzsche's possible influence on Strindberg concentrate on antifeminism and the concept of the "superman" in Strindberg's early, naturalistic work, especially *The Father* (1887) and *Miss Julie* (1888). On this subject see Strecker, *Nietzsche und Strindberg*; McGill, *August Strindberg* 281–83, 296–98; A. Jolivet, "Strindberg et Nietzsche," *Revue de Littérature Comparée* 19 (1939): 390–406; Harold H. Borland, *Nietzsche's Influence on Swedish Literature* (Göteborg, Sweden: Elanders, 1956), 17–46, 151–54; Franklin S. Klaf, *Strindberg: The Origin of Psychology in Modern Drama* (New York: Citadel, 1963), 73–91; and Martin Lamm, *August Strindberg,* trans. Harry G. Carlson (New York: Blom, 1971), 259–65.

McGill denies any strong influence by Nietzsche, although he quotes Strindberg's comment to Brandes regarding "my experiments with Nietzsche, whom I have in part anticipated" (297). Similarly, Borland claims that "Strindberg's intellectual appreciation of Nietzsche was not profound" (153). Klaf, on the other hand, believes that "it was through Strindberg that Nietzsche, a brilliant forerunner of contemporary psychoanalytic theory, exerted his influence on modern dramatic literature" (75).

Other individuals said to have influenced Strindberg include Swedenborg, Maeterlinck, Schopenhauer, Rousseau, Hartmann, Balzac, Baudelaire, and Buddha; see Maurice Valency, *The Flower and the Castle* (New York: Macmillan, 1963), 238–362. The impact of Emanuel Swedenborg seems undeniable. In 1896 Strindberg read *The Wonders of Heaven and Hell* (1758), a vision-book that probably inspired the dream context of *A Dream Play* as well as certain ethical precepts and physical details. Strindberg describes his reaction to this work and to Swedenborg's *Arcana Coelestia* (1749–56) in his *Inferno* (1897), trans. Evert Sprinchorn, Inferno, Alone *and Other Writings* (New York: Doubleday Anchor, 1968), 228, 231: "Everything was to be found there. I recognized my own observations, my own sensations, my own ideas to such an extent that his visions appeared to me to be part of reality, doctrines of authentic human experiences.... We are in hell already. The earth is hell—a prison so constructed by a superior intelligence that I cannot take a single step in it without treading on the happiness of others, and in which my cell mates cannot remain happy without making me suffer. That is how, though possibly without knowing it, Swedenborg describes life on earth in attempting to picture hell."

On Strindberg's use of Hindu myths taken from the Vedas and Upanishads, see Leta Jane Lewis, "Alchemy and the Orient in Strindberg's *A Dream Play*," *Scandinavian Studies* 35 (1963): 208–22. On Strindberg as student of Asian culture, see Walter A. Berendsohn, "The Oriental Studies of August Strindberg," trans. Rudolf Loewenthal, *Central Asian Collectanea* no. 5 (1960): 1–16.

4. Quotations are taken from *A Dream Play*, in *Six Plays of Strindberg*, trans. Elizabeth Sprigge (Garden City, N.Y.: Doubleday Anchor, 1955). For brief comments on repetition in Strindberg, see Alice N. Benston, "From Naturalism to the Dream Play," *Modern Drama* 7 (1964): 383, 396. For discussions of Strindberg's style as the origin of literary expressionism, see C. E. W. L. Dahlström, *Strindberg's Dramatic Expressionism* (Ann Arbor: University of Michigan Press, 1930), esp. ch. 5; and Walter H. Sokel, *The Writer in Extremis* (Stanford: Stanford University Press, 1959), 34–39. Irving Deer, "Strindberg's Dream Vision," *Criticism* 14 (1972): 253–65, discusses Strindberg's techniques in the late plays as a prelude to "cinematic conceptions of form."

5. The Poet and the Officer, two confused, naive males, sound like Strindberg himself in his autobiographical work, *Inferno*, when he longs for a wise, ethereal female guide (like Indra's Daughter) to remedy or at least explain marital discord. For a Freudian interpretation of the play as a "conflict of male and female principles," see Evert Sprinchorn, "The Logic of *A Dream Play*," *Modern Drama* 5 (1962): 352–65.

6. On symbolic associations of plants, trees, and flowers, see (among many others) C. M. Kirtland, ed., *Language and Poetry of Flowers* (Chicago: Belford, Clark, 1884); and Ernst and Johanna Lehner, *Folklore and Symbolism of Flowers, Plants and Trees* (New York: Tudor, 1960). See also Göran Stockenström, "Strindberg's Cosmos in *A Dream Play*," *Comparative Drama* 30 (1996): 72–105.

7. Valency, *The Flower and the Castle* 328, observes that "the Daughter's name, Agnes, was doubtless suggested by Agni the fire-god and heavenly messenger, often associated mythically with Indra, the principal god of the Vedas."

8. On Kafka and dreams, see A. P. Foulkes, *The Reluctant Pessimist* (The Hague: Mouton, 1967), 57–76; and Calvin S. Hall and Richard E. Lind, *Dreams, Life, and Literature: A Study of Franz Kafka* (Chapel Hill: University of North Carolina Press, 1970). On Nietzsche's influence on Kafka (esp. *The Birth of Tragedy, Thus Spoke Zarathustra,* and *The Genealogy of Morals*), see Patrick Bridgwater, *Kafka and Nietzsche* (Bonn: Bouvier, 1974); Bridgwater does not, however, deal with "The Metamorphosis" or the ideas of transformation and recurrence. On parallels between Kafka and Heraclitus, see David Schur, *The Way of Oblivion* (Cambridge: Harvard University Press, 1998).

9. Related studies are by Kurt J. Fickert, "The Window Metaphor in Kafka's *Trial*, *Monatshefte* 58 (1966): 345–52; and A. P. Foulkes, "Kafka's Cage Image," *Modern Language Notes* 82 (1967): 462–71, and *The Reluctant Pessimist: A Study of Franz Kafka* (The Hague: Mouton, 1967), 86–97. Quotations are taken from "The Metamorphosis," *Selected Short Stories of Franz Kafka*, ed. Philip Rahv, trans. Willa and Edwin Muir (New York: Modern Library, 1952).

10. The mechanism whereby a son exaggerates and becomes preoccupied with his father's criticism animates other works by Kafka, notably "The Judgment" (a short story) and the autobiographical "Letter to His Father." The letter, written in 1919, comes close to "The Metamorphosis" in its references to a kind mother, a beloved sister, and a belligerent father, to human "vermin" with a "stammering mode of speech," and to the central character's sense of "worthlessness" (trans. Ernst Kaiser and Eithne Wilkins, New York: Schocken, 1966).

8. Plato's Distrust

1. Translation of the *Republic* by Paul Shorey (Cambridge: Harvard University Press, 1930), reprinted in the *Collected Dialogues of Plato*, ed. Edith Hamilton and Huntington Cairns (New York: Pantheon, 1961). Other dialogues that take up the idea of beauty in connection with literary art include *Laws* bk. 2 and 7: 790–817, concerned chiefly with the collaboration between art and morality in education; *Sophist* esp. 233–37, 264–68, on the concept of imitation; and *Ion*, on the divine inspiration of poets. For exhaustive surveys of Plato's references to poetry, see William Chase Greene, "Plato's View of Poetry," *Harvard Studies in Classical Philology* 29 (1918): 1–75; Carleton Lewis Brownson, *Plato's Studies and Criticisms of the Poets* (Boston: Badger, 1920); Katharine Everett Gilbert and Helmut Kuhn, *A History of Esthetics*, rev. ed. (Bloomington: Indiana University Press, 1953), ch. 2; and G. M. A. Grube, *The Greek and Roman Critics* (London: Methuen, 1965), ch. 4.

2. Do the gods and heroes whose activities are guided by ultimate values *imitate* those values? The answer definitely appears to be "no"; throughout the *Republic*, esp. 10: 595–608, Plato contrasts practical activists, who may deal directly with substance, and poetic imitators, who always deal in semblance.

3. Plato may be reacting against a naturalistic acting style in Athens, but he says very little about the actor's role. He does criticize literary naturalism (3: 395–98), contrasting a sober, monochromatic mode with a less dignified style characterized by exaggerated realism and extreme variation in the pitch and rhythm of language.

4. On Plato's "excessive desire to make what is many one" (157), see Arlene W. Saxonhouse, *Fear of Diversity* (University of Chicago Press, 1992), pt. 2.

5. I agree with Goran Sorbom, *Mimesis and Art* (Stockholm: Bonniers, 1966), 143 ff., that for Plato the arts do *not* realize, directly or indirectly, ultimate truths. On this much-debated subject, see also Greene, "Plato's View"; Bernard Bosanquet, *A History of Aesthetic*, 2nd ed. (London: Allen & Unwin, 1904), ch. 3 and 4; R. G. Collingwood, "Plato's Philosophy of Art," *Mind* 34 (1925): 154–72; Katharine Gilbert, "The Relation of the Moral to the Aesthetic Standard in Plato," *Philosophical Review* 43 (1934): 279–94; G. M. A. Grube, *Plato's Thought* (London: Methuen, 1935), ch. 6; Raphael Demos, *The Philosophy of Plato* (New York: Scribner's, 1939), pt. 3; Richard McKeon, "Literary Criticism and the Concept of Imitation in Antiquity," in *Critics and Criticism*, ed. R. S. Crane (Chicago: University of Chicago Press, 1952), 147–59; W. J. Verdenius, *Mimesis* (Leiden: Brill, 1962); and Joseph P. Maguire, "The Differentiation of Art in Plato's Aesthetics," *Harvard Studies in Classical Philology* 68 (1964): 389–410. Julia Annas comments, in *An Introduction to Plato's* Republic (Oxford: Clarendon Press, 1981), 340, "Plato has gone from accepting that poetry is important and dangerous, to trying to prove that it is really trivial and marginal."

6. Commentators often casually combine this and the next explanation: see, for example, Greene, "Plato's View" 56.

7. Plato has himself been considered a poet, mythmaker, or tragedian: see, among others, J. A. Stewart, *The Myths of Plato* (London: Macmillan, 1905); Helmut Kuhn, "The True Tragedy: On the Relationship between Greek Tragedy and Plato," *Harvard Studies in Classical Philology* 52 (1941): 1–40 and 53 (1942): 37–88; J. Hartland-Swann, "Plato as Poet," *Philosophy* 26 (1951): 3–18, 131–41; and A. A. Krentz, "Dramatic Form and Philosophical Content in Plato's Dialogues," *Philosophy and Literature* 7 (1983): 32–47. But for Plato's distrust of myths, see J. Tate, "Plato and Allegorical Interpretation," *Classical Quarterly* 23 (1929): 142–54. For a sensitive and detailed investigation of contingency and rational self-sufficiency in Greek tragedy, Plato, and Aristotle, see Martha C. Nussbaum, *The Fragility of Goodness* (Cambridge: Harvard University Press, 1986).

8. This is a common tack: see J. Tate, "'Imitation' in Plato's *Republic*," *Classical Quarterly* 22 (1928): 16–23, and "Plato and 'Imitation,'" *Classical Quarterly* 26 (1932): 161–69; R. G. Collingwood, *The Principles of Art* (Oxford: Clarendon Press, 1938), ch. 3; Catherine Rau, *Art and Society* (New York: Smith, 1951); Constantine Cavar-

nos, "Plato's Teaching on Fine Art," *Philosophy and Phenomenological Research* 13 (1953): 487–98; and Darnell Rucker, "Plato and the Poets," *Journal of Aesthetics and Art Criticism* 25 (1967): 167–70. For an unusual variant of this position, to the effect that Plato banished only the *critics* of poetry, see Allan H. Gilbert, "Did Plato Banish the Poets or the Critics?" *Studies in Philology* 36 (1939): 1–19.

9. See, for example, Gilbert and Kuhn, *History of Esthetics* 29–34; and Rau, *Art and Society* 35.

10. This position is taken by Sorbom, *Mimesis and Art* 151.

11. Eric A. Havelock makes this case in his interesting work, *Preface to Plato* (New York: Grosset & Dunlap, 1967), 14–15. For an attack on arguments that attempt to rationalize Plato's strictures against poetry, see Thomas Gould, "Plato's Hostility to Art," *Arion* 3 (1964): 70–91.

12. My thanks to Professor Saul Levin for reviewing this argument with me. I am grateful also to the late Professor Seymour Pitcher for his forceful suggestions.

13. The contention that Plato was dismayed by the contrast between the potential and the practice of poetry is discussed by Greene in "Plato's View," and "The Greek Criticism of Poetry" in *Perspectives of Criticism*, ed. Harry Levin (Cambridge: Harvard University Press, 1950), 19–54; Grube, *Greek and Roman Critics* 54; Werner Jaeger, *Paideia*, trans. Gilbert Highet, 2 vols. (New York: Oxford University Press, 1939, 1943), 2: 360; and J. G. Warry, *Greek Aesthetic Theory* (New York: Barnes & Noble, 1962), 59. Some of these authors cite Plato's *Laws* as a work approving the practice of the arts.

14. That Plato in book 10 extended his definition of imitation to include all types of narration has been argued by, among others, Brownson, *Plato's Studies* 88–94; Collingwood, "Plato's Philosophy" 166; Havelock, *Preface to Plato* 25; Francis Macdonald Cornford, *The Republic of Plato* (New York: Oxford University Press, 1945), 324n; and Gerald F. Else, "Imitation," in *Encyclopedia of Poetry and Poetics*, ed. Alex Preminger (Princeton: Princeton University Press, 1965), 378.

15. Reference to a nonimitative manner is implied in the phrase that begins book 10 (595a), "in refusing to admit at all so much of [poetry] as is imitative . . . ." Are "hymns to the gods and the praises of good men" (10: 607a) nonimitative? Presumably they are, though not necessarily since they are allowed as an exception; Plato does not clarify the point.

16. Gould, "Plato's Hostility" 73. More balanced estimates of Aristotle's debt to Plato may be found in Gilbert and Kuhn, *History of Esthetics* ch. 3; Grube, *Greek and Roman Critics* ch. 5; and Gellrich, *Tragedy and Theory* 94–162. John D. Boyd, *The Function of Mimesis and Its Decline* (Cambridge: Harvard University Press, 1968), 24f., claims that Aristotle changed Plato's application of *mimesis* from a cognitive notion to a "structural concept." See my annotated reference list, "Plato and Aristotle on the Craft of Literature."

17. "The poet must say very little in his own person; for so far as he does that, he ceases to be an imitator" (ch. 24). Aristotle complains that people commonly and mistakenly classify authors "not as poets in virtue of the act of imitating, but

according to the metre used" (ch. 1). References are to the translation by L. J. Potts, *Aristotle on the Art of Fiction*, 2nd ed. (Cambridge: Cambridge University Press, 1959).

18. In *A History of Aesthetic* 28–30, Bosanquet states that Plato's "metaphysical estimate of image-making fine art, . . . although . . . profoundly hostile to the value of the poetic world, is in substance an important foundation-stone of aesthetic theory. . . . The positive result that 'Art has its being in appearance,' not yet extended to the generalization 'that beauty has its being in appearance,' forms [an] element of permanent aesthetic value contained in the metaphysical principle upon which Hellenic theory concerning fine art is founded."

19. Contrary to the prevailing view since Bosanquet, *A History of Aesthetic* (first published in 1892), and S. H. Butcher, *Aristotle's Theory of Poetry and Fine Art* (first published in 1894), some commentators have disputed the idea that poetry for Aristotle involved a process of artistic idealization. For example, see John Crowe Ransom, "The Mimetic Principle," *The World's Body* (New York: Scribner's, 1938), 193–211; and G. N. G. Orsini, "Conceptions of Poetics," in *Encyclopedia of Poetry and Poetics* 636–39. According to Ransom (206), in Aristotle's opinion "the artist interests himself entirely in individuals."

20. Stephen Halliwell, "Aristotle's *Poetics*," in *The Cambridge History of Literary Criticism*, ed. George A. Kennedy (Cambridge: Cambridge University Press, 1989), 1: 149–83, comments that "the indeterminacy of *hamartia* [error, failing, wrongdoing, etc.] lies in the fact that while strongly precluding personal guilt as a cause of tragic events, and replacing it with a notion of human fallibility, [Aristotle] leaves the roots of this fallibility unspecified" (173).

9. Milton's Single-mindedness

1. Quotations are from Paradise Regained, *The Minor Poems and* Samson Agonistes, ed. Merritt Y. Hughes (New York: Odyssey, 1937). In his preface, Milton names as his literary models Aeschylus, Sophocles, Euripides, Dionysus the Elder, Aristotle, Cicero, Seneca, Augustus Caesar, Martial, Plutarch, St. Paul, Gregory Nazianzen, Paraeus, and "the Italians." Discussions of the classical influence on *Samson Agonistes* include Sir Richard C. Jebb, "*Samson Agonistes* and the Hellenic Drama," *Proceedings of the British Academy* 3 (1907–8): 341–48; P. H. Epps, "Two Notes on English Classicism," *Studies in Philology* 13 (1916): 184–96; Wilmon Brewer, "Two Athenian Models for *Samson Agonistes*," *PMLA* 42 (1927): 910–20; P. W. Timberlake, "Milton and Euripides," in *Essays in Dramatic Literature*, ed. Hardin Craig (Princeton: Princeton University Press, 1935), 315–40; William Riley Parker, *Milton's Debt to Greek Tragedy in* Samson Agonistes (Baltimore: Johns Hopkins University Press, 1937); Ann Gossman, "Milton's Samson as the Tragic Hero Purified by Trial," *Journal of English and Germanic Philology* 61 (1962): 528–41; John M. Steadman, "Dalila, the Ulysses Myth, and Renaissance Allegorical Tradition," *Modern Language Review* 57 (1962): 560–65; B. R. Rees, "Aristotle's Theory and Milton's Practice: *Samson Agonistes*" (Birmingham: University of Birmingham, 1972); Martin Mueller, "The Tragedy of Deliverance: *Samson Agonistes*," *Children of Oedipus*

(Toronto: University of Toronto Press, 1980), 193–212; Margaret J. Arnold, "*Graeci Christiani:* Milton's Samson and the Renaissance Editors of Greek Tragedy," *Milton Studies* 18 (1983): 235–54; and John Mulryan, "The Heroic Tradition of Milton's *Samson Agonistes*," *Milton Studies* 18 (1983): 217–34.

2. Classical literature, of course, also presented Milton with instances of character transformation, as in the poetry of Ovid. Among the numberless scholars who have commented on Samson's progression as a Christian legacy are James Holly Hanford, *A Milton Handbook*, 4th ed. (New York: Crofts, 1946); F. Michael Krouse, *Milton's Samson and the Christian Tradition* (Princeton: Princeton University Press, 1949); Arnold Stein, *Heroic Knowledge* (Minneapolis: University of Minnesota Press, 1957); Burton O. Kurth, *Milton and Christian Heroism* (Berkeley: University of California Press, 1959); and Mary Ann Radzinowicz, *Toward* Samson Agonistes (Princeton: Princeton University Press, 1978). Revisionist theories have been proposed by David Loewenstein, *Milton and the Drama of History* (Cambridge: Cambridge University Press, 1990); and Michael Lieb, *Milton and the Culture of Violence* (Ithaca: Cornell University Press, 1994). For Milton's treatment of his biblical sources, see Joseph Anthony Wittreich, *Interpreting* Samson Agonistes (Princeton: Princeton University Press, 1986).

3. H. G. Liddel and Robert Scott, *A Greek-English Lexicon*, rev. ed. (Oxford: Clarendon Press, 1940), 1: 19, define *agonistes* as a "combatant, esp. competitor in the games; pleader, debater; actor; master in any art or science; one who struggles for a thing, champion." Paul R. Sellin, "Milton's Epithet *Agonistes*," *Studies in English Literature, 1500–1900* 4 (1964): 137–62, prefers "actor" or "dissembler." On the argumentative Prolusions, delivered orally by Milton at Christ's College, Cambridge, see Donald Lemen Clark, "Milton's Rhetorical Exercises," *Quarterly Journal of Speech* 46 (1960): 297–307; on Milton's argumentative schemes in the prose pamphlets, see Wilbur Elwyn Gilman, *Milton's Rhetoric: Studies in His Defense of Liberty* (Columbia: University of Missouri, 1939).

Recent articles on the role of Dalila include Joan S. Bennett, "Dalila, Eve, and the 'Concept of Woman,'" in *Arenas of Conflict*, ed. Kristin Pruitt McColgan and Charles W. Durham (Cranbury, N.J.: Associated University Press, 1997), 251–60; and Mary Beth Rose, "Gender and the Heroics of Endurance," *Milton Studies* 33 (1997): 83–109.

4. Sister Miriam Clare, Samson Agonistes: *A Study in Contrast* (New York: Pageant, 1964), believes that "figures of contrast" dominate the rhetoric.

5. *Brachylogia* (sometimes called *synathroesmus*): a series of nonsynonymous words joined by a common intent or meaning. This figure, though unified by a single idea, may involve a genuine variety of meanings. Such differences among items in a series can be illustrated by a passage in Cicero's Eighth Philippic (VIII.iii.10), in *The Philippics*, trans. Walter C. A. Ker (Cambridge: Harvard University Press, 1926), 373: "we undertake to secure to our soldiers liberty, law, rights, courts, the empire of the world, dignity, peace, quiet. The promises therefore of Antonius are bloody, savage, criminal, hateful to gods and men, not lasting or salutory; ours, on the contrary, are honest, upright, noble, full of joy, and full of

patriotism." Each series can be called an example of *brachylogia,* but only the first shows meaningful diversity. Heinrich Lausberg, *Handbuch der Literarischen Rhetorik* (Munich: Hueber, 1960), 331, makes a similar distinction.

6. For a slightly different analysis of this passage, see J. B. Broadbent, "Milton's Rhetoric," *Modern Philology* 56 (1958): 224–42. Broadbent concentrates on Milton's iterative schemes in *Paradise Lost.* On Milton's identical repetitions ("autoplagiarism"), see Edward S. LeComte, *Yet Once More: Verbal and Psychological Pattern in Milton* (New York: Liberal Arts, 1953). Allan H. Gilbert, "Is *Samson Agonistes* Unfinished?" *Philological Quarterly* 28 (1949): 98–106, argues on the basis of uncoordinated "repetition of idea and word" that the play never received its author's final revisions.

On Milton's rhetorical training in grammar school, see Donald Lemen Clark, *John Milton at St. Paul's School* (New York: Columbia University Press, 1948). On rhetoric in England before Milton's time, see Veré L. Rubel, *Poetic Diction in the English Renaissance from Skelton through Spenser* (New York: MLA, 1941); this work contains an excellent glossary of rhetorical figures—my chief source for the definitions in this essay—derived from Puttenham's *The Arte of English Poesie* (London, 1589). These terms and definitions differ in some respects from terminology derived from Peacham's *Garden of Eloquence* (London, 1577), compiled by Sister Miriam Joseph, *Shakespeare's Use of the Arts of Language* (New York: Columbia University Press, 1947), reprinted in modified form as *Rhetoric in Shakespeare's Time* (New York: Harcourt, Brace, 1962). See also Lausberg, *Handbuch der Literarischen Rhetorik.*

7. *Paradox:* a statement apparently self-contradictory or incredible yet true; here and elsewhere I shall not discuss figures irrelevant to my argument.

8. *Comparatio:* comparison of objects ("base degree now" compared with "former servitude"). *Traductio:* a word repeated in different forms ("servile . . . servitude").

9. Despite this rhetorical intricacy, Milton generally avoids the more artificial iterative schemes like *symploce* (consecutive verses beginning and ending with repeated words) and *antimetabole* (repetition of words in inverted order).

10. *The Complete English Poetry of John Milton,* ed. John T. Shawcross (New York: Doubleday, 1963).

10. Shakespeare's Trickery

1. *Venus and Adonis* and *The Rape of Lucrece* in *The Complete Works of Shakespeare,* ed. W. J. Craig (London: Oxford University Press, 1904, 1943). Lines in *King Lear* are quoted from the Alfred Harbage edition (Baltimore: Penguin, 1970)

2. To my knowledge, the linking of equivalent words or word groups has not been explored elsewhere. George T. Wright, "Hendiadys and *Hamlet,*" *PMLA* 96 (1981): 168–93, reviews Shakespeare's use of *hendiadys,* usually two nouns joined by *and.* Wright points out (174) that this figure, which does not occur frequently in *King Lear,* links two terms that are "grammatically parallel [but] not semantically parallel." My focus is upon terms linked by both grammatical and semantic coordination.

Studies of *King Lear* that touch on iterative figures include Paul V. Kreider,

Repetition in Shakespeare's Plays (Princeton: Princeton University Press, 1941); Robert Bechtold Heilman, *This Great Stage: Image and Structure in* King Lear (Baton Rouge: Louisiana State University Press, 1948); and Marvin Rosenberg, *The Masks of Lear* (Berkeley: University of California Press, 1972). On Shakespeare's "logical, even oratorical organization," see Sheldon P. Zitner, "*King Lear* and Its Language," *Some Facets of* King Lear, ed. Rosalie L. Colie and F. T. Flahiff (London: Heinemann, 1974), 3–22.

3. Authors commenting on Lear's and Goneril's commands include Hazel Sample Guyol, "A Temperance of Language: Goneril's Grammar and Rhetoric," *English Journal* 55 (1966): 316–19; Paul A. Jorgensen, *Lear's Self-Discovery* (Berkeley: University of California Press, 1967), 72–73; and Madeleine Doran, "Command, Question, and Assertion in *King Lear*," in *Shakespeare's Art*, ed. Milton Crane (Chicago: University of Chicago Press, 1973), 53–78.

4. Editors disagree in glossing "property": for example, Alexander Schmidt, *Shakespeare-Lexicon*, rev. Gregor Sarrizan, 5th ed. (Berlin: de Gruyter, 1962), takes the word to denote here "ownership" rather than "particular quality." If he is correct, the addition (now wholly nonsynonymous) should read 1+2+3.

5. Here and following, an arrow signifies "causes," "results in," "leads to" (1→2), or "is caused by" (1←2). A slash indicates contrast, antithesis, or exception (1/2).

6. See Manfred Weidhorn, "The Relation of Title and Name to Identity in Shakespearean Tragedy," *Studies in English Literature* 9 (1969): 306–9.

7. Among the many other references to "nothing," there is a similar exchange between Kent, Lear, and the Fool (I.iv.122–26):

Kent: This is nothing, fool.

Fool: Then 'tis like the breath of an unfee'd lawyer—you gave me nothing for't. Can you make no use of nothing, nuncle?

Lear: Why, no, boy. Nothing can be made out of nothing.

Both these passages combine a form of addition (repeating a word with a single meaning) with *antistasis* or *antanaclasis* (repeating a word in different senses). In this essay I concentrate on the first; on *antanaclasis* see Stephen Booth, *An Essay on Shakespeare's Sonnets* (New Haven: Yale University Press, 1969), 90–96, 204–7, *Shakespeare's Sonnets* (New Haven: Yale University Press, 1977), and King Lear, Macbeth, *Indefinition, and Tragedy* (New Haven: Yale University Press, 1983), 1–58. On the multiple senses of "nothing" in *King Lear*, see Edward W. Taylor, "*King Lear* and Negation," *English Literary Renaissance* 20 (1990): 17–39.

8. See Jerry Wasserman, "'And Every One Have Need of Other': Bond and Relationship in *King Lear*," *Mosaic* 9.2 (1976): 15–30.

9. Other statements in the first scene on the divorce between love and speech are made by Cordelia (224–33), Kent (152–54, 182–83), and France (235–37). Edgar's later request to "speak what we feel, not what we ought to say" (V.iii.325) addresses this impasse. On the inadequacy of verbal expression, see Richard D. Fly, "Revelations of Darkness: The Language of Silence in *King Lear*," *Bucknell Review* 20.3 (1972): 73–92.

10. On the shift to generalization, see Martha Andresen, "'Ripeness is All': Sen-

tentiae and Commonplaces in *King Lear*," in Colie and Flahiff, *Some Facets of* King Lear 145–68. Essays that discuss the play's pessimism include Barbara Everett, "The New King Lear," *Critical Quarterly* 2 (1960): 325–39; Nicholas Brooke, *Shakespeare:* King Lear (London: Arnold, 1963), and "The Ending of *King Lear,*" *Shakespeare, 1564–1964*, ed. Edward A. Bloom (Providence: Brown University Press, 1964); William R. Elton, King Lear *and the Gods* (San Marino, Cal.: Huntington Library, 1966); Brower, *Hero and Saint* 383–415; A. L. French, *"King Lear,"* in *Shakespeare: Select Bibliographical Guides*, ed. Stanley Wells (Oxford: Oxford University Press, 1973), 171–88; S. L. Goldberg, *An Essay on* King Lear (Cambridge: Cambridge University Press, 1974); Joyce Carol Oates, "'Is This the Promised End?': The Tragedy of King Lear," *Journal of Aesthetics and Art History* 33 (1974): 19–32; Paul Delany, *"King Lear* and the Decline of Feudalism," *PMLA* 92 (1977): 429–40; John Reibetanz, *The Lear World* (Toronto: University of Toronto Press, 1977); and G. R. Hibbard, "*King Lear:* A Retrospect, 1939–79," *Shakespeare Survey* 33 (1980): 1–12.

11. On characters in the play, most prominently Lear, who replicate traits or experiences of others, see Elton, King Lear *and the Gods* 267–338; and Thomas McFarland, *Tragic Meanings in Shakespeare* (New York: Random House, 1966), 127–71.

12. In act 1, characters besides Goneril ("Old fools are babes again") who take Lear's poor judgment to indicate a metamorphosis or reversal of identity include Regan ("such unconstant starts"), Kent ("when Lear is mad"), France ("your . . . affection /Fall'n into taint"), Gloucester ("the King falls from bias of nature"), and the fool ("Thou wouldst make a good fool"). On Ovidian metamorphosis in *King Lear, Othello,* and *Antony and Cleopatra*, see Jonathan Bate, *Shakespeare and Ovid* (Oxford: Clarendon Press, 1993), 181–214.

13. "There are two countermovements of personality," Robert B. Heilman writes in "Manliness in the Tragedies: Dramatic Variations," *Shakespeare, 1564–1964,* 19–37: "the holding back of the self, or the ruthless assertion of the self over others" (28). On Shakespearean "contrariety," "paradox," "inconsistency," and "unpredictable mobility," see Rosalie L. Colie, *Paradoxia Epidemica: The Renaissance Tradition of Paradox* (Princeton: Princeton University Press, 1966), 232–51, 461–81; and Robert Grudin, *Mighty Opposites: Shakespeare and Renaissance Contrariety* (Berkeley: University of California Press, 1979).

14. On the trial structure, see Dorothy C. Hockey, "The Trial Pattern in *King Lear*," *Shakespeare Quarterly* 10 (1959): 389–95.

Summary and Speculation

1. Thanks to William Coughlan and Howard Oliker for an intense, competitive debate on this subject. On the origins of dualistic thinking in Greek philosophy, see G. E. R. Lloyd, *Polarity and Analogy* (Cambridge: Cambridge University Press, 1966); see also John Peter Anton, *Aristotle's Theory of Contrariety* (New York: Humanities Press, 1957).

Further Reference

The Theory of Tragedy

Twentieth-century literary critics and theorists have displayed an insatiable interest in the nature of tragedy. To limit the scope of a checklist dealing with their vast production, I have generally excluded works on individual playwrights or novelists; on theorists writing before 1900, except Hegel and Nietzsche; and on the preliterary origins of tragic drama in religious myth, ritual, and hero cult. This list is confined to articles and books published in English, and for the most part it does not draw upon reference works, unpublished dissertations, or collections of reprinted material.

Abel, Lionel. "Is There a Tragic Sense of Life?" *Theatre* (Lincoln Center, New York) 2 (1965): 29–42.
———. *Metatheatre*. New York: Hill and Wang, 1963.
Adamczewski, Zygmunt. *The Tragic Protest*. The Hague: Nijhoff, 1963.
Adolf, Helen. "The Essence and Origin of Tragedy." *Journal of Aesthetics and Art Criticism* 10 (1951): 112–25.
Alexander, Peter. *Hamlet, Father and Son*. Oxford: Clarendon Press, 1955. 40–114.
Anderson, Maxwell. "The Essence of Tragedy." *The Essence of Tragedy and Other Footnotes and Papers*. Washington, D.C.: Anderson House, 1939. 1–14.
Anderson, Michael. "Dionysus and the Cultured Policeman." *Tulane Drama Review* 11 (Summer 1967): 99–104.
Anton, John P. "Mythos, Katharsis, and the Paradox of Tragedy." *Proceedings of the Boston Area Collegium in Ancient Philosophy* 1 (1986): 299–325.
Arnott, W. Geoffrey. "Nietzsche's View of Greek Tragedy." *Arethusa* 17 (1984): 135–49.
Auden, W. H. "The Christian Tragic Hero." *New York Times*, December 16, 1945, sec. 7: 1, 27.
Aylen, Leo. "The Vulgarity of Tragedy." *Classical Drama and Its Influence*. Ed. M. J. Anderson. London: Methuen, 1965. 85–100.
Ballard, Edward G. "On Good and Evil in the Philosophy of Art and Aesthetic Theory." *Southern Journal of Philosophy* 7 (1969): 273–87.

Barbour, John D. *Tragedy as a Critique of Virtue*. Chico, Cal.: Scholars Press, 1984.

Barker, Stephen. *Autoaesthetics*. Atlantic Highlands, N.J.: Humanities Press, 1992. 214–27 (Nietzsche).

Barnet, Sylvan. "Some Limitations of a Christian Approach to Shakespeare." *English Literary History* 22 (1955): 81–92.

Barrack, Charles M. "Nietzsche's Dionysus and Apollo." *Nietzsche Studien* 3 (1974): 114–29.

Beaumont, Albert. *The Hero: A Theory of Tragedy*. London: Routledge, 1925.

Bell, Charles G. "Tragedy." *Diogenes* 7 (Summer 1954): 12–32.

Bennett, Benjamin. "Nietzsche's Idea of Myth." *PMLA* 94 (1979): 420–33.

Bentley, Eric. "Tragedy." *The Life of the Drama*. New York: Atheneum, 1964. 257–94.

Berke, Bradley. *Tragic Thought and the Grammar of Tragic Myth*. Bloomington: Indiana University Press, 1982.

Berkowitz, Peter. "The Ethics of Art: *The Birth of Tragedy*." *Nietzsche: The Ethics of an Immoralist*. Cambridge: Harvard University Press, 1995.

Berlin, Normand. *The Secret Cause*. Amherst: University of Massachusetts Press, 1981.

Berndtson, Arthur. "Tragedy as Power: Beyond Nietzsche." *Bucknell Review* 15 (December 1967): 97–107.

Bernstein, Richard J. "Why Hegel Now?" *Review of Metaphysics* 31 (1977): 29–60.

Birenbaum, Harvey. *Tragedy and Innocence*. Washington, D.C.: University Press of America, 1983.

———. "*The Birth of Tragedy*: A Checklist of Criticism, 1872–1972." *Malahat Review* 24 (1972): 177–82.

Boas, George. "The Evolution of the Tragic Hero." *Carleton Drama Review* 1 (1955): 5–21.

Bodkin, Maud. "Archetypal Patterns in Tragic Poetry." *Archetypal Patterns in Poetry*. London: Oxford University Press, 1934. 1–25.

Bolen, Frances E. *Irony and Self-Knowledge in the Creation of Tragedy*. Salzburg: Institut für Englische Sprache und Literatur, 1973.

Bosanquet, Bernard. *A History of Aesthetic*. 2nd ed. London: Allen and Unwin, 1904. 334–62 (Hegel).

Bouchard, Larry D. *Tragic Method and Tragic Theology*. University Park: Pennsylvania State University Press, 1989.

Bradley, A. C. "Hegel's Theory of Tragedy." *Hibbert Journal* 2 (1903): 662–80. Rpt. in *Oxford Lectures on Poetry*. London: Macmillan, 1909.

Breazeale, Daniel. "The Hegel-Nietzsche Problem." *Nietzsche Studien* 4 (1975): 146–64.

Bredvold, Louis I. "The Modern Temper and Tragic Drama." *Quarterly Review* 61 (1955): 207–13.

Brereton, Geoffrey. *Principles of Tragedy*. Coral Gables: University of Miami Press, 1969.

Brown, John Mason. "The Tragic Blueprint." *European Theories of the Drama*. 1940. Ed. Barrett H. Clark. Rev. ed. New York: Crown, 1947. 553–57.

Brueck, Katherine T. *The Redemption of Tragedy.* Albany: State University of New York Press, 1995.
Bubner, Rüdiger. "Hegel's Aesthetics—Yesterday and Today." Steinkraus and Schmitz, *Art and Logic* 15–34.
Buchanan, Scott. "Tragedy and Comedy." *The Critical Performance.* 1929. Ed. Stanley Edgar Hyman. New York: Vintage, 1956. 81–94.
Bungay, Stephen. *Beauty and Truth: A Study of Hegel's Aesthetics.* Oxford: Oxford University Press, 1984.
Burke, Kenneth. "Dialectic of Tragedy." *A Grammar of Motives.* Englewood Cliffs, N.J.: Prentice-Hall, 1945. 38–41.
———. "On Tragedy." *Counter-Statement.* Los Altos, Cal.: Hermes, 1953. 252–55.
Butler, John Francis. "Tragedy, Salvation, and the Ordinary Man." *London Quarterly Review* 162 (1937): 489–97.
Calarco, N. Joseph. "Tragedy as Demonstration." *Educational Theatre Journal* 18 (1966): 271–74.
———. *Tragic Being: Apollo and Dionysus in Western Drama.* Minneapolis: University of Minnesota Press, 1969 (Nietzsche).
Callahan, Virginia Woods. "Recent Views on Tragedy Ancient and Modern." *Traditio* 15 (1959): 443–48.
Campbell, Brenton. "Free Will and Determinism in the Theory of Tragedy: Pérez de Ayola and Ortega y Gasset." *Hispanic Review* 37 (1969): 375–82.
Campbell, Lewis. "On Climax in Tragedy." *Fortnightly Review* ns 74 (1900): 83–91.
Camus, Albert. "On the Future of Tragedy." 1955. Trans. Ellen Conroy Kennedy. *Lyrical and Critical Essays.* Ed. Philip Thody. New York: Vintage, 1970. 295–310.
Carritt, E. F. *The Theory of Beauty.* 1914. 2nd ed. London: Methuen, 1923. 82–101 (Nietzsche), 149–78 (Hegel).
Carson, Herbert L. "The Tragic Quest." *Personalist* 44 (1963): 309–21.
Carter, Curtis L. "A Re-examination of the 'Death of Art' Interpretation of Hegel's Aesthetics." Steinkraus and Schmitz, *Art and Logic* 83–102.
Cartwright, David E. "Reversing Silenus' Wisdom." *Nietzsche Studien* 20 (1991): 309–13.
Casson, T. E. "Tragedy and the Infinilte." *Poetry Review* 30 (1939): 363–70.
Christensen, Parley A. "Tragedy as Religious Paradox." *Western Humanities Review* 12 (1958): 39–50.
Chu, Kwang-Tsien. *The Psychology of Tragedy.* Strasbourg: Libraire Université d'Alsace, 1933.
Clark, Richard C. "Hegel: Bibliographical Spectrum." *Review of National Literatures* 1 (1970): 273–92.
Clay, J. H. "A New Theory of Tragedy." *Educational Theatre Journal* 8 (1956): 295–305.
Coffman, George R. "Tragedy and a Sense of the Tragic." *Sewanee Review* 50 (1942): 26–34.
Cole, Susan Letzler. *The Absent One.* University Park: Pennsylvania State University Press, 1985.

Coolidge, Mary L. "Ethics—Apollonian and Dionysian." *Journal of Philosophy* 38 (1941): 449–65 (Nietzsche).
Cordle, Thomas R. "Malraux and Nietzsche's *Birth of Tragedy*." *Bucknell Review* 8 (1959): 89–104.
Coulter, James A. "Nietzsche and Greek Studies." *Greek, Roman and Byzantine Studies* 3 (Winter 1960): 46–51.
Courtney, W. L. "Fate and the Tragic Sense." *Transactions of the Royal Society of Literature* 28 (1908): 201–33.
———. *The Idea of Tragedy in Ancient and Modern Drama*. London: Constable, 1900.
Croce, Benedetto. *What Is Living and What Is Dead of the Philosophy of Hegel*. Trans. Douglas Ainslie. London: Macmillan, 1915.
Crocker, Lester G. "Mr. Bell on Tragedy." *Diogenes* 15 (Fall 1956): 112–20.
Currie, R. Hector. "The Energies of Tragedy." *Centennial Review* 2 (1967): 220–36.
Dahl, Mary Karen. *Political Violence in Drama*. Ann Arbor: University of Michigan Press, 1987.
Dahlström, Carl E. W. L. "An Approach to Tragedy." *Modern Drama* 1 (1958): 35–49, 71–83.
Danto, Arthur C. "Art and Irrationality." *Nietzsche as Philosopher* New York: Macmillan, 1965. 36–67.
DeGennaro, Angelo A. "Croce and Hegel." *Personalist* 44 (1963): 302–8.
Del Caro, Adrian. *Dionysian Aesthetics*. Frankfurt am Main: Lang, 1981 (Nietzsche).
———. *Nietzsche Contra Nietzsche*. Baton Rouge: Louisiana State University Press, 1989.
de Man, Paul. "Genesis and Genealogy in Nietzsche's *The Birth of Tragedy*." *Diacritics* 11.4 (1972): 44–53.
Den Ouden, Bernard. *Essays on Reason, Will, Creativity, and Time*. Washington, D.C.: University Press of America, 1982 (Nietzsche).
Desmond, William. *Art and the Absolute: A Study of Hegel's Aesthetics*. Albany: State University of New York Press, 1986.
Dickens, Robert S. "Unamuno on Tragedy, Agony and the Tragic Sense of Life." *Journal of Existentialism* 8 (1967): 161–77.
Dixon, W. Macneile. *Tragedy*. London: Arnold, 1924.
Dodd, Wayne. "Tragedy and the Mortal Condition." *Centennial Review* 12 (1968): 314–33.
Donougho, Martin. "The Semiotics of Hegel." *Clio* 11 (1982): 415–30.
Drew, Elizabeth. "Tragedy." *Discovering Drama*. New York: Norton, 1937. 173–211.
Drost, Mark P. "Nietzsche and Mimesis." *Philosophy and Literature* 10 (1986): 309–17.
Earle, William. "Being Versus Tragedy." *Chicago Review* 14 (1960): 107–14.
Eberhart, Richard. "Tragedy as Limitation: Comedy as Control and Resolution." *Tulane Drama Review* 6 (June 1962): 3–14.
Elder, Lucius Walter. *A Criticism of Some Attempts to Rationalize Tragedy*. Diss. University of Pennsylvania, 1915. Privately printed, 1915.
Ellerman, Carl P. "Nietzsche's Madness: Tragic Wisdom." *American Imago* 27 (1970): 338–57.

Ellis, Robert Richmond. *The Tragic Pursuit of Being: Unamuno and Sartre.* Tuscaloosa: University of Alabama Press, 1988.
Ellis-Fermor, Una. *The Frontiers of Drama.* London: Methuen, 1948. 127–47.
Engel, S. Morris. *The Problem of Tragedy.* Fredericton: Brunswick Press, 1960.
Faas, Ekbert. *Tragedy and After.* Montreal: McGill-Queen's University Press, 1984.
Falk, Eugene H. *Renunciation as a Tragic Focus.* Minneapolis: University of Minnesota Press, 1954.
Fallon, C. "Tragic Fact." *Imago Mundi* 75 (1947): 24–31.
Farley, Wendy. *Tragic Vision and Divine Compassion.* Louisville: Westminster/Knox Press, 1990.
Farnham, Willard. "Tragic Prodigality of Life." *Essays in Criticism* 2 (1934): 185–98.
Feagin, Susan L. "The Pleasures of Tragedy." *American Philosophical Quarterly* 20 (1983): 95–104.
Feibleman, James K. "The Meaning of Tragedy." *Aesthetics.* New York: Humanities Press, 1968. 62–80.
Fergusson, Francis. *The Idea of a Theater.* Princeton: Princeton University Press, 1949.
Fiet, Lowell A. "'The Tragic Fallacy' Revisited." *Journal of Aesthetic Education* 10 (1976): 61–74.
Figes, Eva. *Tragedy and Social Evolution.* London: Calder, 1976.
Fitts, Dudley. "Tragic Emotion, and the Hero." *Essays—Yesterday and Today.* Ed. Harold L. Tinker. New York: Macmillan, 1934. 627–42.
Flaccus, Louis William. *Artists and Thinkers.* New York: Longmans Green, 1916. 104–39 (Hegel), 161–200 (Nietzsche).
Ford, David F. "Tragedy and Atonement." *Christ, Ethics, and Tragedy.* Ed. Kenneth Surin. Cambridge: Cambridge University Press, 1989. 117–30.
Foss, Martin. *Death, Sacrifice, and Tragedy.* Lincoln: University of Nebraska Press, 1966.
Fouconnier, R. L. "Tragedy and the Modern Theatre." *Queen's Quarterly* 55 (1948): 327–32.
Fowkes, William I. *A Hegelian Account of Contemporary Art.* Ann Arbor, Mich.: UMI Research Press, 1981.
Frye, Northrop. "The Mythos of Autumn: Tragedy." *Anatomy of Criticism.* 1957. New York: Atheneum, 1967. 206–22.
Frye, Prosser Hall. *Romance and Tragedy.* 1922. 2nd ed. Lincoln: University of Nebraska Press, 1961.
Gall, Robert S. "Tragedy or Religion?" *Philosophy Today.* 29 (1985): 110–20.
Gallagher, Kent G. "Emotion in Tragedy and Melodrama." *Educational Theatre Journal* 17 (1965): 215–19.
Gardner, Helen. "Concepts of Tragedy." *Religion and Literature.* Oxford: Oxford University Press, 1971. 13–37.
Gassner, John. "Catharsis and the Modern Theater." *European Theories of the Drama.* 1937. Ed. Barrett H. Clark. Rev. ed. New York: Crown, 1947. 549–52.
———. "The Possibilities and Perils of Modern Tragedy." *Tulane Drama Review* 1 (May 1957): 3–14.

———. "Tragedy in the Modern Theatre." *The Theatre in Our Times.* New York: Crown, 1954. 51–74.

———. "Tragic Perspectives." *Tulane Drama Review* 2 (May 1958): 7–22.

Gearhart, Suzanne. *The Interrupted Dialectic.* Baltimore: Johns Hopkins University Press, 1992.

Gellrich, Michelle. *Tragedy and Theory.* Princeton: Princeton University Press, 1988.

Gelven, Michael. "The Dionysian Sources in Philosophy." *Man and World* 10 (1977): 173–93 (Nietzsche).

———. "An Existential Theory of Tragedy." *Man and World* 21 (1988): 145–69.

Georgopoulos, N., ed. *Tragedy and Philosophy.* New York: St. Martin's Press, 1993 (ten essays, several on Hegel and Nietzsche).

———. "The Tragic Form." *Man and World* 10 (1977): 137–45.

Gilbert, Katharine Everett, and Helmut Kuhn. *A History of Esthetics.* Rev. ed. Bloomington: Indiana University Press, 1953. 436–54 (Hegel), 516–23 (Nietzsche).

Girard, René. *Violence and the Sacred.* 1972. Trans. Patrick Gregory. Baltimore: Johns Hopkins University Press, 1977.

Glicksberg, Charles I. "The Modern Playwright and the Absolute." *Queen's Quarterly* 65 (1958): 459–71.

———. *The Tragic Vision in Twentieth-Century Literature.* Carbondale: Southern Illinois University Press, 1963.

Goedert, Georges. "The Dionysian Theodicy." Trans. Robert M. Helm. *Studies in Nietzsche and the Judeo-Christian Tradition.* Ed. James C. O'Flaherty, et al. Chapel Hill: University of North Carolina Press, 1985. 319–40.

Goldmann, Lucien. "The Tragic Vision." *The Hidden God.* 1956. Trans. Philip Thody. London: Routledge and Kegan Paul, 1964. 3–88.

Goodman, Paul. "Serious Plots." *The Structure of Literature.* Chicago: University of Chicago Press, 1954. 26–79.

Gould, Thomas. "The Innocence of Oedipus and the Nature of Tragedy." *Massachusetts Review* 10 (1969): 281–300.

Green, Andre. *The Tragic Effect: The Oedipus Complex in Tragedy.* 1969. Trans. Alan Sheridan. Cambridge: Cambridge University Press, 1979.

Green, Paul. "Tragedy—Playwright to Professor." *Dramatic Heritage.* New York: French, 1953. 81–91.

Griffin, Drew E. "Nietzsche on Tragedy and Parody." *Philosophy and Literature* 18 (1994): 339–47.

Groth, J. H. "Wilamowitz-Möllendorf on Nietzsche's *Birth of Tragedy.*" *Journal of the History of Ideas* 11 (1950): 179–90.

Guha, Praphulla Kumar. *Tragic Relief.* London: Oxford University Press, 1932.

Haar, Michael. "Heidegger and the Nietzschean 'Physiology of Art'." Krell and Wood, *Exceedingly Nietzsche* 13–30.

Hadow, William Henry. *The Use of Comic Episodes in Tragedy.* London: Oxford University Press, 1915.

Haecker, Theodor. "Theodicy and Tragedy." Trans. Alexander Dru. *Criterion* 13 (1934): 371–81.

Hale, Edward Everett, Jr. "Our Idea of Tragedy." *Dramatists of To-day*. New York: Holt, 1905. 176–202.
Hall, Robert W. "Being and Tragedy." *Chicago Review* 14 (1960): 99–106.
Hallman, Ralph J. *Psychology and Literature: A Study of Alienation and Tragedy*. New York: Philosophical Library, 1961.
Hanna, Thomas. "The Compass Points of the Comic and Pathetic." *British Journal of Aesthetics* 8 (1968): 284–94.
Harries, Karsten. "Hegel on the Future of Art." *Review of Metaphysics* 27 (1974): 677–96.
Harris, H. S. "The Resurrection of Art." *Owl of Minerva* 16 (1984): 5–20 (Hegel).
Harris, Mark. *The Case for Tragedy*. New York: Putnam's, 1932.
Hasenclaver, Walter. "The Nature of Tragedy." *English Review* 33 (1921): 403–4.
Hathorn, Richard Y. *Tragedy, Myth, and Mystery*. Bloomington: Indiana University Press, 1962.
Hausman, Carl R. "Sophocles and the Metaphysical Question of Tragedy." *Personalist* 47 (1966): 509–19.
Heckman, Peter. "The Role of Music in Nietzsche's *Birth of Tragedy*." *British Journal of Aesthetics* 30 (1990): 351–60.
Heilman, Robert B. "Melpomene as Wallflower; or, The Reading of Tragedy." *Sewanee Review* 55 (1947): 154–66.
———. "Tragedy and Melodrama." *Texas Quarterly* 3 (Summer 1960): 36–50.
———. *Tragedy and Melodrama*. Seattle: University of Washington Press, 1968.
Heller, Erich. "Yeats and Nietzsche." *Encounter* 33 (December 1969): 64–72.
Heller, Peter. "Nietzsche." *Dialectics and Nihilism*. Amherst: University of Massachusetts Press, 1966. 69–147.
Henderson, Robert L. "Chopin and the Expressionists." *Music and Letters* 41 (January 1960): 38–45 (Nietzsche).
Henn, T. R. *The Harvest of Tragedy*. London: Methuen, 1956.
Henrichs, A. "The Modern View of Dionysus from Nietzsche to Girard." *Harvard Studies in Classical Philology* 88 (1984): 205–40.
Hester, D. A. "Sophocles the Unphilosophical." *Mnemosyne* 24 (1971): 11–59 (Hegel).
Hinden, Michael. "Ritual and Tragic Action." *Journal of Aesthetics and Art Criticism* 32 (1973–74): 357–73 (Nietzsche).
Hofstadter, Albert. "Art: Death and Transfiguration." *Review of National Literatures* 1 (1970): 149–64 (Hegel).
———. "On Artistic Knowledge." *Beyond Epistemology*. The Hague: Nizhoff, 1974. 58–97 (Hegel).
Hollingdale, R. J. *Nietzsche*. London: Routledge and Kegan Paul, 1965. 96–104.
Hook, Sydney. "Pragmatism and the Tragic Sense of Life." *Commentary* 30 (August 1960): 139–49.
Houlgate, Stephen. "Hegel and Nietzsche on Tragedy." *Hegel, Nietzsche and the Criticism of Metaphysics*. Cambridge: Cambridge University Press, 1986. 182–220.
Hoy, Cyrus. "Comedy, Tragedy, and Tragicomedy." *Virginia Quarterly Review* 36 (1960): 105–18.

———. *The Hyacinth Room.* New York: Knopf, 1964.
Hunt, Barbara Joan. *The Paradox of Christian Tragedy.* Troy, N.Y.: Whitson, 1985.
Huxley, Aldous. "Tragedy and the Whole Truth." *Virginia Quarterly Review* 7 (1931): 176–85.
Hyman, Stanley Edgar. "Freud and the Climate of Tragedy." *Partisan Review* 28 (1956): 198–214.
Jacobs, Carol. "The Stammering Text." *The Dissimulating Harmony.* Baltimore: Johns Hopkins University Press, 1978. 1–22.
Jarrett, James L. "'Tragedy'." *ETC* 12 (1954): 189–97.
Jarrett-Kerr, Martin. "The Conditions of Tragedy" *Comparative Literature Studies* 2 (1965): 363–74.
Jaspers, Karl. *Tragedy Is Not Enough.* 1947. Trans. Harald A. T. Reiche, Harry T. Moore, and Karl W. Deutsche. Boston: Beacon, 1952.
Jepsen, Laura. *Ethical Aspects of Tragedy.* Gainesville: University Press of Florida, 1953.
Kainz, Howard P. "Hegel's Theory of Aesthetics in the *Phenomenology.*" *Idealistic Studies* 2 (1972): 81–94.
Kallen, Horace M. "The Essence of Tragedy." *Indecency and the Seven Arts.* New York: Liveright, 1930. 207–46.
———. *Liberty, Laughter and Tears.* De Kalb: Northern Illinois University Press, 1968.
———. "The Meaning of Tragedy in the Freedom of Man." *Journal of Philosophy* 55 (1958): 772–80.
Kaminsky, Jack. *Hegel on Art.* Albany: State University of New York Press, 1962.
Karelis, Charles. "Hegel's Concept of Art." *Hegel's Introduction to Aesthetics.* Trans. T. M. Knox. Oxford: Clarendon Press, 1979. xi–lxxvi.
Kaufmann, R. J. "Tragedy and Its Validating Conditions." *Comparative Drama* 1 (1967): 3–18.
Kaufmann, Walter. "Art and History." *Nietzsche.* Princeton: Princeton University Press, 1950. 99–110.
———. "Freud and the Tragic Virtues." *American Scholar* 29 (1960): 469–81.
———. "Hegel's Ideas about Tragedy." *New Studies in Hegel's Philosophy.* Ed. Warren E. Steinkraus. New York: Holt, Rinehart and Winston, 1971. 201–20.
———. "Nietzsche between Homer and Sartre." *Revue Internationale de Philosophie* (Brussels) 67 (1964): 50–73.
———. *Tragedy and Philosophy.* Garden City, N.Y.: Doubleday, 1968.
Kelly, Henry Ansgar. *Ideas and Forms of Tragedy from Aristotle to the Middle Ages.* Cambridge: Cambridge University Press, 1993.
Kemal, S. "Nietzsche, Creativity, and the Redundancy of Literary Value." *Nietzsche Studien* 21 (1992): 63–80.
Kerényi, Charles. "Birth and Rebirth of Tragedy." Trans. Edith Cooper. *Diogenes* 28 (1959): 18–39.
Kerr, Walter. *Tragedy and Comedy.* New York: Simon and Schuster, 1967.
Kimmelman, George. "The Concept of Tragedy in Modern Criticism." *Journal of Aesthetics and Art Criticism* 4 (1946): 141–60.

Kitto, H. D. F. "Religious Drama and Its Interpretation." *Form and Meaning in Drama.* 2nd ed. London: Methuen, 1964. 231–45.

Klapp, Orrin E. "Tragedy and the American Climate of Opinion." *Centennial Review* 2 (1958): 396–413.

Knight, A. H. J. "The Philosophy of Dionysus." *Some Aspects of the Life and Work of Nietzsche.* Cambridge: Cambridge University Press, 1933. 67–92.

Knox, Israel. *The Aesthetic Theories of Kant, Hegel, and Schopenhauer* New York: Columbia University Press, 1936.

———. "The Comic, the Tragic, and the Cynical." *Ethics* 62 (1952): 210–14.

Knox, T. M. "The Puzzle of Hegel's Aesthetics." Steinkraus and Schmitz, *Art and Logic* 1–10.

Koelb, Clayton. "'Tragedy' and 'the Tragic'." *Genre* 13 (1980): 275–86 (Hegel).

Kofman, Sarah. *Nietzsche and Metaphor.* 1983. Trans. Duncan Large. Palo Alto: Stanford University Press, 1993.

Kohok, Erazim. "The Person in a Personal World." *Independent Journal of Philosophy* 1 (1977): 51–64.

Kojève, Alexandre. "Notes on Hegel's Theory of Tragedy." Trans. Lionel Abel. *Moderns on Tragedy.* Ed. Lionel Abel. Greenwich, Conn.: Fawcett, 1967. 295–98.

Kouzel, Daisy Fornacca. "The Hegelian Influence in the Literary Criticism of Francesco De Sanctis." *Review of National Literatures* 1 (1970): 214–31.

Krell, David Farrell. *Lunar Voices.* Chicago: University of Chicago Press, 1995 (Nietzsche).

Krell, David Farrell, and David Wood, eds. *Exceedingly Nietzsche.* London: Routledge, 1988.

Krieger, Murray. "Tragedy and the Tragic Vision." *Kenyon Review* 20 (1958): 281–99.

———. *The Tragic Vision.* New York: Holt, Rinehart and Winston, 1960.

Krook, Dorothea. *Elements of Tragedy.* New Haven: Yale University Press, 1969.

Krukowski, Lucien. "Hegel." *Aesthetic Legacies.* Philadelphia: Temple University Press, 1992. 65–88, 118–34.

———. "Hegel, 'Progress,' and the Avant-Garde in Europe." *Art and Concept.* Amherst: University of Massachusetts Press, 1987. 10–28.

Krutch, Joseph Wood. "The Tragic Fallacy." *The Modern Temper.* New York: Harcourt Brace, 1929. 115–43.

Kuhns, Richard. *Tragedy: Contradiction and Repression.* Chicago: University of Chicago Press, 1991.

LaBelle, Maurice M. "H. L. Mencken's Comprehension of Friedrich Nietzsche." *Comparative Literature Studies* 7 (1970): 43–49.

Lamb, Sidney. *Tragedy: Six Radio Lectures.* Toronto: Canadian Broadcasting Corp., 1965.

Langer, Susanne K. "The Tragic Rhythm." *Feeling and Form.* New York: Scribner's, 1953. 351–66.

Lea, F. A. "The Hellenist." *The Tragic Philosopher.* London: Methuen, 1957. 30–48 (Nietzsche).

Leaska, F. R. *The Voice of Tragedy.* New York: Speller, 1963.

Leavis, F. R. "Tragedy and the 'Medium'." *The Importance of Scrutiny*. Ed. Eric Bentley. New York: Stewart, 1948. 214–26.
Lee, Lawrence. "The Present Status of Tragedy." *Classical World* 56 (1963): 237–40.
Leech, Clifford. "The Implications of Tragedy." *Shakespeare's Tragedies and Other Studies in Seventeenth Century Drama*. London: Chatto and Windus, 1950. 3–20.
———. *Tragedy*. London: Methuen, 1969.
Lenson, David. *Achilles' Choice*. Princeton: Princeton University Press, 1975 (Hegel and Nietzsche).
———. *The Birth of Tragedy*. Boston: Twayne, 1987 (Nietzsche).
Lerner, Laurence. "Tragedy: Religious and Humanist." *Review of English Literature* (Leeds) 2 (October 1961): 28–37.
Lesser, Simon O. "Tragedy, Comedy and the Esthetic Experience." *Literature and Psychology* 6 (1956): 131–39. Expanded in *Fiction and the Unconscious*. Boston: Beacon, 1957. 269–93.
Levi, Albert William. "The Problem of Tragedy and the Nature of Peace." *Literature, Philosophy, and the Imagination*. Bloomington: Indiana University Press, 1962. 273–316.
Levin, David Michael. "The Spacing of Comedy and Tragedy." *Journal of the British Society for Phenomenology* 11 (1980): 16–36.
Lewisohn, Ludwig. "A Note on Tragedy." *The Drama and the Stage*. New York: Harcourt Brace, 1922. 19–23.
Leyburn, Ellen Douglass. "Comedy and Tragedy Transposed." *Yale Review* 53 (1963): 553–62.
Loewenberg, J. *Dialogues from Delphi*. Berkeley: University of California Press, 1949.
Löwith, Karl. *From Hegel to Nietzsche*. 1941. Trans. David E. Green. New York: Holt, Rinehart and Winston, 1964.
———. "Nietzsche's Revival of the Doctrine of Eternal Recurrence." *Meaning in History*. Chicago: University of Chicago Press, 1949. 214–22.
Lucas, R. S. "A Problem of Hegel's Aesthetics." *Renaissance and Modern Studies* 4 (1960): 82–118.
Lynch, William F. "Confusion in Our Theater." *Thought* 26 (1951): 342–60.
———. "Tragedy." *Christ and Apollo*. New York: Sheed and Ward, 1960. 65–90.
Mackay, L. A. "Antigone, Coriolanus, and Hegel." *Transactions of the American Philological Association* 93 (1962): 166–74.
Madigan, Patrick. *Aristotle and His Modern Critics*. Scranton: University of Scranton Press, 1996.
Magnus, Bernd, Stanley Stewart, and Jean-Pierre Mileur. *Nietzsche's Case: Philosophy as/and Literature*. New York: Routledge, 1993.
Mandel, Oscar. *A Definition of Tragedy*. New York: New York University Press, 1961.
Martin, Nicholas. *Nietzsche and Schiller: Untimely Aesthetics*. Oxford: Clarendon Press, 1996.
Mason, H. A. *The Tragic Plane*. Oxford: Clarendon Press, 1985.
Maxwell, J. C., and Clifford Leech. "The Presuppositions of Tragedy." *Essays in Criticism* 5 (1955): 175–81.

May, Keith M. *Nietzsche and the Spirit of Tragedy.* New York: St. Martin's Press, 1990.
McArthur, Herbert. "Tragic and Comic Modes." *Criticism* 3 (1961): 36–45.
McCollom, William G. *Tragedy.* New York: Macmillan, 1957.
McEachran, F. "Humanism and Tragedy." *Nineteenth Century and After* 106 (1929): 70–81.
McGahey, Robert. *The Orphic Moment.* Albany: State University of New York Press, 1994. 1–74 (Nietzsche).
McGinn, Robert E. "Culture as Prophylactic: Nietzsche's *Birth of Tragedy* as Culture Criticism." *Nietzsche Studien* 4 (1975): 75–138.
McLaughlin, Peter. "The Elements of Tragedy." *Queen's Quarterly* 71 (1964): 103–11.
Meager, R. "Tragedy." *Proceedings of the Aristotelian Society* (supp. vol.) 34 (1960): 165–86.
Megill, Allan. "Nietzsche as Aestheticist." *Philosophy and Literature* 5 (1981): 204–25. Expanded as "Friedrich Nietzsche as Aestheticist." *Prophets of Extremity.* Berkeley: University of California Press, 1985. 27–102.
Michel, Laurence. "The Possibility of a Christian Tragedy." *Thought* 31 (1956): 403–23.
———. *The Thing Contained: Theory of the Tragic.* Bloomington: Indiana University Press, 1970.
———. "Yardsticks for Tragedy." *Essays in Criticism* 5 (1955): 81–88.
Miller, Arthur. "Tragedy and the Common Man." *New York Times,* February 27, 1949, sec. 2: 1, 3.
Milstead, John. "The Structure of Modern Tragedy." *Western Humanities Review* 12 (1958): 365–69.
Mitias, Michael H. "Hegel on the Art Object." Steinkraus and Schmitz, *Art and Logic* 67–76.
Morawski, Stefan. "On the Tragic." *Essays on Aesthetics.* Ed. John Fisher. Philadelphia: Temple University Press, 1983. 278–92.
Moretti, Franco. "The Great Eclipse: Tragic Form as the Deconsecration of Sovereignty." *Signs Taken for Wonders.* Trans. S. Fischer, D. Forgacs, and D. Miller. London: New Left Books, 1983. 42–82.
Morgan, George Allen. "Art and Artist." *What Nietzsche Means.* Cambridge: Harvard University Press, 1941. 206–37.
Morgan, Margery M. "Shaw, Yeats, Nietzsche, and the Religion of Art." *Komos* 1 (March 1967): 24–34.
Morreall, John. "Enjoying Negative Emotions in Fictions." *Philosophy and Literature* 9 (1985): 95–103.
Morrell, Roy. "The Psychology of Tragic Pleasure." *Essays in Criticism* 6 (1956): 22–37.
Morris, Ivor. *Shakespeare's God.* New York: St. Martin's, 1972 (ch. 6–19, theory of tragedy).
Moss, Leonard. "The Unrecognized Influence of Hegel's Theory of Tragedy." *Journal of Aesthetics and Art Criticism* 28 (1969): 91–97.
Mueller, Gustav Emil. "The Dialectical Development of Hegel's Aesthetics." *Origins and Dimensions of Philosophy.* New York: Pageant, 1965. 445–54.

———. "The Function of Aesthetics in Hegel's Philosophy." *Journal of Aesthetics and Art Criticism* 5 (1946): 49–53.

Mueller, Martin. *Children of Oedipus and Other Essays on the Imitation of Greek Tragedy 1550–1800.* Toronto: University of Toronto, 1980.

Muller, Herbert Joseph. *The Spirit of Tragedy.* New York: Knopf, 1956.

Myers, Henry Alonzo. *Tragedy: A View of Life.* Ithaca: Cornell University Press, 1956.

Naas, Michael. "The Tragedy of Renown: Nietzsche, Aeschylus, and Might Have Been." *Philosophy Today* 35 (1991): 277–90.

Napieralski, Edmund A. "The Tragic Knot." *Journal of Aesthetics and Art Criticism* 31 (1973): 441–50.

Nelson, Robert J. "Tragedy and the Tragic." *Arion* 2.4 (1963): 86–95.

Nicoll, Allardyce. "Tragedy." *The Theatre and Dramatic Theory.* New York: Barnes and Noble, 1962. 95–115.

———. "Tragedy." *The Theory of Drama.* London: Harrap, 1931. 103–74.

Niebuhr, Reinhold. "Christianity and Tragedy." *Beyond Tragedy.* New York: Scribner's, 1937. 153–69.

Nussbaum, Martha C. *The Fragility of Goodness.* Cambridge: Cambridge University Press, 1986. 63–79 (Hegel).

Nuttall, A. D. *Why Does Tragedy Give Pleasure?* Oxford: Clarendon Press, 1996.

O'Connor, William Van. *Climates of Tragedy.* Baton Rouge: Louisiana State University Press, 1943.

O'Flaherty, James C. "Eros and Creativity in Nietzsche's *Birth of Tragedy.*" *Studies in German Literature of the Nineteenth and Twentieth Centuries.* Ed. Siegfried Mews. Chapel Hill: University of North Carolina Press, 1970. 83–104.

O'Flaherty, James C., et al., eds. *Studies in Nietzsche and the Classical Tradition.* Chapel Hill: University of N. Carolina Press, 1976.

Olson, Elder. *Tragedy and the Theory of Drama.* Detroit: Wayne State University Press, 1961.

Orage, A. R. "Apollo or Dionysos?" *Friedrich Nietzsche.* Chicago: McClurg, 1911. 25–44.

Osborne, Harold. "The Concept of Tragedy." *British Journal of Aesthetics* 15 (1975): 287–93.

Oudemans, T. C. W. and A. P. M. H. Lardinois. *Tragic Ambiguity.* Leiden, The Netherlands: Brill, 1987. 110–17 (Hegel), 223–29 (Nietzsche).

Packer, Mark. "Dissolving the Paradox of Tragedy." *Journal of Aesthetics and Art Criticism* 47 (1989): 211–20.

Palmer, Richard H. *Tragedy and Tragic Theory.* Westport, Conn.: Greenwood, 1992.

Paolucci, Anne. "Bradley and Hegel on Shakespeare." *Comparative Literature* 16 (1964): 211–25.

Paolucci, Anne, and Henry Paolucci. Introduction. *Hegel on Tragedy.* Garden City, N.Y.: Anchor, 1962. xi–xxxi.

Paolucci, Henry. "The Poetics of Aristotle and Hegel." *Review of National Literatures* 1 (1970): 165–213.

Pasley, Malcolm, ed. *Nietzsche: Imagery and Thought*. Berkeley: University of California Press, 1978.
Pavel, Thomas G. "Tragedy and the Sacred." *Poetics* 10 (1981): 231–42.
Peacock, Ronald. "Tragedy, Comedy and Civiliation." *The Poet in the Theatre*. London: Routledge, 1946. 125–32.
Perkins, Robert L. "Hegel and Kierkegaard." *Review of National Literatures* 1 (1970): 232–54.
Pfeffer, Rose. *Nietzsche*. Lewisburg, Penn.: Bucknell University Press, 1972.
Philipson, M. H. "Some Reflections on Tragedy." *Journal of Philosophy* 55 (1958): 197–202.
Pietercil, Raymond. "Antigone and Hegel." *International Philosophical Quarterly* 18 (1978): 289–310.
Pollard, Richard N., and Hazel M. Pollard. *From Human Sentience to Drama*. Athens: Ohio University Press, 1974. 10–79 (tragedy).
Pottle, Frederick A. "Catharsis." *Yale Review* 40 (1950): 621–41.
Prior, Moody E. *The Language of Tragedy*. New York: Columbia University Press, 1947.
Pütz, Peter. "Nietzsche: Art and Intellectual Inquiry." Pasley, *Nietzsche* 1–32.
Quinton, A. M. "Tragedy." *Proceedings of the Aristotelian Society* (supp. vol.) 34 (1960): 145–65. Rpt. in *Aesthetics and the Philosophy of Criticism*. Ed. Marvin Levich. New York: Random House, 1963. 185–203.
Rai, Alok. "The Idea of Tragedy." *Quest* 56 (1968): 38–40.
Raphael, D. D. *The Paradox of Tragedy*. Bloomington: Indiana University Press, 1960.
Rehder, Helmut. "Of Structure and Symbol: The Significance of Hegel's Phenomenology for Literary Criticism." *A Hegel Symposium*. Ed. D. C. Travis. Austin: University of Texas Press, 1962. 115–37.
Reid, B. L. *William Butler Yeats: The Lyric of Tragedy*. Norman: University of Oklahoma Press, 1961. 3–44.
Reiss, Timothy J. *Tragedy and Truth*. New Haven: Yale University Press, 1980.
Remes, Carol. "Walter Kaufmann and Some Problematics in the Definition of Tragedy." *Science and Society* 33 (1969): 340–47.
Rethy, Robert. "The Tragic Affirmation of the *Birth of Tragedy*." *Nietzsche Studien* 17 (1988): 1–44.
Reyburn, H. A., et al. *Nietzsche*. London: Macmillan, 1948. 119–47.
Richards, I. A. "The Imagination." *Principles of Literary Criticism*. London: Kegan Paul, 1924. 239–53.
Roberts, Patrick. *The Psychology of Tragic Drama*. London: Routledge and Kegan Paul, 1975.
Robson, John M. "Tragedy and Society." *Queen's Quarterly* 71 (1964): 419–33.
Rosenberg, Marvin. "Tragedy—Departures from Aristotelian Imitation." *Proceedings of the IVth Congress of the International Comparative Literature Association* 2: 730–36. Ed. François Yost. The Hague: Mouton, 1966.
Rosenstein, Leon. "Metaphysical Foundations of the Theories of Tragedy in Hegel and Nietzsche." *Journal of Aesthetics and Art Criticism* 28 (1970): 521–33.

Ruprecht, Louis A., Jr. *Tragic Posture and Tragic Vision*. New York: Continuum, 1994 (Hegel and Nietzsche).
Sallis, John. *Crossings: Nietzsche and the Space of Tragedy*. Chicago: University of Chicago Press, 1991.
———. "Dionysus—In Excess of Metaphysics." Krell and Wood, *Exceedingly Nietzsche* 3–12.
———. "The Play of Tragedy." *Tulane Studies in Philosophy* 19 (1970): 89–108.
Santayana, George. "Tragic Philosophy." 1936. *Literary Opinion in America* Ed. Morton Dauwen Zabel. New York: Harper, 1951.
Santoro, Liberato. "Hegel's Aesthetics and 'the End of Art'." *Philosophical Studies* 30 (1984): 62–72.
Saunders, Thomas. "Religion and Tragedy." *Dalhousie Review* 24 (1944): 283–97.
Schacht, Richard. "Nietzsche on Art in *The Birth of Tragedy*." *Aesthetics*. Ed. George Dickie and R. J. Sclafani. New York: St. Martin's, 1977. 269–313.
Schechner, Richard. "Approaches to Theory/Criticism." *Tulane Drama Review* 10 (Summer 1966): 20–53.
Scheler, Max. "On the Tragic." Trans. Bernard Stambler. *Cross Currents* 4 (1953): 178–91.
Schier, Flint. "The Claims of Tragedy." *Philosophical Papers* 18 (1989): 7–26.
Schipper, Edith Watson. "The Wisdom of Tragedy." *Journal of Aesthetics and Art Criticism* 24 (1965): 533–37.
Schlesinger, Alfred Cary. *Boundaries of Dionysus: Athenian Foundations for the Theory of Tragedy*. Cambridge: Harvard University Press, 1963.
———. "Can We Moderns Write Tragedy?" *Transactions of the American Philological Association* 77 (1946): 1–21.
———. "Tragedy and the Moral Frontier." *Transactions of the American Philological Association* 84 (1953): 164–75.
Schrade, Leo. *Tragedy in the Art of Music*. Cambridge: Harvard University Press, 1964.
Schwartz, Elias. "Detachment and Tragic Effect." *College English* 18 (1956): 153–56.
———. "The Possibilities of Christian Tragedy." *College English* 21 (1960): 208–13.
———. "The Problem of Literary Genres." *Criticism* 13 (1971): 113–30.
Scott, Nathan A., Jr., ed. *The Tragic Wisdom and the Christian Faith*. New York: Association, 1957.
Sefler, George F. "The Existential *vs.* the Absurd." *Journal of Aesthetics and Art Criticism* 32 (1974): 415–21 (Nietzsche).
Sewell, Richard B. "The Tragic Form." *Essays in Criticism* 4 (1954): 345–58.
———. "The Vision of Tragedy." *Review of Metaphysics* 10 (1956): 193–200.
———. *The Vision of Tragedy*. New Haven: Yale University Press, 1959.
Shapiro, Gary. "Hegel on Implicit and Dialectical Meanings of Poetry." Steinkraus and Schmitz, *Art and Logic* 35–54.
———. "Hegel's Dialectic of Artistic Meaning." *Journal of Aesthetics and Art Criticism* 35 (1976): 23–35.
Shearman, Hugh. *The Purpose of Tragedy*. Wheaton, Ill.: Theosophical Press, 1954.

Shoben, Edward Joseph, Jr. "A Clinical View of the Tragic." *Colorado Quarterly* 11 (1963): 352–63.
Shumaker, Wayne. "The Major Literary Types: Tragedy." *Literature and the Irrational*. Englewood Cliffs, N.J.: Prentice-Hall, 1960. 155–88.
Silk, M. S., and J. P. Stern. *Nietzsche on Tragedy*. Cambridge: Cambridge University Press, 1981.
Simon, Bennett. *Tragic Drama and the Family*. New Haven: Yale University Press, 1988.
Simon, Ulrich. *Pity and Terror: Christianity and Tragedy*. New York: St. Martin's Press, 1989.
Sleinis, E. E. "Aesthetic Values." *Nietzsche's Revaluation of Values*. Urbana: University of Illinois Press, 1994. 123–50.
Smart, John S. "Tragedy." *Essays and Studies* (Eng. Assoc., London) 8 (1922): 9–36.
Smith, John E. "Nietzsche: Conquest of the Tragic through Art." Scott, *Tragic Wisdom* 211–37.
Snyder, John. *Prospects of Power: Tragedy, Satire, the Essay, and the Theory of Genre*. Lexington: University Press of Kentucky, 1991.
Soll, Evan. "Pessimism and the Tragic View of Life: Reconsiderations of Nietzsche's *Birth of Tragedy*." *Reading Nietzsche*. Ed. Robert C. Solomon and Kathleen M. Higgins. New York: Oxford University Press, 1988.
Spanos, William V. "The Paradox of Anguish: Some Notes on Tragedy." *Journal of Aesthetics and Art Criticism* 24 (1966): 525–32.
Spears, Monroe K. *Dionysus and the City*. London: Oxford University Press, 1970 (Nietzsche).
Spivak, Charlotte K. "Tragedy and Comedy." *Bucknell Review* 9 (1960): 212–23.
Stace, W. T. *The Philosophy of Hegel*. London: Constable, 1924. 443–83.
Stambaugh, Joan. *Nietzsche's Thought of Eternal Return*. Baltimore: Johns Hopkins University Press, 1972.
Staten, Henry. "*The Birth of Tragedy* Reconstructed." *Studies in Romanticism* 29 (1990): 9–37. Rpt. in *Nietzsche's Voice*. Ithaca: Cornell University Press, 1990. 187–216.
States, Bert O. *Irony and Drama*. Ithaca: Cornell University Press, 1971.
Stein, Walter. *Criticism as Dialogue*. London: Cambridge University Press, 1969.
———. "Tragedy and the Absurd." *Dublin Review* 233 (1959): 363–82.
Steiner, George. *Antigones*. New York: Oxford University Press, 1984. 19–42 (Hegel).
———. *The Death of Tragedy*. New York: Knopf, 1961.
Steinhauer, H. "Pleasure Found in Witnessing a Tragedy." *Queens's Quarterly* 36 (1929): 470–81.
Steinkraus, Warren E., and Kenneth I. Schmitz, eds. *Art and Logic in Hegel's Philosophy*. Atlantic Highlands, N.J.: Humanities Press, 1980.
Sterling, M. C. "Recent Discussions of Eternal Recurrence." *Nietzsche Studien* 6 (1977): 261–91.
Stern, Alfred. "Tragedy and Human Value." *Personalist* 44 (1963): 164–74.
Stern, J. P. "Nietzsche and the Idea of Metaphor." Pasley, *Nietzsche* 64–82.

---. *A Study of Nietzsche.* Cambridge: Cambridge University Press, 1979. 171–201.

Stoll, Elmer Edgar. "The Tragic Fallacy, So-Called." *University of Toronto Quarterly* 5 (1935): 457–81.

Stolnitz, Jerome. "Notes on Comedy and Tragedy." *Philosophy and Phenomenological Research* 16 (1955): 45–60.

Stratman, Carl J. "Unpublished Dissertations in the History and Theory of Tragedy, 1889–1957." *Bulletin of Bibliography* 22 (1958–59): 161–64, 190–92, 214–16, 237–40; 23 (1960): 15–20, 162–65, 187–92.

Strong, Tracy B. "Aesthetic Authority and Tradition: Nietzsche and the Greeks." *History of European Ideas* 11 (1989): 989–1007.

---. "Nietzsche's Political Aesthetics." *Nietzsche's New Seas.* Chicago: University of Chicago Press, 1988. 153–74.

Symons, Arthur. "Nietzsche on Tragedy." *Academy* 63 (August 30, 1902): 220.

---. "Nietzsche on Tragedy." *Plays, Acting and Music.* New York: Dutton, 1909. 11–16.

Szondi, Peter. *On Textual Understanding and Other Essays.* Trans. Harvey Mendelsohn. Minneapolis: University of Minnesota Press, 1986. 43–56 (Hegel).

Tarvin, William L. "Tragic Closure and 'Tragic Calm'." *Modern Language Quarterly* 51 (1990): 5–24 (Hegel).

Taubes, Susan B. "The Nature of Tragedy." *Review of Metaphysics* 7 (1953): 193–206.

Terzakis, Angelos. *Homage to the Tragic Muse.* Trans. Athan H. Anagnostopoulos. Boston: Houghton Mifflin, 1978.

Thatcher, David S. *Nietzsche in England, 1890–1914.* Toronto: University of Toronto Press, 1970.

---. "A Scholar's Departure: Nietzsche's *Birth of Tragedy.*" *Malahat Review* 24 (1972): 30–44.

Thompson, Alan Reynolds. "Melodrama and Tragedy." *PMLA* 43 (1928): 810–35.

---. "Melodrama and Tragedy" and "The Dilemma of Modern Tragedy." *The Anatomy of Drama.* 2nd ed. Berkeley: University of California Press, 1946. 238–315.

Thorndike, Ashley H. *Tragedy.* Boston: Houghton Mifflin, 1908.

Traschen, Isadore. "The Elements of Tragedy." *Centennial Review* 6 (1962): 215–29.

Tree, Sir Herbert Beerbohm. "Humor in Tragedy." *English Review* 21 (1915): 353–74.

Tsanoff, Radoslav A. "Tragedy and Comedy." *Forum* (University of Houston) 3 (Fall 1960): 19–22.

Tymieniecka, Anna-Teresa, ed. *The Existential Coordinates of the Human Condition: Poetic-Epic-Tragic.* Dordrecht: Reidel, 1984.

Unamuno, Miguel de. *The Tragic Sense of Life.* 1913. Trans. J. E. Crawford Flitch. London: Macmillan, 1921.

Vaughan, C. E. *Types of Tragic Drama.* London: Macmillan, 1908.

Vernant, Jean-Pierre, and Pierre Vidal-Naquet. *Myth and Tragedy in Ancient Greece.* 1972, 1986. Trans. Janet Lloyd. New York: Zone, 1988.

Versényi, Laszlo. "Dionysus and Tragedy." *Review of Metaphysics* 16 (1962): 82–97.

Vivas, Eliseo. "Atrabilious Thoughts on a Theory of Tragedy." *Papers in Dramatic*

Theory and Criticism. Ed. David M. Knauf. Iowa City: University of Iowa Press, 1969. 9–23.

———. "The Substance of Tragedy." *The Artistic Transaction and Essays on the Theory of Literature.* Columbus: Ohio State University Press, 1963. 117–39.

Volkelt, Johannes. "The Philosophical Implications of Tragedy." Trans. Ludwig Lewisohn. *A Modern Book of Criticism.* New York: Modern Library, 1919. 55–59.

Wakeman, Mary K. "Dynamics of the Tragic Catharsis." *Literature and Psychology* 9 (1959): 39–41.

Waldek, Peter B. *Weighing Delight and Dole.* New York: Lang, 1989.

Warshow, Robert. "Film Chronicle: The Gangster as Tragic Hero." *Partisan Review* 15 (1948): 240–44.

Wasserman, E. R. "The Pleasures of Tragedy." *English Literary History* 14 (1947): 283–307.

Watson, Shawn. "Shakespeare's Problem Comedies: An Hegelian Approach to Genre." *Drama and Philosophy.* Ed. James Redmond. Cambridge: Cambridge University Press, 1990. 61–71.

Watt, Lauchlan Maclean. *Attic and Elizabethan Tragedy.* Port Washington, N.Y.: Kennikat, 1908.

Watts, Harold H. "Myth and Drama." *Cross Currents* 5 (1955): 154–70.

Weber, Carl J. "Tragedy and the Good Life." *Dalhousie Review* 25 (1945): 225–33.

Weinberg, Kurt. "Nietzsche's Paradox of Tragedy." *Yale French Studies* 38 (1967): 251–66.

Weisinger, Herbert. *Tragedy and the Paradox of the Fortunate Fall.* East Lansing: Michigan State University Press, 1953.

Weitz, Morris. "Tragedy." *The Opening Mind.* Chicago: University of Chicago Press, 1977. 91–104.

Wellek, René. "A. C. Bradley, Shakespeare, and the Infinite." *Philological Quarterly* 54 (1975): 85–103 (Hegel).

———. *A History of Modern Criticism, 1750–1950.* New Haven: Yale University Press, 1955, 1965. Vol. 2: 318–34 (Hegel); vol. 4: 336–56 (Nietzsche).

Wells, George A. *"The Birth of Tragedy." Trivium* 3 (1968): 59–75.

West, Elinor J. M. "Euripides' *Hippolytus* and Nietzsche's 'Death of Tragedy'." *Arethusa* 3 (1970): 23–47.

White, Alan. "Tragedy." *Within Nietzsche's Labyrinth.* New York: Routledge, 1990. 26–38.

White, Richard. "Art and the Individual in Nietzsche's *Birth of Tragedy.*" *British Journal of Aesthetics* 28 (1988): 59–67.

———. "The Individual and the Birth of Tragedy." *Nietzsche and the Problem of Sovereignty.* Urbana: University of Illinois Press, 1997. 54–77.

Whitmore, Charles Edward. "The Nature of Tragedy." *PMLA* 34 (1919): 341–45.

———. *The Supernatural in Tragedy.* Cambridge: Harvard University Press, 1915.

Wicks, Robert. "Hegel's Aesthetics." *The Cambridge Companion to Hegel.* Ed. Frederick C. Beiser. Cambridge: Cambridge University Press, 1993. 348–77.

———. *Hegel's Theory of Aesthetic Judgment.* New York: Lang, 1994.

Willet, Cynthia. "Hegel, Antigone, and the Possibility of Ecstatic Dialogue." *Philosophy and Literature* 14 (1990): 268–83.
Williams, Francis Howard. "The Tragic Touch." *Lippincott's* 74 (1904): 463–68.
Williams, Raymond. "A Dialogue on Tragedy." *New Left Review* 13 (January 1962): 22–35.
———. *Modern Tragedy*. London: Chatto and Windus, 1966.
———. "Tragic Resignation and Sacrifice." *Critical Quarterly* 5 (1963): 5–19.
Williams, Robert R. "Theology and Tragedy." *New Perspectives on Hegel's Philosophy of Religion*. Ed. David Kolb. Albany: State University of New York Press, 1992. 39–58.
Winfield, Richard Dien. "Rethinking the Particular Forms of Art." *Owl of Minerva* 24 (1993): 131–44 (Hegel).
———. *Stylistics*. Albany: State University of New York Press, 1996 (Hegel).
Worsfold, W. Basil. "The Motive of Tragedy." *Cornhill* ns 11 (1901): 490–501.
Yeats, William Butler. "The Tragic Theatre." *Mask* 3 (October 1910): 77–81. Rpt. in *Essays*. New York: Macmillan, 1924. 294–303.
Young, Julian. *Nietzsche's Philosophy of Art*. Cambridge: Cambridge University Press, 1992.
Zink, Sidney. "The Moral Effect of Art." *Ethics* 60 (1950): 261–74.

Plato and Aristotle on the Craft of Literature (Annotated)

This listing is limited to twentieth-century works published in English and concerned with the theories of poetic literature proposed by Plato and Aristotle, especially their ideas on imitation, Plato's rejection of poetry, and the relationship between Plato and the *Poetics*. Included also are essays about Plato as aesthete, aesthetician, mythmaker, or tragedian. The voluminous commentary on Aristotle's concepts of tragic error, reversal, recognition, and catharsis has been indexed elsewhere.

Adkins, Arthur W. H. "Aristotle and the Best Kind of Tragedy." *Classical Quarterly* 16 (1966): 78–102. "*Poetics* 13 has really no relevance at all to . . . extant Greek tragedy."
Adler, Mortimer J. *Poetry and Politics*. Revision of *Art and Prudence*, 1937. Pittsburgh: Duquesne University Press, 1965. 1–51. Aristotle and Plato offer radically different solutions to the question "Of what practical use is art in the state?"
Annas, Julia. *An Introduction to Plato's Republic*. Oxford: Clarendon Press, 1981. 335–44. "So the poet as imitator is the person who neither makes nor uses what he is talking about, not the person who has no grasp of a Form."
Anton, John P. "Tragic Vision and Philosophic *Theoria* in Classical Greece." *Philosophy and the Civilizing Arts*. Ed. Craig Walton and John P. Anton. Athens, O.: Ohio University Press, 1974. 1–23. "Plato became convinced that philosophy could supplant tragedy not only by taking over its sweeping themes . . . but also by showing how mimesis and catharsis . . . take on greater significance when treated in the light of the new method, the dialectic."

Ardley, Gavin. "Plato as Tragedian." *Philosophical Studies* (Ireland) 12 (1963): 7–24. Plato was sympathetic to the concerns of tragedy.

Atkins, J. W. H. *Literary Criticism in Antiquity*. 1934. New York: Smith, 1952. Vol. 1: 33–119. Plato, favoring rational interrogation, distrusted the poets' aphoristic approach to truth.

Barish, Jonas. *The Antitheatrical Prejudice*. Berkeley: University of California Press, 1981. 5–37. "Platonic attitudes toward art form a complex of negative injunctions. . . . Whatever tends to widen the individual's range . . . imperils the stability of the social order."

Battin, M. Pabst. "Aristotle's Definition of Tragedy in the *Poetics*." *Journal of Aesthetics and Art Criticism* 33 (1974–75): 155–70, 293–302. "The definition does not correspond precisely to the classification upon which it is based."

Beardsley, Monroe C. *Aesthetics from Classical Greece to the Present*. New York: Macmillan, 1966. 30–68. A general review of Plato's and Aristotle's views on beauty and the arts.

Belfiore, Elizabeth. "Plato's Greatest Accusation against Poetry." *New Essays on Plato*. Ed. Francis Jeffry Pelletier and John King-Farlow. Guelph, Ont.: Canadian Assoc. for Publishing in Philosophy, 1983. 39–62. "The poet does not merely give us false beliefs, as a sophist does, he attacks the very order of the soul."

———. "A Theory of Imitation in Plato's *Republic*." *Transactions of the American Philological Association* 114 (1984): 121–46. "Plato maintains a clear and consistent view of the relationships and distinctions among the visual and poetic imitative arts."

———. *Tragic Pleasures: Aristotle on Plot and Emotion*. Princeton: Princeton University Press, 1992. 44–70. Summary and analysis of Aristotle on *mimesis*.

Bosanquet, Bernard. *A History of Aesthetic*. 2nd ed. London: Allen and Unwin, 1904. 16–76. Plato implies the possibility of an allegorical, expressive function in art; Aristotle's position on imitation was similar.

Boyd, John D. *The Function of Mimesis and Its Decline*. Cambridge: Harvard University Press, 1968. *Mimesis* has been interpreted as cognitive, structural, or stylistic: "in making what is imitative in poetry essentially a structural concept, Aristotle turned the notion of *mimesis* in a fresh and new direction."

Brownson, Carleton Lewis. *Plato's Studies and Criticisms of the Poets*. Boston: Badger, 1920. An exhaustive, intelligent survey of Plato's references to and criticisms of poetry.

Butcher, S. H. *Aristotle's Theory of Poetry and Fine Art*. 1895. 4th ed. London: Macmillan, 1907. For Aristotle, art represents a union of the particular and universal. An influential, now dated, commentary.

Bywater, Ingram. *Aristotle on the Art of Poetry*. Rev. ed. Oxford: Clarendon Press, 1909. Rivaled Butcher's translation and commentary for definitive status at the turn of the century.

Cameron, Alister. *Plato's Affair with Tragedy*. Cincinnati: University of Cincinnati, 1978. Plato was himself a great tragic poet.

Castellani, Victor. "Drama and Aristotle." *Drama and Philosophy*. Ed. James Redmond. Cambridge: Cambridge University Press, 1990. 21–36. "Very many of the ethical, personal data that Aristotle used, both the things and the names for them, came from dramatic types, and especially from comedy."

Cavarnos, Constantine. "Plato's Teaching on Fine Art." *Philosophy and Phenomenological Research* 13 (1953): 487–98. Plato condemns only "pseudo art," not "true art."

Collingwood, R. G. "Plato's Philosophy of Art." *Mind* 34 (1925): 154–72. Poetry, according to Plato, can be valuable even though its imitations are inferior products.

———. *The Principles of Art*. Oxford: Clarendon Press, 1938. 42–56. Plato banished only "representational" (imitative and amusement-oriented) poetry.

Cornford, F. M. *Principium Sapientiae: The Origins of Greek Philosophical Thought*. Cambridge University Press, 1952. The "quarrel between philosophy and poetry" cited in the *Republic* represents a splitting apart of functions originally unified by ancient wisdom figures.

Cross, R. C., and A. D. Woozley. *Plato's Republic*. New York: St. Martin's, 1964. 270–88. Repeats the position argued by Tate (q.v.) that Plato attacked only *inferior* poetry.

Daiches, David. *Critical Approaches to Literature*. Englewood Cliffs, N.J.: Prentice-Hall, 1956. 3–49. On Aristotle's "solution" to the dilemma in which Plato placed the arts.

Demos, Raphael. *The Philosophy of Plato*. New York: Scribner's, 1939. 197–252. The best art, in Plato's opinion, may "represent a definite achievement of value."

Dewey, Ernest W. "Aristotle's Aesthetics: A Fulfillment of the Platonic Position." *Darshana Quarterly* 6 (1966): 75–84. Aristotle, like Plato, placed a high value on the "esthetic experience."

Dorter, Kenneth. "The *Ion:* Plato's Characterization of Art." *Journal of Aesthetics and Art Criticism* 32 (1973): 65–78. *Ion* gives to Plato's ideas "a unity, completeness, and unbiased perspective that is not found elsewhere."

Downer, Alan S., ed. *English Institute Essays 1951*. New York: Columbia University Press, 1952. Essays on the *Poetics* and its relevance to modern criticism by Elder Olson (q.v.), Philip Wheelwright (q.v.), and others.

Dyson, M. "Poetic Imitation in Plato *Republic* 3." *Antichthon* 22 (1988): 42–53. Plato's criteria for proper literature are most relevant to "corrected epic."

Eden, Kathy. *Poetic and Legal Fiction in the Aristotelian Tradition*. Princeton: Princeton University Press, 1986. "It is Aristotle who first formulates the logical and psychological arguments in poetry's defense."

Edmundson, Mark. "An Ancient Quarrel." *Literature against Philosophy, Plato to Derrida*. Cambridge: Cambridge University Press, 1995. 1–17. "If the proposed analogy between Plato's critique of poetry and current critical practices suggests anything, it is never to underestimate the hostility that literary critics may nurse toward literature."

Elias, Julius A. *Plato's Defense of Poetry*. Albany: State University of New York Press, 1984. Plato the poet and mythmaker did not condemn poetry; in fact, "every system proposed must contain some terms that are primitive, undemonstrable, asserted on faith, [and show] . . . a touch of the poet."

Else, Gerald F. *Aristotle's Poetics: The Argument*. Cambridge: Harvard University Press, 1963. A structuralist approach: art offers a way of "making" governed by the principles operative in natural processes.

———. "'Imitation' in the Fifth Century." *Classical Philology* 53 (1958): 73–90. Attacks Hermann Koller, *Die mimesis in der antike* (Berne, 1954), on the etymology of *mimesis:* the term originally meant "miming" with body and voice, later referred to painting and sculpture.

———. *Plato and Aristotle on Poetry*. Ed. Peter Burian. Chapel Hill: University of North Carolina Press, 1986. "Plato's treatment of poetry in the *Republic* . . . was incomplete and unsatisfactory." Aristotle saw "the poem as a construct and the poet as a constructor. This runs squarely counter to Plato's deepest intuition . . . that poetry is a communication from one soul to another."

Ferrari, G. R. F. "Plato and Poetry." Kennedy, *Cambridge History of Literary Criticism* 1: 92–148. "'Theatricality' is a major target of Plato's hostility."

Freeman, Kathleen. "Plato: The Use of Inspiration." *Greece and Rome* 9 (1940): 137–49. A critique of Plato's doctrine of inspiration in the *Ion*.

Friedlander, Paul. *Plato*. Trans. Hans Meyerhoff. Princeton: Princeton University Press, 1969. Vol. 3: 75–79, 85–87, 132–33. Brief references to Plato's comments on the arts.

Gadamer, Hans-Georg. "Plato and the Poets." Trans. P. Christopher Smith. *Dialogue and Dialectic*. New Haven: Yale University Press, 1980. 39–72. "Plato's censorship of poetry seems to betray the moralistic bias of an intellectual purist."

Gassner, John. Introduction: "Aristotelian Literary Criticism." *Aristotle's Theory of Poetry and Fine Art*. By S. H. Butcher. New York: Dover, 1951. xxxvii–lxxi. Aristotle was an antimoralistic reformer of Plato's dogmas on the arts: he replaced the idea of imitation as literal copying with the concept of an idealized symbolism.

Gellrich, Michelle. *Tragedy and Theory*. Princeton: Princeton University Press, 1988. 94–162. Original comments relating the *Poetics* to Plato's views: Aristotle "not only provides an alternative . . . but implicitly excludes consideration of issues that troubled Plato and that cluster around the dramatization of conflict and crisis."

Gilbert, Allan H. "Did Plato Banish the Poets?" *Medieval and Renaissance Studies* 2 (1968): 35–55. It was not Plato but Socrates, a fictional persona, who rejected the poets.

———. "Did Plato Banish the Poets or the Critics?" *Studies in Philology* 36 (1939): 1–19. Plato outlawed not poets but rather the ignorant *critics* of poetry.

Gilbert, Katharine Everett. "Aesthetic Imitation and Imitators in Aristotle." *Philosophical Review* 45 (1936): 558–73. An earlier version of the chapter on Aristotle in *A History of Esthetics* (q.v.).

———. "The Relation of the Moral to the Aesthetic Standard in Plato." *Philosophical Review* 43 (1934): 279–94. For Plato, moral standards such as honesty and benevolence dictate aesthetic standards such as clarity and simplicity.

Gilbert, Katharine Everett, and Helmut Kuhn. *A History of Esthetics*. Rev. ed. Bloomington: Indiana University Press, 1953. 19–86. An excellent survey. According to Plato, artists have no monopoly on beauty; on the contrary, the philosopher is better able to envision it. Aristotle's "approach to art was the biologist's": he studied its natural origins and functions.

Gill, Christopher. "Plato on Falsehood—not Fiction." *Lies and Fiction in the Ancient World*. Ed. Christopher Gill and T. P. Wiseman. Austin: University of Texas Press, 1993. 38–87. "The distinction between factual and fictional discourse, which is familiar to us, has no obvious equivalent in Plato's framework."

Givens, Terryl L. "Aristotle's Critique of Mimesis: The Romantic Prelude." *Comparative Literature Studies* 28 (1991): 121–36. "Aristotle confirms that imitation is inessential as a characteristic of art ... [which] is freed from any ... reference to an external model." Art does, however, embody nonmaterial models.

Golden, Leon. *Aristotle on Tragic and Comic "Mimesis."* Atlanta: Scholars Press, 1992. "While Aristotle adopted Plato's view of the power of *mimesis* to illuminate ultimate reality, he expanded the role of art well beyond the narrow limits allowed by Plato's strictly applied moral vision."

———. "Mimesis and Catharsis." *Classical Philology* 64 (1969): 145–53. For both Plato and Aristotle the concepts of mimesis and catharsis are closely related; in fact, the first brings about the second and produces "an important learning experience."

———. "Plato's Concept of *Mimesis*." *British Journal of Aesthetics* 15 (1975): 118–31. "Plato actually believed that art ... 'can reveal something of the reality behind the shadow'."

———. "Toward a Definition of Tragedy." *Classical Journal* 72 (1976): 21–33. This essay "suggests a way of expanding the Aristotelian definition of tragedy so that it effectively illuminates both high and pathetic tragedy."

Goldstein, Harvey D. "Mimesis and Catharsis Reexamined." *Journal of Aesthetics and Art Criticism* 24 (1966): 567–77. For Aristotle mimetic art duplicates nature's creative "mode of making," a principle of structural organization. Follows Else (q.v.).

Gomme, A. W. *The Greek Attitude to Poetry and History*. Berkeley: University of California Press, 1954. 49–72. Neither Plato nor Aristotle took "imitation" to denote the making of exact copies.

Gould, Thomas. *The Ancient Quarrel between Poetry and Philosophy*. Princeton: Princeton University Press, 1990. A thorough analysis of the idea of pathos, unmerited and catastrophic suffering: Plato understood it more accurately than Aristotle, which made him deny it as "counterrational."

———. "The Innocence of Oedipus: The Philosophers on *Oedipus the King*." *Arion* 4 (1965): 363–86, 582–611; 5 (1966): 478–525. In order to reconcile his acceptance of tragedy with Plato's rejection, Aristotle mistakenly proposed that the protagonist's fall must be brought about by some imperfection of character; but Oedipus, at least, is blameless. An ingenious, controversial argument.

———. "Plato's Hostility to Art." *Arion* 3 (1964): 70–91. Rejects scholarly "attempts to reduce the harshness of Plato's questioning of art and literature": Plato *was* hostile to art.

Greene, William C. "The Greek Criticism of Poetry." *Perspectives of Criticism*. Ed. Harry Levin. Cambridge: Harvard University Press, 1950. 19–54. Because perfect poetry is inconceivable, Plato decided to accept imperfect products so long as they were regulated by the proper authorities.

———. "Plato's View of Poetry." *Harvard Studies in Classical Philology* 29 (1918): 1–75. Plato sets up different standards for the arts in the differing contexts of his dialogues; in general, the artist strives to realize the ideal through a sensuous dialectic. An excellent discussion of Plato's ideas on beauty in all relevant dialogues.

Grey, D. R. "Art in the *Republic*." *Philosophy* 27 (1952): 291–310. Plato inconsistently adopted both a "mimetic and an educative theory of art."

Griswold, Charles. "The Ideas and the Criticism of Poetry in Plato's *Republic*, Book 10." *Journal of the History of Philosophy* 19 (1981): 135–50. "Socrates' criticism of the imitative poets is also a caricature of their imitations."

Grube, G. M. A. *The Greek and Roman Critics*. London: Methuen, 1965. 46–102. A clear, thorough exposition of the major passages in Plato and Aristotle dealing with art.

———. "Plato's Theory of Beauty." *Monist* 37 (1927): 269–88. "As Plato grew older, his appreciation of art—by which he especially means poetry and music—declined."

———. *Plato's Thought*. London: Methuen, 1935. 179–215. Plato condemned the practice of art, but he praised art as it might be; he conceived poetic models composed of "the particular phenomena of the world of sense."

Hagberg, Garry. "Aristotle's *Mimesis* and Abstract Art." *Philosophy* 59 (1984): 365–71. "Non-representational art [does not] constitute a refutation of any theory of art based upon *mimesis* or imitation."

Halliwell, Stephen. *Aristotle's* Poetics. London: Duckworth: 1986. 109–37, 331–36. Of the five categories of imitation— visual (image-making), behavioral, impersonation, vocal, and metaphysical—Aristotle emphasized image-making and impersonation.

———. "Aristotle's *Poetics*." Kennedy, *Cambridge History of Literary Criticism* 1: 149–83. For Aristotle, "mimesis defines the poems themselves not in terms of an inward relation to the poet's mind, but as the (preferably dramatic) representation of patterns of positive reality." A sensible treatment of the subject.

———. "The Importance of Plato and Aristotle for Aesthetics." *Proceedings of the Boston Area Colloquium in Ancient Philosophy* 5 (1991): 321–48. "What Aristotle offers is an appraisal of the relation between 'technical,' inherent matters of art and . . . truth and goodness."

———. "Plato and Aristotle on the Denial of Tragedy." *Proceedings of the Cambridge Philological Society* 210 (1984): 49–71. The author points to "the fundamental difference between tragedy and [both] philosophers' ethical systems, for tragedy typically pictured a world in which the relation of virtue to happiness is far from secure."

Hardison, O. B., Jr. *Aristotle's* Poetics. Englewood Cliffs, N.J.: Prentice-Hall, 1968. 281–96. In contrast to Plato's view of imitation as copying an original model, Aristotle believed that poetic narratives "universalize" history and nature.

Harriott, Rosemary. *Poetry and Criticism before Plato*. London: Methuen, 1969.

78–91. Plato presented a new concept of inspiration in his traditional language and imagery.

Havelock, Eric A. *Preface to Plato.* Cambridge: Harvard University Press, 1963. A stimulating treatment of Plato's rejection of poetry in light of an attack conducted by literate Greek rationalists against the oral tradition of Homer and other "image-thinkers."

Hight, George Ainslie. "Plato and the Poets." *Mind* 47 (1922): 195–99. Plato condemned only "debased art" and uncouth realism; in any case, "we must not unduly press consistency upon Plato."

House, Humphrey. *Aristotle's* Poetics. London: Hart-Davis, 1956. 112–25. Discusses Aristotle's emphasis on the formal principles of tragedy as a corrective to the misguided Plato.

Ingarden, Roman. "A Marginal Commentary on Aristotle's *Poetics.*" Trans. Helen R. Michejda. *Journal of Aesthetics and Art Criticism* 20 (1961): 163–74, 273–85. For Aristotle imitation denotes the creation of a plausible *illusion,* one that does not necessarily correspond in all respects to reality.

Jaeger, Werner. *Paideia: The Ideals of Greek Culture.* Trans. Gilbert Highet. New York: Oxford University Press, 1943. Vol. 2: 211–30, 358–65. Plato's hostility to poetry follows from his role as reformer of traditional Greek education.

Janaway, Christopher. *Images of Excellence: Plato's Critique of the Arts.* Oxford: Clarendon Press, 1995. "The truth is that Plato wanders in his descriptions of the poetry he criticizes. Sometimes it is 'all poetry,' sometimes Homer and the tragedians, sometimes something called 'mimetic poetry,' sometimes the kind of poetry whose aim is pleasure."

Jones, John. *On Aristotle and Greek Tragedy.* New York: Oxford University Press, 1962. 11–62. "When . . . Aristotle came to reject the heaven of real forms, . . . he formulated in its place a principle of indwelling form."

Kaufmann, Walter. *Tragedy and Philosophy.* Garden City, N.Y.: Doubleday, 1968. 1–74. *Both* Plato and Aristotle failed to understand the spiritual significance of tragedy!

Kennedy, George A., ed. *The Cambridge History of Literary Criticism.* Cambridge: Cambridge University Press, 1989. Volume 1 contains essays on Plato and Aristotle.

Keuls, Eva C. *Plato and Greek Painting.* Leiden, The Netherlands: Brill, 1978. 9–32. Plato found no "feud" between philosophy and painting: "the true target in *Republic* 10 is poetry."

Kirby, John T. "Mimesis and Diegesis: Foundations of Aesthetic Theory in Plato and Aristotle." *Helios* 18.2 (1991): 113–28. "We must adopt . . . modes of diegesis (narrative) in order to appropriate mimesis mentally."

Kosman, L. A. "Silence and Imitation in the Platonic Dialogues." *Oxford Studies in Ancient Philosophy,* Supp. vol. (1992): 73–92. "Despite Socrates' profession of the preferability of narration to *mimesis* there is no authorial, no non- mimetic narrative voice [in the *Republic*]. . . . All the dialogues are mimetic or imitative."

Kuhn, Helmut. "The True Tragedy: On the Relationship between Greek Tragedy and Plato." *Harvard Studies in Classical Philology* 52 (1941): 1–40; 53 (1942): 37–88. Extensive correspondences between the dialogues and the tragedies.
LaDrière, Craig. "The Problem of Plato's *Ion*." *Journal of Aesthetics and Art Criticism* 10 (1951): 26–34. "The problem of the *Ion* is not poetry, and not the recitation of poetry, but the criticism of poetry as Ion practises it."
Levinson, Ronald B. *In Defense of Plato*. Cambridge: Harvard University Press, 1953. 26–37. Plato's creation of Socrates as a character is a literary masterpiece.
Lodge, Rupert C. *Plato's Theory of Art*. New York: Humanities Press, 1953. A thoughtful but overelaborate explanation of the origins of each philosophical tendency in Plato's theory of art.
Lucas, F. L. *Tragedy and Serious Drama in Relation to Aristotle's* Poetics. London: Hogarth, 1927. "Tragedy is simply one fruit of the human instinct to tell stories, to reproduce and recast experience."
Maguire, Joseph P. "Beauty and the Fine Arts in Plato." *Harvard Studies in Classical Philology* 70 (1966): 171–93. On the consequences of Plato's conclusion that "art has a . . . pedagogical function of suggesting Ideas."
———. "The Differentiation of Art in Plato's Aesthetics." *Harvard Studies in Classical Philology* 68 (1964): 389–410. For Plato the uniqueness of the artwork as an imitation lies in the representation of "moral Ideas for a pedagogical purpose."
McGahey, Robert. *The Orphic Moment*. Albany: State University of New York Press, 1994. 27–49. Though he banned the poets, Plato himself was a great intuitive poet, listening through Socrates to the music of his inner self.
McKeon, Richard. "Literary Criticism and the Concept of Imitation in Antiquity." *Modern Philology* 34 (1936): 1–35. Plato gives *imitation* an expandable definition; Aristotle limits the term to a single application.
McMahon, A. Philip. *Preface to an American Philosophy of Art*. Chicago: University of Chicago Press, 1945. 106–16, 135–48. Elementary facts about the views of Plato and Aristotle on the arts.
Moravcsik, Julius. "On Correcting the Poets." *Oxford Studies in Ancient Philosophy* 4 (1986): 35–47. "Plato is right in claiming that the poets can be corrected on matters of human nature and agency."
Moravcsik, Julius, and Philip Temko, eds. *Plato on Beauty, Wisdom and the Arts*. Totowa, N.J.: Rowman and Littlefield, 1982. Relevant essays by Julia Annas, "Plato on the Triviality of Literature," 1–28; Julius Moravcsik, "Noetic Inspiration and Artistic Inspiration," 29–46; Alexanger Nehamas, "Plato on Imitation and Poetry in *Republic* 10," 47–78; Martha Craven Nussbaum, "'This Story Isn't True': Poetry, Goodness, and Understanding in Plato's *Phaedrus*," 79–124; James O. Urmson, "Plato and the Poets," 125–36; and Paul Woodruff, "What Could Go Wrong with Inspiration? Why Plato's Poets Fail," 137–50.
Moss, Leonard. "Plato and the *Poetics*." *Philological Quarterly* 50 (1971): 533–42. Despite important differences, Plato and Aristotle are intimately related on the subject of imitation.

Mueller, Gustav E. *Plato: The Founder of Philosophy as Dialectic*. New York: Philosophical Library, 1965. 140–57. Plato did not exclude art from the state; the true artist, however, must lead a "responsible life."

Murdoch, Iris. *The Fire and the Sun: Why Plato Banished the Artists*. Oxford: Oxford University Press, 1977. "Beauty as a spiritual agent, in Plato, excludes art."

Murphy, N. R. *The Interpretation of Plato's Republic*. Oxford: Clarendon Press, 1951. 224–37. Plato held beauty to be a cardinal value but did not believe that poetry could achieve it.

Murray, Penelope. Introduction. *Plato on Poetry*. Cambridge: Cambridge University Press, 1996. 1–32. Brief comments on imitation and other salient points.

Nahm, Milton C. *Aesthetic Experience and Its Presuppositions*. New York: Harper, 1946. 5–36, 89–119, 280–314. Plato pointed out that the limitations of art interfered with its goals; for Aristotle, catharsis "resolved the antimony."

Nehamas, Alexander. "Plato and the Mass Media." *The Monist* 71 (1988): 214–34. Plato's "attack on poetry is better understood as a specific social and historical gesture than as an attack on poetry."

Nettleship, Richard Lewis. *Lectures on the Republic of Plato*. 2nd ed. Ed. Godfrey R. Benson. London: Macmillan, 1901. 77–123, 340–54. Summary of Plato's views on the arts.

Nolte, Fred O. "Imitation as an Aesthetic Norm." *Studies in Honor of Frederick W. Shipley*. St. Louis: Washington University Press, 1942. 289–301. "Whereas Aristotle rationalizes beauty, Plato beautifies reason."

Oates, Whitney J. *Plato's View of Art*. New York: Scribner's, 1972. "The creative artist must . . . become a 'mystico-philosophical' creative artist."

Olson, Elder, ed. *Aristotle's* Poetics *and English Literature*. Chicago: University of Chicago Press, 1965. Fourteen essays on the *Poetics* and its reception.

———. "The Poetic Method of Aristotle." In Downer, *English Institute Essays: 1951*. 70–94. "The method of the *Poetics* is precisely the method of productive science or art as Aristotle conceives it."

Osborne, Catherine. "The Repudiation of Representation in Plato's *Republic* and Its Repercussions." *Proceedings of the Cambridge Philological Society* 213 (1987): 52–73. "Plato was right to see art as dangerous and influential."

Oudemans, T. C. W. and A. P. M. H. Lardinois. *Tragic Ambiguity*. Leiden, The Netherlands: Brill, 1987. 206–15. "Plato refers to tragic persons not only as being in contradiction with themselves but as being many-coloured, diversified, double-edged as well. Such self-contradictory and ambiguous people are dangerous."

Pappas, Nickolas. "The *Poetics'* Argument against Plato." *Southern Journal of Philosophy* 30.1 (1992): 83–100. In the *Poetics*, "plot is meant to show the cognitive value of tragedy, against Plato's charge of its irrationality."

Partee, Morriss Henry. "Inspiration in the Aesthetics of Plato." *Journal of Aesthetics and Art Criticism* 30 (1971): 87–95. Plato's attitude toward inspiration in the *Ion* justifies the enjoyment of poetry, but the inspired poet has no real knowledge.

———. "Plato's Banishment of Poetry." *Journal of Aesthetics and Art Criticism* 29

(1970): 209–22. Plato's attack on the poets "is consistent with his attack on empty rhetoric and misguided literary criticism."

———. *Plato's Poetics.* Salt Lake City: University of Utah Press, 1981. Plato "could not . . . treat poetry as a thing irrelevant to truth and to human excellence. . . . He forces us to seek [that relevance] in his partial statements."

Patterson, Richard. "The Platonic Art of Comedy and Tragedy." *Philosophy and Literature* 6 (1982): 76–93. In *Laws, Philebus,* and *Symposium,* Plato defines tragedy both positively (as educative) and negatively (as deluded).

Peltz, Richard. "Classification and Evaluation in Aesthetics: Weitz and Aristotle." *Journal of Aesthetics and Art Criticism* 30 (1971): 69–78. "Aristotle treats evaluation as classfication."

Philip, J. A. "Mimesis in the *Sophistês* of Plato." *Transactions and Proceedings of the American Philological Association* 92 (1961): 453–68. In the *Sophist* Plato distinguishes between two kinds of imitation—artistic craftsmanship and acting (impersonation).

Pitcher, Seymour M. "The Concepts of Originality and Imitation in Plato and Aristotle." *Proceedings of the Fourth Congress of the International Comparative Literature Association.* The Hague: Mouton, 1966. Vol. 2: 721–29. Actors experience a "loss of selfhood" during their imitative performance.

Potts, L. J. *Aristotle on the Art of Fiction.* Cambridge: Cambridge University Press, 1953. 1–15, 62–87. "Poetry is a species of imitation, and the myth (rather than character or language) is the essence of tragedy."

Preminger, Alex, ed. *Encyclopedia of Poetry and Poetics.* Princeton: Princeton University Press, 1965. Two entries—"Imitation," by Gerald F. Else, 378–81, and "Conceptions of Poetics," by G. N. G. Orsini, 636–39—illustrate the diversity of opinion on the term *imitation*. Orsini disagrees with those who, like Else, believe that Aristotle saw "the poem as a self-developing organism governed by its own principles."

Preston, Raymond. "Aristotle and the Modern Literary Critic." *Journal of Aesthetics and Art Criticism* 21 (1962): 57–71. The *Poetics* should be read in the context of other writings by Aristotle that relate poetry to psychology, ethics, education, and metaphysics.

Randall, John Herman, Jr. *Aristotle.* New York: Columbia University Press, 1960. 272–93. Art realizes potentials inherent in nature, especially "nature's productive activities."

———. "Plato as the Philosopher of the Aesthetic Experience." *American Scholar* 37 (1968): 502–11. Revised in *Plato: Dramatist of the Life of Reason.* New York: Columbia University Press, 1970. 122–45. Refutes popular misconceptions of Plato's attitude toward beauty and the arts: Plato possessed an artistic imagination.

Ransom, John Crow. "The Mimetic Principle." *The World's Body.* New York: Scribner's, 1938. 193–211. Rebuts Bosanquet (q.v.) and Butcher (q.v.), who find a "concrete universal" in the *Poetics*.

Rau, Catherine. *Art and Society: A Reinterpretation of Plato.* New York: Smith, 1951. Interprets Plato as an apologist for didactic art.

Ritter, Constantine. *The Essence of Plato's Philosophy.* Trans. Adam Alles. London: Allen and Unwin, 1933. 357–69. Summarizes Plato's "philosophy of art."

Robinson, Richard. *Plato's Earlier Dialectic.* 2nd ed. Oxford: Clarendon Press, 1953. 218–22. Plato is generally negative on the subject of images and imitation.

Rorty, Amélie Oksenberg, ed. *Essays on Aristotle's* Poetics. Princeton: Princeton University Press, 1992. Contains twenty-one essays.

Rosen, Stanley. *The Quarrel between Philosophy and Poetry.* New York: Routledge, 1988. 1–26. For Plato "the philosophical investigation of the good life is much more like poetry than it is like mathematics."

Rucker, Darnell. "Plato and the Poets." *Journal of Aesthetics and Art Criticism* 25 (1967): 167–70. "Plato does not denigrate art as such—only art . . . which claims to be more than it is."

Saintsbury, George. "Aristotle." *A History of Criticism.* Edinburgh: Blackwood, 1900. Vol. 1: 29–59. A summary and critique of the *Poetics* and the *Rhetoric.*

Salkever, Stephen G. "Tragedy and the Education of the *Demos:* Aristotle's Response to Plato." *Greek Tragedy and Political Theory.* Ed. J. Peter Euben. Berkeley: University of California Press, 1986. 274–303. "Whereas Plato holds that the many as such are not open to the sort of persuasion at which good laws and education aim," for Aristotle "the tragic art is crucial to the successful actualization of a good democracy."

Saxonhouse, Arlene W. *Fear of Diversity.* Chicago: University of Chicago Press, 1992. 132–46. "Socratic censorship becomes a countermodel to the multiplicity . . . to which the Platonic dialogue drives us."

Schaper, Eva. *Prelude to Aesthetics.* London: Allen and Unwin, 1968. 20–118. "Aristotle like Plato thinks that there is a fundamental distinction between artistic creation and discursive reasoning, . . . [but he] does not therefore hold that the non-theoretical must belong to the irrational."

Schipper, Edith Watson. "*Mimesis* in the Arts in Plato's *Laws.*" *Journal of Aesthetics and Art Criticism* 22 (1963): 199–202. *Mimesis* in *Laws* refers not to the literal representation of appearances but to the "rightness inherent in the [art] work."

Sikes, E. E. *The Greek View of Poetry.* London: Methuen, 1931. A very general survey.

Simpson, Peter. "Aristotle on Poetry and Imitation." *Hermes* 116 (1988): 279–91. "Actions and the imitations of actions are somehow primary for all poetry, not just dramatic and narrative kinds."

Skillen, Anthony. "Fiction Year Zero: Plato's *Republic.*" *British Journal of Aesthetics* 32 (1992): 201–8. "It is in relation to truth that, like other rhetorical practices, art is to be judged."

Sorbom, Goran. *Mimesis and Art.* Stockholm: Bonniers, 1966. An inventory of usage of the term in Greek writing.

Steven, R. G. "Plato and the Art of his Time." *Classical Quarterly* 27 (1933): 149–55. Plato's "philosophy compelled him to condemn [painting] utterly."

Stewart, J. A. *The Myths of Plato*. London: Macmillan, 1905. Plato as mythmaker—a literary as well as philosophical genius.

Stockton, David. "Plato's Quarrel with the Poets." *Durham University Journal* 14 (1952): 64–70. Plato's criticism was directed against poetry only and did not involve other art forms.

Tarrant, Dorothy. "Plato as Dramatist." *Journal of Hellenic Studies* 75 (1955): 82–89. Plato entertains subjects and techniques usually considered to be theatrical.

Tatarkiewicz, Wladyslaw. *History of Aesthetics*. The Hague: Mouton, 1970. Vol. 1: 112–27, 138–55. Imitation for Plato was merely copying appearances; Aristotle, following the Pythagoreans, added to this the expression of inner character, and following the Hedonists he saw art giving pleasure.

Tate, J. "'Imitation' in Plato's *Republic*." *Classical Quarterly* 22 (1928): 16–23. In *Republic* 10 Plato excludes only bad poets, who imitate appearances rather than realities.

———. "Plato and Allegorical Interpretation." *Classical Quarterly* 23 (1929): 142–54. Plato placed little trust in myths, which often were false, ugly, and obscure.

———. "Plato and 'Imitation'." *Classical Quarterly* 26 (1932): 161–69. Plato did not contradict himself in the *Republic*; he ejected only *bad* poets.

Trench, W. F. "Mimesis in Aristotle's Poetics." *Hermathena* 48 (1933): 1–24. For Aristotle, *mimesis* denotes a mathematical-organizational-formal principle, one that refers to artistic process, not content.

Trimpi, Wesley. *Muses of One Mind*. Princeton: Princeton University Press, 1983. "At its best [as in the *Poetics*], literary theory articulates the ways to achieve and maintain the delicate balance between the cognitive, the judicative, and the formal intentions of literature." Cf. Boyd, *Function of Mimesis*.

Urmson, James O. "Plato and the Poets." *Plato's* Republic. Ed. Richard Kraut. Lanham, Md.: Rowman and Littlefield, 1997. 223–34. "So far from Plato's charges being obsolete, they are directed against a view of serious imaginative literature that is still very common in modern times."

Valency, Maurice. "The Poetics." *Tragedy*. New York: New Amsterdam Press, 1991. 49–122. Summarizes Aristotle's work.

Verdenius, W. J. *Mimesis: Plato's Doctrine of Artistic Imitation*. Leiden, The Netherlands: Brill, 1962. Good art, according to Plato, "refers to an ideal pattern of beauty."

Warry, J. G. *Greek Aesthetic Theory*. London: Methuen, 1962. 52–118. "Plato was as concerned about theatrical performances as many reflecting persons are today about the influence of television programmes."

Webster, T. B. L. "Greek Theories of Art and Literature down to 400 B.C.." *Classical Quarterly* (1939): 166–79. Surveys the historical origins of Greek views of art: the main tendencies are the monument theory (art as moralistic, religious, and commemorative) and the mimetic theory (art as hedonistic, technical, and realistic).

———. "Plato and Aristotle as Critics of Greek Art." *Symbolae Osloensis* 29 (1952):

8–23. On the critical standards by which Plato and Aristotle judged contemporary painting.

Wheelwright, Philip. "Mimesis and Katharsis: An Archetypal Consideration." In Downer, *English Institute Essays: 1951* 3–30. "Mimesis and katharsis are valid critical concepts . . . provided that they are reinterpreted with attention to all levels of meaning, all relevant overtones of allusion."

Wiegmann, Hermann. "Plato's Critique of the Poets." Trans. Henry W. Johnstone Jr. *Philosophy and Rhetoric* 23 (1990): 109–24. "The so-called critique of the poets by Plato is exclusively aimed at dividing domains of knowledge, and . . . [has no] ethical, political, or pedagogical intent."

Will, Frederic. "Aristotle and the Source of the Art-Work." *Phronesis* 5 (1960): 152–68. Imitation in the *Poetics* refers to a subjective or inner-directed process of aligning the artistic creator with the divine creator.

Wimsatt, William K., Jr., and Cleanth Brooks. *Literary Criticism: A Short History*. New York: Knopf, 1957. 3–76. Plato's "mathematical" orientation contrasts with Aristotle's "biological" approach to the arts.

Woodruff, Paul. "Aristotle on *Mimesis*." Rorty, *Essays on Aristotle's* Poetics. 73–95. "Aristotle is no clearer than his predecessors as to what place mimesis has in the family that includes likeness, image, sign, reproduction, impersonation, and the rest."

Index

Aeschylus: and Aristotle, 104; debate format, 49–52; and Euripides, 27, 30; female stereotype in, 33, 35, 41, 45; and Hegel, x, 13, 17–19, 36, 76, 80–81; and Heraclitus, 76; and Homer, viii, 9, 18; male stereotype in, 9, 20, 25, 27, 29–31, 53, 55, 151; and Milton, 114–16, 120–21; and Nietzsche, x, 73, 75–81; politics in, 9; and Seneca, x, 81–82, 84, 114; and Shakespeare, 58, 61–63, 66, 151; and Sophocles, 20, 23, 30, 51
—Works:
  Agamemnon: and choric viewpoint in, 13, 38–39; debate format of, 49–52; and Euripides' *Bacchae*, 36; and Euripides' *Medea*, 43–46; female stereotype in, 18–19, 36–39, 41–46; imagery in, x, 76–79; madness in, 53; narrative format of, 47–49, 52; and *Prometheus Bound*, 18–19, 36, 79; and Shakespeare, 58, 66, 151
  Eumenides, The: choric viewpoint in, 14; debate format of, 49–52; and Hegel, 81; female stereotype in, 40; imagery in, 80–81; madness in, 53; narrative format of, 49; and Nietzsche, 80–81
  Libation Bearers, The: debate format of, 49, 52; female stereotype in, 34; imagery in, 80; narrative format of, 49; and Sophocles' *Electra*, 41, 43–44
  Oresteia, 40; imagery in, 76, 80–81; narrative format of, 47–49, 52; and Nietzsche, 76–77, 81; and *Prometheus Bound*, 18–19, 36; and Seneca's *Oedipus*, xi, 81–82, 84, 114
  Prometheia, 19, 52
  Prometheus Bound: and *Agamemnon*, 18–19, 36, 79; choric viewpoint in, 19–20, 27–28; debate format of, 49–52; and Euripides' *Bacchae*, 18, 27–29; and Hegel, 17–19; and Homer's *Iliad*, 18; madness in, 53; male stereotype in, 17–23, 25, 29–30, 41; narrative format of, 47–49, 52; and Nietzsche, 73–74; and Shakespeare, 58, 61, 63, 66; and Sophocles' *Philoctetes*, 20–23, 25
  Prometheus Unbound, 23, 52, 120
  Seven against Thebes, 10
  Suppliant Maidens, The, 35
Aesthetics. *See* Hegel, G.W.F.
Agamemnon. See Aeschylus
Ajax. See Sophocles
Alcestis (Euripides), 15
Antigone. See Sophocles
Antony and Cleopatra. See Shakespeare, William

Aristotle, *Poetics:* and Aeschylus, 104; and Euripides, 104; and Hegel, 3, 7–8, 113; and Homer, 104; and Milton, 114–16, 119; and Nietzsche, 113; and Plato, ix–x, 104, 110–13, 157; and Shakespeare, 61, 104, 146, 154; and Sophocles, 104; and Strindberg, 90; and tragic drama, x, 3, 155, 159
Arrowsmith, William, 163n.10
Athens: oratory and rhetoric in, 63, 116–18, 123–24; politics in, 9, 17, 26, 163n.1, 165n.9. *See also* tragic drama

Bacchae, The. *See* Euripides
Beckett, Samuel, *Waiting for Godot*, 87
Bible, the, 105, 116, 119, 150. *See also* Christian allegory; Ecclesiastes; Jesus
Birth of Tragedy, The (Nietzsche), 74–75, 85, 87, 93
Bosanquet, Bernard, 178nn.18, 19
Bradley, A. C., 3, 5, 161n.1
Brandes, Georg, 88
Burke, Kenneth, 3

Christian allegory, 58, 114, 116, 119–21, 123. *See also* Bible, the; Jesus; Milton, John
Cicero, 116, 186. *See also* Rome; Seneca
Conrad, Joseph, *Lord Jim*, vi, viii, 158
Coriolanus. *See* Shakespeare, William
Coughlan, William, 182n.1

Death of a Salesman (Miller), 87, 93
Derrida, Jacques, 161n.4
Dostoyevsky, Fyodor, 93
Dream Play, A. *See* Strindberg, August
DuBoulay, Juliet, 167n.1

Early Greek Philosophy (Nietzsche), 75, 92
Ecce Homo (Nietzsche), 75, 87
Ecclesiastes, 27. *See also* Bible, the
Electra. *See* Euripides; Sophocles

Eumenides, The. *See* Aeschylus
Elizabethan tragedy, 58, 67, 73. *See also* Shakespeare
Euripides: and Aeschylus, 27, 30; and Aristotle, 104; debate format of, 49–52; female stereotype in, 33, 41; and Hegel, 6, 55, 75–76; and Homer, viii, 9; male stereotype in, viii, 27, 30, 54; and Milton, 116, 121; and Nietzsche, 75–76, 98; politics in, 9; and Shakespeare, 58, 66, 68, 139, 151; and Sophocles, 27–28, 30, 41, 45
—Works:
  Alcestis, 15
  Bacchae, The: and Aeschylus' *Agamemnon*, 36; and Aeschylus' *Prometheus Bound*, 18, 27–29; choric viewpoint in, 14; debate format of, 49–52; female stereotype in, 28–29, 36, 43, 98; male stereotype in, 18, 27–30, 54, 98; narrative format of, 47–49, 52; and Shakespeare, 58, 63, 68, 139, 151; and Sophocles' *Ajax*, 28; and Sophocles' *Oedipus Rex*, 28; and Sophocles' *Philoctetes*, 29
  Electra: female stereotype in, 34–44; male stereotype in, 27; narrative format of, 47–48
  Hecuba: female stereotype in, 32, 59; madness in, 54–55; male stereotype in, 10, 54–55, 139; narrative format of, 47–49, 52, 85; and Shakespeare's *King Lear*, 138; and Sophocles' *Philoctetes*, 54
  Heracleidae, The 34
  Hippolytus: choric viewpoint in, 15; female stereotype in, 34; male stereotype in, 27; narrative format of, 47–49, 52
  Ion, 35
  Iphigenia in Aulis, 15
  Iphigenia in Tauris, 35
  Medea: and Aeschylus' *Agamemnon*,

43–46; choric viewpoint in, 15; female stereotype in, 34–36, 43–46; male stereotype in, 27, 158; narrative format of, 47–49, 52; and Nietzsche, 98; and Shakespeare, 58, 66, 68; and Sophocles' *Ajax*, 45; and Sophocles' *Electra*, 43–45
Orestes, 35
The Suppliant Women, 34

Gellrich, Michelle, 56, 162n.7, 165n.7, 168n.4

Hamlet. *See* Shakespeare, William
Hecuba. *See* Euripides
Hegel, G. W. F., *Aesthetics:* and Aeschylus, x, 13, 17–19, 36, 76, 80–81; and Aristotle, 3, 7–8, 113; and Athenian tragedy, 5–13, 16–17, 30, 32, 47, 56, 72–74, 76, 159; choric viewpoint in, 13–15; and Euripides, 6, 55, 75–76; female stereotype in, 32–33; and Homer, 8; and Kafka, 98; and Milton, 114–15, 120; narrative format of, 47, 52, 56; and Nietzsche, 5, 73–74, 76, 85–86, 93, 113; and Plato, 103–4, 113, 156–59; and Seneca, 82, 84; and Shakespeare, 5–8, 16, 33, 57, 59–61, 63–64, 66, 68–69, 85, 104, 122–23, 127, 145, 147, 151–56, 158–59; and Sophocles, 21–22, 24–25, 41, 53, 157–58, 169n.2; and Strindberg, 91, 93, 98; and tragic drama, ix–xi, 3–8, 16–17, 30, 56, 155, 157–59
Henry IV, Part 1 (Shakespeare), 139
Heracleidae, The (Euripides), 34
Heraclitus: and Aeschylus, 76; and Kafka, 94, 175n.8; and Nietzsche, 75–76, 87, 92, 94, 103; and Seneca, 82; and Strindberg, 92
Hester, D. A., 164n.4
Hippolytus. *See* Euripides

Hitler, Adolf, 87
Homer: and Aeschylus, 18; and Aristotle, 104; and Athenian tragedy, viii, 9; and Hegel, 8; *Iliad*, viii, 11, 18; male stereotype in, 9, 21, 50; and Plato, 105, 107, 109, 112; and Shakespeare, 60, 62, 170n.1; and Sophocles, 9
Hook, Sidney, 5

Iliad. *See* Homer
Ion (Euripides), 35
Ion (Plato), 175n.1
Iphigenia in Aulis (Euripides), 15
Iphigenia in Tauris (Euripides), 35

"Judgment, The" (Kafka), 175n.10
Jesus, 121. *See also* Bible, the; Christian allegory
Julius Caesar. *See* Shakespeare, William

Kafka, Franz, "The Metamorphosis": and Athenian tragedy, 93, 95, 98–99; and Hegel, 98; and Heraclitus, 94, 175n.8; imagery in, ix–x, 94–98; and "The Judgment," 175n.10; and "Letter to His Father," 175n.10; and Nietzsche, ix–x, 93–98, 175n.8; and Seneca, 93; and Shakespeare, 93–95, 97–99, 132; and Strindberg, 93, 98
Kierkegaard, Sören, 161n.4
King Lear. *See* Shakespeare, William

Laws (Plato), 175n.1
Left Hand of Darkness, The (LeGuin), vi
LeGuin, Ursula K., *The Left Hand of Darkness*, vi
"Letter to His Father" (Kafka), 175n.10
Levin, Saul, xi, 177n.12
Libation Bearers, The. *See* Aeschylus
Lord Jim (Conrad), vi, viii, 158

Macbeth. *See* Shakespeare, William
Mao Zedong, 87

Medea. See Euripides
"Metamorphosis, The." See Kafka, Franz
Miller, Arthur, *Death of a Salesman*, 87, 93
Milton, John: ethical purpose, 104, 178nn.1, 2
—Works:
　Paradise Lost, 120
　Samson Agonistes: and Aeschylus, 114–16, 120–21; and Aristotle, 114–16, 119; Athenian tragedy in, 114–16; Christian allegory in, 114, 116, 119, 121, 123; and Cicero, 116; debate format of, 116; and Euripides, 116, 121; and Hegel, 114–15, 120; and Jesus, 121; and Nietzsche, 114, 120; and the Phoenix, 121; and Plato, x, 104, 114–16, 118, 121, 123; rhetoric in, x, 116–21, 124, 179n.4, n.5, 180n.6; and Seneca, 114, 116–17, 119; and Shakespeare, 114–15, 118, 122–25, 127–28, 131, 136, 141, 147, 149; and Sophocles, 116, 120–21
Mourning Becomes Electra (O'Neill), 87
Mueller, Gustav E., 162nn.5, 7

Nietzsche, Friedrich: and Aeschylus, x, 73–81; and Aristotle, 113; and Athenian tragedy, 73–74, 76, 98–99; and Euripides, 75–76, 98; and Hegel, 5, 73–74, 76, 85–86, 93, 113; and Heraclitus, 75–76, 87, 92, 94, 103; and Kafka, ix–x, 93–98, 175n.8; and Milton, 114, 120; and Plato, 103–4, 113, 157–58; and Seneca, x, 82–84, 86; and Shakespeare, 73–74, 85–86, 98–99, 104, 122–23, 137, 143, 147, 151, 153–54, 159; and Sophocles, 75–75; and Strindberg, ix–x, 87–93, 98, 157, 173nn.2, 3; and tragic drama, ix–x, 74–75, 85–93, 155, 157–59

—Works:
　The Birth of Tragedy, 74–75, 85, 87, 93
　Early Greek Philosophy, 75, 92
　Ecce Homo, 75, 87
　Twilight of the Gods, 75
　Will to Power, The, 74–75, 85, 87

OED (*Oxford English Dictionary*), 119
Oedipus. See Seneca
Oedipus at Colonus. See Sophocles
Oedipus Rex. See Sophocles
Oliker, Howard, 182n.1
O'Neill, Eugene: *Long Day's Journey into Night*, 87; *Mourning Becomes Electra*, 41
Oresteia. See Aeschylus
Orestes (Euripides), 35
Othello. See Shakespeare, William
Ovid, 170n.1

Paradise Lost (Milton), 120
Pericles (Shakespeare), 57
Philoctetes. See Sophocles
Phoenix, 121
Pitcher, Seymour, 177n.12
Plato, ix–x, 103
—Works:
　Ion, 175n.1
　Laws, 175n.1
　Republic: and Aristotle, ix–x, 104, 110–13, 157; and Hegel, 103–4, 113, 156–59; and Heraclitus, 103; and Homer, 105, 107, 109, 112; and Milton, x, 104, 114–16, 118, 121, 123; and Nietzsche, 103–4, 113, 157–58; and Shakespeare, 104, 122–23, 127, 132, 145, 147, 151, 153–54, 159; and Sophocles, 103; and tragic drama, ix–x, 103–13, 155–60, 176nn.2, 5, 177nn.14, 17
　Sophist, 175n.1
Plutarch, 170n.1
Poe, Edgar Allan, 93
Poetics. See Aristotle

Prometheia (Aeschylus), 19, 52
Prometheus Bound. See Aeschylus
Prometheus Unbound (Aeschylus), 23, 52, 120

Rape of Lucrece, The (Shakespeare), 123
Raphael, D. D., 3
Republic. See Plato
Rome, oratory and rhetoric, 63, 116–18, 123–24. *See also* Cicero; Seneca
Romeo and Juliet (Shakespeare), 59

Samson Agonistes. See Milton, John
Schelling, Friedrich von, 163n.9
Schiller, Johann Cristoph von, 163n.9
Schlegel, Friedrich, 163n.9
Seneca, *Oedipus:* and Aeschylus, xi, 81–82, 84, 114; and Athenian tragedy, 81–82, 84; and Hegel, 82, 84; and Heraclitus, 82; imagery in, x, 81–84; and Kafka, 93; and Milton, 114, 116–17, 119; and Nietzsche, x, 82–84, 86; and Shakespeare, 64, 68, 123; and Sophocles' *Oedipus Rex,* 82; and tragic drama, 84, 86, 98. *See also* Cicero; Rome
Seven against Thebes (Aeschylus), 10
Shakespeare, William: and Aeschylus, 58, 61–63, 66, 151; and Aristotle, 61, 104, 146, 154; and Athenian tragedy, 57–64, 66, 68–69, 73–74, 98, 132, 139, 142, 146–49, 151, 153, 155–56, 158–59; Christian allegory in, 58; and Euripides, 58, 66, 68, 139, 151; female stereotype in, 57–60, 64–65, 68–69; and Hegel, 5–8, 16, 33, 57, 59–61, 63–64, 66, 68–69, 85, 104, 122–23, 145, 147, 155–56, 158–59; and Homer, 60, 62, 170n.1; and Kafka, 93–95, 97–99, 132; and male stereotype in, viii–xi, 57–61, 64, 151–54, 159–60; and Milton, 114–15, 118, 122–25, 127–28, 131, 136, 142, 147, 149; narrative format in, x, 57–69, 147; and Nietzsche, 73–74, 85–86, 98–99, 104, 122–23, 137, 143, 147, 151, 153–54, 159; and Plato, 104, 122–23, 132; rhetoric in, 122–25; and Seneca, 64, 68, 123; and Sophocles, 58, 61, 66, 151; and Strindberg, 90, 132
—Works:
Antony and Cleopatra: female stereotype in, 58, 60–61, 63; and Milton's *Samson Agonistes,* 118, 122; narrative format of, 60–61, 63, 65–67
Coriolanus: female stereotype in, 58, 60–62; narrative format of, 60–62, 64–66
Hamlet: female stereotype in, 65, 67–69; and Kafka's "Metamorphosis," 93, 98; narrative format of, 64, 67–69, 154
Henry IV, Part 1, 139
Julius Caesar: female stereotype in, 59, 61–62, 65; narrative format of, 60–62, 64–66
King Lear: and Aristotle, 147, 154; and Athenian tragedy, 132, 139, 142–48, 151, 153; and the Bible, 150; and Euripides' *Hecuba,* 138; female stereotype in, 65, 68–69; and Hegel, 122–23, 127, 145, 147, 151–54, 158–59; imagery in, 139–40, 154; and Kafka's "Metamorphosis," 93–95, 97–99, 132; and Milton's *Samson Agonistes,* 114–15, 122–25, 127–28, 131, 136, 141, 147; narrative format of, 64–65, 68–69, 154, 159; and Nietzsche, 98–99, 122–23, 137, 143, 147, 151, 153–54, 159; and Plato, 122, 127, 132, 145, 147, 151, 153–54, 159; rhetoric in, x–xi, 114, 122–54, 158–59
Macbeth: female stereotype in, 65–69; and Kafka's "Metamorphosis," 97–99; narrative format

218 / Index

Shakespeare—*continued*
    of, 64–69, 153–54; rhetoric in, 122
    Othello: female stereotype in, 64, 66–69; and Kafka's "Metamorphosis," 93–94, 97–99; narrative format of, 64–69, 154; rhetoric in, 122
    Pericles, 57
    Rape of Lucrece, The 123
    Romeo and Juliet, 59
    Venus and Adonis, 123. See also Elizabethan tragedy
Shelley, Percy Bysshe, 164n.5
Sophist (Plato), 175n.1
Sophocles: and Aeschylus, 20, 23, 30, 51; debate format of, 49–52; and Aristotle, 104; and Euripides, 27–28, 30, 41, 45; female stereotype in, 33, 35, 41, 45; and Hegel, 21–22, 24–25, 41, 43, 157–58, 169n.2; and Homer, viii, 9; and Milton, 116, 120–21; narrative format of, 47–49, 52, 55; and Nietzsche, 75–76; and Plato, 27–28, 30, 41, 103; politics in, 9, 26–27; and Shakespeare, 58, 61, 66, 151
—Works:
    Ajax: and Aeschylus' *Agamemnon*, 37; and Aeschylus' *Prometheus Bound*, 24–25; and *Antigone*, 25; choric viewpoint in, 11, 14, 27; debate format of, 49–52; and *Electra*, 41; and Euripides' *Bacchae*, 28; and Euripides' *Medea*, 45; female stereotype in, 34; madness in, 53; male stereotype in, 11, 14, 20–21, 24–27, 30–31; narrative format of, 47–49; and Shakespeare, 58, 61, 66; and Sophocles' *Electra*, 66
    Antigone: and Hegel, 157, 169n.2; madness in, 53; male stereotype in, 20, 25; narrative format of, 47–49, 52; and Shakespeare, 58
    Electra: and Aeschylus' *Agamemnon*, 41–43; and Aeschylus' *Libation Bearers*, 41, 43–44; and Euripides' *Medea*, 43–45; female stereotype in, 35–36, 41–44; narrative format of, 47–49, 52; and O'Neill's *Mourning Becomes Electra*, 41
    Oedipus at Colonus: debate format of, 49–52; and Homer's *Iliad*, viii; male stereotype in, 10, 20; and Milton's *Samson Agonistes*, 120; narrative format of, 47–49, 55
    Oedipus Rex: and Euripides' *Bacchae*, 28; madness in, 53, 55; male stereotype in, 20, 28; narrative format of, 47–49, 52, 55; and Seneca's *Oedipus*, 82
    Philoctetes: and Aeschylus' *Prometheus Bound*, 20–23, 25; and Aeschylus' *Prometheus Unbound*, 23, 52, 120; debate format of, 49–52; and *Electra*, 41; and Euripides' *Bacchae*, 29, and Euripides' *Hecuba*, 54; female stereotype in, 41; and Homer's *Iliad*, viii, 21; and Kafka's "The Metamorphosis," 95; madness in, 53; male stereotype in, 20–27, 29–30, 54; and Milton's *Samson Agonistes*, 121; narrative format of, 47–49, 52; and Plato's *Republic*, 103
    Women of Trachis, The 20
Stalin, Josef, 87
Strindberg, August, *A Dream Play*: and Aristotle, 90; and Athenian tragedy, 95; and Hegel, 91, 93, 98; and Heraclitus, 92; imagery in, x, 89, 91–93, 98, 157, 175n.6; and Kafka, 93, 98; and Nietzsche, ix–x, 87–93, 98, 157, 173nn.2, 3; and Shakespeare, 90, 132
Study of History, A (Toynbee), 47, 169n.1

Suppliant Maidens, The (Aeschylus), 35
Suppliant Women, The (Euripides), 34
Swedenborg, Emanuel, 174n.3

Toynbee, Arnold, *A Study of History*, 47, 169n.1
tragic drama: choric viewpoint in, 13–15; debate format of, 49–52; female stereotype in, x, 32–36, 43–44, 46; and Hegel, 5–13, 16–17, 30, 32, 47, 56, 72–74, 76, 159; and Kafka, 93, 95, 98–99; madness in, 53–55; male stereotype in, viii–x, 9–13, 16–17, 26–27, 30–31, 155–56, 158–60; and Milton, 114–16; narrative format of, 47–49, 52, 55; and Nietzsche, 73–74, 76, 98–99; and Seneca, 81–82, 84; and Shakespeare, 57–64, 66, 68–69, 73–74, 98, 132, 139, 142, 146–49, 151, 153, 155–56, 158–59; and Strindberg, 95; and the supernatural, 29–30, 55
Twilight of the Idols (Nietzsche), 75

Venus and Adonis (Shakespeare), 123
Virgil, 170n.1

Waiting for Godot (Beckett), 87
Will to Power, The (Nietzsche), 74–75, 85, 87
Women of Trachis (Sophocles), 20

Leonard Moss, professor emeritus of comparative literature at the State University of New York at Geneseo, currently edits the journal of the Rhode Island Jewish Historical Association in Providence. He is the author of *Arthur Miller* (1967, 1980) and many articles on tragic drama.